"Prepare to be surprised and delighted, and ultimately, roused to action. *Ready or Not* is a primer for any Christian leader wanting to step into a future that takes innovation seriously."

MARK BATTERSON, *New York Times* bestselling author of *The Circle Maker*; lead pastor, National Community Church, Washington, DC

"This book has come at just the perfect moment! Innovative, refreshing, different, and *possible* ... Doug Paul invites the church to actually do what it was born for ... reimagine the future. Let this book challenge and inspire you toward kingdom come!"

DANIELLE STRICKLAND, author; speaker; leader

"Doug is a pioneer with a passion to bring others along. It's easy to deconstruct the past, but it takes a true revolutionary to paint a vision for the future."

GABE LYONS, president, Q Ideas; co-author of *Good Faith*

"Innovative? Creative? These are not the words that most associate with church, are they? Doug Paul is going to change all of that. Filled with compelling stories and practical instructions, *Ready or Not* teaches us how to rediscover Christianity's core DNA of innovative creativity—and at just the right time. I will be recommending this book to every pastor or leadership team I coach."

TOD BOLSINGER, author of *Canoeing the Mountains* and *Tempered Resilience*

"Provocative and compelling, this is an essential book to help us meet the moment. The stories and insights, practice and application, are all woven together to surprise, delight, and help you lean into becoming the innovative leader God has uniquely created you to be."

WILL MANCINI, co-author of *Future Church*; founder, the Future Church Company

"*Ready or Not* will serve as a navigational guide into the steps of innovation you need to take. In compelling, entertaining, and brilliant form, Doug Paul has captured the patterns of some of the most interesting innovations and distilled them into a process for leaders and teams to follow."

JEFF VANDERSTELT, author; lead teaching pastor, Doxa Church

"Some leadership books are so boringly technical I just can't get through them, but Doug Paul's *Ready or Not* is different. It's a rollicking gallop through the recent history of innovation, chock-full of fascinating stories from a variety of fields of endeavor. Never before has a step-by-step process for innovation been presented with this much verve. *Ready or Not* is a roller-coaster ride—exhilarating and inspiring."

MICHAEL FROST, Morling College, Sydney

"*Ready or Not* is a road map to break the church out of its sleepy programs and break it into the holy art of kingdom innovation. As eccentric as it is practical, you'll want to reread it and start trying it—I recommend both."

JUSTIN WHITMEL EARLEY, lawyer; author of *The Common Rule*

"In *Ready or Not*, Doug Paul offers an invaluable, transcendent work that offers not just inspiration and hope for an innovative future, but tested tools for the church to get free of old forms and join in God's risky and adventurous mission."

LUCAS PULLEY, director, Tampa Underground Network

"Doug Paul has thrown us a life-preserver with a jetpack attached. *Ready or Not* will be returned to again and again to find fresh insights and recalibration toward innovation in the church for a very long time."

CAESAR KALINOWSKI, founder, Everyday Disciple; author of *Transformed* and *The Gospel Primer*

"Doug Paul has provided an essential road map for innovation that incarnates the gospel in any context."

DAVID M. BAILEY, founder and director, Arrabon; co-author of *Race, Class, and the Kingdom of God*

"This book is loaded: practical tools, helpful illustrations, and timely insights that make for a great resource. I know it will help all of us produce more fruit for the kingdom."

PATRICK O'CONNELL, global director, NewThing

"This is a book that not only you, but your entire leadership team needs to read and implement together. The future of the church can be changed by this book!"

GREG NETTLE, president, Stadia Church Planting

"This is Malcolm Gladwell worthy and so refreshing. Besides Doug being brilliant, it is blasted practical. You will want to buy copies for every serious leader you know."

JEREMIE KUBICEK, CEO, GiANT; co-author of *5 Voices, 5 Gears,* and *The 100X Leader*

"Doug Paul provides a simple, scalable, and practical framework to move us from being averse to change, to being agents of change."

WILL PLITT, executive director, Christ Together

"Everyone loves to talk about innovation. But few people know what it actually looks like or how it's produced. Doug Paul has written a book that will help you lead your team and organization into the future with innovations that further your stated mission rather than simply breaking the mold for the fun of it."

LARRY OSBORNE, pastor, North Coast Church, California; author

"Hopeful, inspirational, and practical—in equal parts! What a joy to read a book that gives us a process and tools, but trusts leaders to follow the Spirit."

PAUL HARCOURT, national leader, New Wine England

"In the style of Malcolm Gladwell, Doug pulls together what, at first, may seem like disparate puzzle pieces. Page by page, the pieces snap together into a picture of stunning insight and clarity. This book is a masterclass."

ROB WEGNER, founder, Kansas City Underground; co-author of *Made for More*

"*Ready or Not* opens our minds to welcome innovation in the now. It is time for us to boldly go forward with creativity and hope, unrestrained by outdated paradigms."

NEIL COLE, author of *Organic Church, Church 3.0, Primal Fire,* and *Rising Tides*

"Everyone is talking about the need for innovation, but few tell you how to make it happen. In *Ready or Not*, Doug Paul provides a brilliant framework to help you navigate what's next for your church."

MAC LAKE, author of *Leading Others*

"I've spent my life encouraging innovation in the church, both as a lay-person and a pastor. What a timely and helpful read Doug has gifted the church. You don't want to miss this one. It's arriving at a critical season in the church."

RON EDMONDSON, pastor; leadership consultant; author

"If you are ready to boldly embrace what God can do among you, then this is the book for you."

KELLY KANNWISCHER, CEO, Younique

"Doug Paul is the best ministry strategist I know. Read this book and not only will you see why, but you'll find yourself more prepared than you can imagine to lead in new and innovative ways."

JR ROZKO, national director, Missio Alliance

"So many resources are cookie-cutter, prescriptive approaches. *Ready or Not* goes much deeper and helps the reader understand the dynamics that lead to breakthrough innovation."

DANA ALLIN, synod executive, ECO: A Covenant Order of Evangelical Presbyterians

"At a time when many leaders are stuck in status-quo thinking, *Ready or Not* invites readers into a world of kingdom possibility. If you're looking to unlock the door of innovation, let this extraordinary book be your guide."

STEVE COCKRAM, co-founder, GiANT; co-author of *5 Voices, 5 Gears,* and *The 100X Leader*

"This is a terrific book. If you read it superficially, you will come out with some terrific stories that you can use in your own leadership context. If you read it seriously, it will help you codify what you do well so that you can multiply it in a God-sized way."

JOHN CHANDLER, author; director, Uptick

"As we think about what needs to change and the church's role, I'm grateful for the strategies Doug brilliantly breaks down in *Ready or Not*. I hope the world is ready for a sequel ... voices joined and clear vision as we proclaim 'here we come!'"

KEVIN DAVIS, director, NewThing North America

"If innovation is the path ahead, *Ready or Not* is your guide. This book will not only inspire you to action; it will provide you with a step-by-step process for kingdom innovation."

RYAN & LAURA HAIRSTON, directors, Forge America

"I recognize this book as a must-read for anyone leading a church, movement, business, or organization that is seeking to do a new thing in the world."

LUKE DOOLEY, president, OCEAN Programs

"Doug has done a fantastic job of providing a challenge and a framework for your church to accelerate innovation to accomplish the Great Commission *right now*. Read it. Then do it!"

DOUG PARKS, CEO, co-founder, Intentional Churches; co-author of *Intentional Churches*

"Honestly, this is the most inspiring read placed in my hands in a very long time!" Doug Paul has written a game-changer! It delivers on courage. It inspires with story. It offers tools to innovate a future church."

GAIL FICKEN, co-executive leader, PLI

"Doug has gone ahead for us and marked out a road map—a way to not only help us identify why and where change needs to happen, but how we can implement and multiply it for the benefit of others. An insightful, valuable, and timely rallying cry for us all in this moment that we find ourselves in—whether we are ready or not."

RICH ROBINSON, team leader, Catalyse Change

"In *Ready or Not*, Doug has given us the why and how to dream and innovate for the glory of God. Through narrative examples, visuals, and practical tools, this book is like a breath of fresh air that is spot-on relevant for exactly the current times we find ourselves in."

JASON LANTZ, vision leader, RiverTree Christian Church

"Filled with interesting stories, witty banter, thoughtful ideas, and practical tools, my friend Doug Paul is helping us all think, un-think and re-think the process of innovation at its core. He pulls us in with his charm and pushes us forward with his tenacity."

DAVE RHODES, co-founder, Younique

"Through historical accounts, wild stories, and brilliant examples, Doug Paul offers a compelling and practical road map for how any leader can embrace five phases of kingdom innovation in their context."

GUY WASKO, pastor, Sanctuary Church, New York City

"*Ready or Not* demystifies the potentially intimidating notion of innovation and makes you think, 'I can do this. I need to do this.' What a timely book!"

KEITH NIX, head of school, Veritas School, Richmond, Virginia

"Full of Gladwell-esque real life and historic examples, this is a book for its time."

NIC HARDING, director, Kairos Connexion

"Applicable in every area of your life, *Ready or Not* is the book you need to work out how to leverage the current disruption and bring about scalable transformative solutions for the common good."

DUNCAN MCFADZEAN, co-founder, CREO Collective

"Gladwell-esque stories wrapped around piercing insights and layered with practical next steps. *Ready or Not* is a brilliant book on the process of innovation. You and your team will love it!"

ALEX ABSALOM, co-founder, Dandelion Resourcing

"Finally, a book about innovation with a kingdom perspective, written by a practitioner and not a mere theorist. In *Ready or Not*, Doug Paul puts master tools in our hands to reclaim our role as innovators with an eternal impact."

PAUL ANDREW, lead pastor, Liberty Church, New York City

"In every generation the church has had to find ways to adapt and innovate in order to fulfil its purpose. *Ready or Not* calls us to be part of that heritage and history that makes us joyfully fit for purpose today."

JOHN HARDING, senior pastor, Frontline Church, Liverpool, England

"Paul helps us to find ways to stay in the game of innovation—or even enter it for the first time. Leaders of all kinds will benefit—take up and read!"

DR. VINCENT BACOTE, associate professor of theology; director, Center for Applied Christian Ethics, Wheaton College

"*Ready or Not* is a well-timed book when the need for innovation has never been greater. Doug Paul has a pioneering mind and bold vision to see the gospel advance in our day."

AARON GRAHAM, lead pastor, The District Church, Washington, DC

"In *Ready or Not*, Doug Paul pulls out new brushes and paints with a vivid palette. His writing style keeps you turning the pages, his approach to the topic makes it easy to digest, and his encouragement will invigorate all to believe that you, even you, could be a world-shaking innovator."

JOHNSON BOWIE, lead pastor, Victory Church, Atlanta

"Take some manure, subtract a naked mathematician ... and you're just at the start of a book that will entertain, educate, and energize you for the church of the future that's just getting (re) started."

ANTHONY DELANEY, senior leader, Ivy Church Network, Manchester, England; movement leader, NewThing Europe

READY OR NOT

READY OR NOT

KINGDOM INNOVATION

FOR A BRAVE NEW WORLD

DOUG PAUL

100
MOVEMENTS
PUBLISHING

First published in 2020 by 100 Movements Publishing
www.100mpublishing.com

Cover design by Sean O'Brien
Typeset and designed by Revo Creative Ltd

ISBN 978-1-7333727-8-7

For my beloved wife, Elizabeth: This is our story.
You are evidence of God's grace each and every day.

Access the Ready or Not Training Lab

Because you've purchased *Ready or Not*, you now have access to the various resources and training mentioned throughout the book:

- A video training on each of the five Master Tools
- Downloadable Small Group Discussion Guide
- Downloadable Case Studies
- An in-depth video exploring the Scalability Tool (Phase 5)
- Curated videos and resources referred to in the book
- And much more ...

Find everything at:
DougPaul.org/ReadyorNotLab

Contents

4: MOBILIZATION

5: MULTIPLICATION

HOW THEN SHALL WE LEAD?

Foreword

A book like this is so good that it requires a foreword from two people! Besides, there's a connection between the two of us: Both our ministries are based in Chicagoland, and over the last few years, we've seen an amazing level of collaboration among church leaders for church planting. We're also seeing some of what Doug is describing in *Ready or Not*.

I (Dave) had heard of Doug's skilled work developing practical tools for leaders to advance their mission, but it wasn't until he started helping out the NewThing team that I really got to know him. It was through Doug's leadership with our LARN (Launching a Reproducing Network) cohorts that I began to appreciate the tremendous value he brings to all his efforts. Doug helped NewThing double the number of church planting networks in the United States from twenty to forty-one in just over a year. He also brought thought leadership, creativity, and an uncanny knack for making complex things simple. You will discover each of those traits in this book.

The first time I (Daniel) met Doug was when he spoke at the national NewThing conference hosted by Dave at the Yellow Box in Naperville, Illinois. The meeting was brief but meaningful—enough so to eventually put us all together in a foxhole when the COVID-19 pandemic hit. On March 16, 2020, Doug sent an email to me with the subject line: *Collaborating on Coronovirus Response?* Here's a snippet from his email:

> We've thought about starting temporary coaching groups of pastors that would last for six weeks. Our thought is most pastors are underprepared for the leadership that's necessary in this, their churches aren't currently built to respond effectively, and they will need encouragement and

practical coaching on a weekly basis. (This is also an amazing opportunity to use the crisis to pioneer new forms of church expressions.) These temporary coaching groups would be online and free.

In these few sentences, you gain a little insight into the person of Doug Paul. We know him to be responsive, collaborative, pastoral, futuristic, and generous. Along with Todd Milby and the Catapult team, Doug knew the world had changed, and churches needed to get ready. Their team surmised the best thing to do was pivot away from regular day-to-day work in order to serve churches and leaders without expecting anything in return. They were kingdom-minded, collaborative, and innovative—exactly what this book is all about.

There are three kinds of leaders in Christian mission. The first kind is a *mission theologian*. Mission is intrinsically a theological concept. When we study it properly, mission is really about the nature of God and his purposes. Therefore, a mission theologian deals with all of Scripture and the common themes in systematic theology. A mission theologian is driven by an attempt to understand God's revelation of himself to humankind as both the motivator of mission and the mode for mission.

Second, there are *mission theorists*. Theorists differ from theologians in that they are primarily motivated to describe and model missional ideas. They remind us that sometimes the mission needs to be reimagined in order for better strategies to be proposed. Mission theorists push churches and networks to define kingdom opportunities, to identify expiring models and paradigms, and to be innovative in their thinking.

Third, there are *mission strategists*. This group is the most practical of all mission leaders. Strategists go beyond theological foundations and theoretical models, and with an accurate assessment of culture, they create an imaginative game plan to execute in a ministry context. A strategist deploys a kingdom vision so that others can work toward creating sustainable churches that are missionally mature and contextually appropriate.

In this book, Doug has compressed these three kinds of mission leaders into one voice, in order to motivate church leaders and practitioners toward better thinking for now, and for the future. With all the thrill and suspense of a Malcom Gladwell book, *Ready or Not* cuts through some of the modern tensions we have in mission theory by seeing today from the future, adding a much-needed perspective on our current times. This book encourages its readers to think strategically and locally about this unique moment in history and the necessity to adapt not just our methods but how we think about mission and ministry in the twenty-first century.

Sometimes our knowledge and expertise can trick us into thinking there is such a thing as best practice for the future church. We think Doug might convince you otherwise. While we can learn some good lessons from yesteryear, the future is created by pioneering and persevering practitioners.

We genuinely appreciate Doug's friendship and thought leadership, especially in the area of mission innovation in North America and beyond. The first three months into the COVID-19 pandemic fast-tracked our friendship and admiration for his passion for innovation. We have seen his love for the local church and his dream for a new generation of leaders. And it's contagious!

Whether you're ready or not, God is doing a new thing, and this book gives us an imagination for how it might be happening.

Let's get ready then.

DAVE FERGUSON
Visionary Leader, NewThing

DANIEL YANG
Director, Send Institute

Introduction

"IF YOU LOVE THE FORM, YOU HAVE EVERYTHING TO LOSE.
IF YOU LOVE WHAT GIVES IT ITS FORM, YOU'RE FREE TO
RECEIVE WHATEVER IT IS TURNING INTO."

1.

Manure.

In 1894, that word, coupled with the word *crisis*, hit the headlines of *The Times*, Britain's premier newspaper of the day. As you can imagine, it caught the public's attention, and copies of the daily periodical flew off the shelves. In painstaking detail, *The Times* laid out the problem facing the people of London. It was a simple issue, really. Increased population and the Industrial Revolution caused accelerated growth in urban centers, and London was leading the way. Not since before the fall of Rome had a city housed more than a million people, and the problems of overpopulation were mounting.

Maybe you can see where this is going. You have a lot of people in a small landmass, and the predominant mode of transportation (other than walking) is by horse or horse-drawn carriage. More people equals more horses, and more horses equals more manure.

In the late 1800s, London had more than fifty thousand horses, and your average horse deposits around thirty pounds of manure each day (and don't even get me started on the two pints of urine).

"In fifty years," *The Times* claimed, "every street in London will be buried under nine feet of manure." It was just math: Project the population in fifty years' time, work out the equivalent increase in horses, and figure out the proportionate rise in manure.

Across the pond, the situation was even worse. Though New York City had a smaller population than London, it had far more horses in a much smaller landmass. City officials shifted the manure into vacant lots, and the dung often towered forty to sixty feet in the air.

To call this a crisis was an understatement.

As the issue grew with each passing year, a group assembled in an attempt to solve the problem. Great thinkers, scientists, and civic professionals came together and gathered for the first "Global Urban Planning Conference." It was scheduled to last ten days, and the topic du jour was manure.

But after only three days, the conference shut down and the group disbanded their efforts. Not only did they fail to find agreement on virtually anything, they couldn't perceive any possible way forward. They exited the halls of London, leaving the fate of the urban world in the hands of their lessers.

2.

Friday the thirteenth, March 2020. Reports of COVID-19 outbreaks were pouring in from New York City and Seattle, while similar outbreaks were appearing in high-density cities across the world. State governors were openly discussing the implications for their cities—social distancing, closures of schools and non-essential businesses, swamped hospitals, and shelter-in-place orders—and how these measures were necessary until all states could collectively flatten the exponential curve that was spiking at a terrifying rate.

I've never been someone who suffers from anxiety, much less panic. But on that Friday afternoon in March, I felt an intense level of existential dread. My panic didn't come from the reports themselves but rather from the potential ripple effects. For about twenty minutes, my mind, body, and spirit simultaneously began to absorb all that would fall if these first few dominoes started to tip.

Each thought and realization brought another. And another. And another, in this intuitive chain reaction of events. I spent some time in prayer with the Lord and in the Word, specifically returning to the promises of Jesus in the book of Luke, and the anxiety began to subside. I eventually got to sleep that night a little after midnight.

A few hours later, my eyes flew open. I was wide awake and there was a pressing burden to pray. Now, to be very clear, this has *never* happened to me. I've always heard about people who have these middle-of-the-night prayer experiences; I've just never been one of them. And to be honest ... I haven't felt the need to be. I'm a man who needs his sleep! But there I was, walking down the stairs to my living room, where I spent the next three hours on my knees as the Lord brought peace and rest to my weary, doubting soul.

The next night it happened again: 3 a.m. Wide awake.

This time, the Lord brought me to 2 Corinthians 11 where Paul talks about the internal pressure and concern he feels for the churches he's working with. I felt this deep sense to intercede for the church, starting with the local church I help lead in the city center of Richmond, Virginia. I pushed in hard for three hours, with a mental picture of Jesus interceding for his church etched on my mind.

Night three. 3 a.m. Wide awake.

I trudged downstairs, my body starting to feel the effects of three nights of very little sleep. Unlike the other two nights, I didn't know what the Lord was specifically asking me to pray for. I started in the Psalms and used this ancient prayer text to help me. As three more hours of prayer came to a close, I simply sat in the presence of God, meditating on the prayers of the past and his promises for today.

While sitting quietly in this moment, out of nowhere I was hit by a freight train of ideas and insights. I grabbed my paper and began to write everything down. After five minutes, I stopped and looked over what I'd written. It was a simple and scalable way to innovate for this moment in time. It was just a sketch, but the scaffolding was there.

Standing up, I grabbed my phone and sent out some texts to a few leaders: "I got something in prayer this morning. Let's get a few people on a Zoom call. Let's talk. All of us together."

Five weeks later, over ten thousand churches had joined the coaching groups we started together. Kingdom innovation was happening left, right, and center, as those leaders and their teams met the moment head on. Not surviving the crisis. Not running away from it. Running into the storm.

3.

In the pages to come, I'll introduce you to rock stars who got it wrong, iconoclasts with a cultural mandate, alcoholic movement-makers, world creators, research geeks, posh Brits with revolutionary chops, and middle-aged men in dad jeans who are not-so-loudly changing the world. We'll explore why some denominations are skyrocketing after decades of decline, and we'll see how a group of moms made a plan to take over (and did).

This book is about how we find, activate, and multiply fresh innovation for the sake of gospel transformation. It's about how, ready or not, we recover our imagination for innovation in the church again.

I'm going to challenge some of the fundamental assumptions we have about how innovation happens and why Christian leaders can sometimes be so resistant to change.

We'll look at a simple initiative in a south side neighborhood of Chicago that's ending generations of poverty; a church planting movement that's living up to the hype; and the true history of Civil Rights. We're going to see radical prison reform, and a Bible reading movement that's as beautiful on the page as it is in its simplicity. We'll discover why (and how) WWJD become a worldwide phenomenon, and what that has to do with the band Weezer. And we'll unpack the story of a reproducible discipleship system that came out of nowhere. Each and every one of them done boldly in the name of Jesus: They are kingdom innovations.

We're going to look at stories of wild breakthrough and epic collapse. We'll debunk myths that have built the temple of our collective cultural understanding of how innovation occurs. We'll unpack theories that have proved true in practice.

Most importantly, we'll ask: *How does kingdom innovation happen and how can we make it normal?*

The history of God's people is marked by innovators and pioneers in all sectors of society. It's in our lifeblood. In fact, the last two thousand years paints an astonishing picture of followers of Jesus innovating in social movements, art, technology, architecture, biological sciences, church life, psychological development, movement multiplication (and that's barely scratching the surface). And yet today, rather than being on the forefront of innovation, both within and outside of church life, Western Christianity seems stuck.

The COVID-19 pandemic, in particular, has provided an opportunity for the church to see where we stand and what we're missing. It became pretty clear that when you remove weekly live worship services, church (which is always a people and not a place) isn't necessarily sure what to do or even why it exists. Like a string of old Christmas lights, unplug one bulb, and the whole string of lights goes dead.

In the world in which we now live, the people of God either need to innovate or simply close up shop and stop fighting a war of attrition. That is why, for Christian leaders, missing the tool of kingdom innovation is the equivalent of a carpenter missing a hammer. In this book, we'll explore how leaders, whether in the church, in business, or within the social sector, can learn to wield the skill of kingdom innovation, regardless of how fast the world is spinning. This is a story about adaptation and flexibility, imagination and persistence, creativity and selflessness, and it's a story that began thousands of years ago.

The prophet Isaiah said, "See, I am doing a new thing! Now it springs up; do you not perceive it? I am making a way in the wilderness and streams in the wasteland." God has never left the business of bringing new hope and healing to the wilderness and the wastelands of humanity.

What, you may ask, is a kingdom innovation? It's simply this: *It's new, it works, and it brings glory to Jesus.*

When kingdom innovation *works*, it means God's will is becoming a reality here "on earth as it is in heaven." The transformational promise of the gospel is colliding with our world, continuing to adapt and change to the needs of the current moment. Think of it this way: When the Reformation happened, there wasn't a sense that reformation had happened, as a once and for all occurrence. The leaders were supposed to *keep reforming.* These continual changes were meant to spread into all domains of human life and existence! Why? Well as theologian Abraham Kuyper once said: "There is not a square inch in the whole domain of our human existence over which Christ, who is Sovereign over all, does not cry, Mine!'" Yet somehow that became past tense. We stopped actively *reforming* and, instead, a tribe of Christianity became *reformed.*

Because of God's faithfulness, we don't need to worry about the survival of the church or the endurance of the gospel. So while the gospel is never at risk, what *is* at risk is our own faithfulness to what Jesus has called us to. As leaders, will we be faithful in leading the people of God into the uncertain and tumultuous waters of the future? As Andy Crouch wrote in *Culture Making,* "Why aren't we known as creators—people who dare to think and do something that has never been thought or done before, something that makes the world more welcoming and thrilling and beautiful?"

What if we embraced that calling again? What if God chose to use us to ensure every child received an excellent education, regardless of where they were born? What if we became the place people went to when they had crippling anxiety? What if Christians innovated new practices to defeat isolation and loneliness in the digital age that led to millions coming to faith in Jesus? What if we were finally planting enough churches to not only keep up with general population increase, but far exceeding it? What if all of these possibilities of heaven colliding with earth could make earth a little more like heaven? You see, the more we talk about innovation, the more we see the enormity and the transformative nature of the gospel. It's why the Reformers wanted to keep reforming.

4.

On a Saturday morning in 1947, retired teacher Dr. Ethel Percy Andrus received a call that would change the remainder of her life.

On the other end of the phone was a local man requesting help. He had recently read a newspaper article about a former teacher living in poor conditions and hoped Dr. Andrus might be able to assist. Hearing his pleas, Andrus finished the call and drove the thirty miles outside of Los Angeles to try to locate the destitute woman.

"It was a cold, drizzly day," she recalled, "such as sometimes comes to Southern California." She checked with a neighbor next to the address she'd received to see if there was anyone who might match the description, but it didn't ring any bells. "Just as he was dismissing me, he recalled that there was an old woman who lived next door, 'in back,' in the chicken house. Perhaps she was the one I sought."

Going out back to the chicken coop, Andrus knocked on the sagging door, and a voice from the other side invited her to come in, where she finally placed eyes on the woman she was looking for: "Stockily built, with short grey hair, in an old coat much the worse for both age and wear, a woman withered of skin, with sunken cheeks but with the bluest and merriest of eyes, she looked me over—smiling at me, putting me at my ease."

Dr. Ethel Andrus learned this teacher had planned her retirement for years, carefully saving and calculating, but had lost everything in the Great Depression. She was now using the forty dollars a month she received as pension to cover all of her needs. Yes, it meant living in a chicken coop, but she could survive.

Later that day, as Andrus drove back to Los Angeles, a slow, gnawing feeling began to creep into the pit of her stomach.

Not long after, she had a conversation with her ninety-year-old mother who said:

> Old age, Ethel, needs care as youth needs care, but it needs something more. It needs the desire to live, to continue planning, and striving hopefully, to keep working at something worthwhile, and then when at last old age becomes dependent, it needs someone to still care or, if there is no one to care, there should be community care which can make it easy to help those who now cannot help themselves to keep their dignity and their self-respect.

Later that same year, Andrus started experimenting with the launch of the National Retired Teachers Association. Annual dues were just one dollar. A little more than a decade later, she launched the group that now, over sixty years later, has more than thirty-eight million members: the AARP, a collective of aging Americans aimed at empowering individuals to choose how they live as they age. Many years after its inception, it continues to be one of the largest and most effective lobbying groups in Washington. Have no doubt—this was a significant social innovation, bringing with it a leap forward in the quality of life for aging Americans. Without the AARP, the physical and emotional welfare of some of our most vulnerable would be in grave jeopardy.

Dr. Andrus, a woman in a chicken coop, and a conversation with an aging mother might not seem likely catalysts for innovation, but as we will see, *kingdom innovation* rarely starts in expected places or with expected people.

In fact, when we left off with our manure story, the best and the brightest had just slinked off in miserable defeat. And indeed they did. But before we ask *why* they failed, perhaps there is another question we should ask: Were they really the best suited people to solve the Great Manure Crisis of 1894?

You see, what no one saw coming was something happening somewhere on the margins—not just a new invention, but a new *innovation*—a new spin on current technology that would revolutionize the entire world and, unintentionally, solve the Great Manure Crisis of 1894.

That innovation was the *car.*

5.

By 1912, the number of cars operating in New York City exceeded the number of horses, and by 1917, the last horse-drawn streetcar in the city that never sleeps was officially removed from circulation. The manure crisis had all but disappeared.

Maybe you've heard the famous quote attributed to Henry Ford: "If I had asked people what they wanted, they would have said faster horses."

These words hint at Ford's single-minded focus to deliver on the vivid idea that captivated his mind: a Model T automobile parked in every driveway. Ford's vision resonates with the spark of creativity in all of us and is an inspiring example of the possibilities that can open up when we wholeheartedly pursue an idea or innovation.

A few years ago, Patrick Vlaskovits, writing for the *Harvard Business Review*, went digging to find out if Ford ever spoke those oft-quoted words:

> Let me dispel with the suspense; it doesn't appear that Henry Ford ever actually uttered this famous and polarizing phrase. However, even if Ford didn't verbalize his thoughts on customers' ostensible inability to communicate their unmet needs for innovative products—history indicates that Henry Ford most certainly did think along those lines— and his tone-deafness to customers' needs (explicit or implicit), had a very costly and negative impact on the Ford Motor Company's investors, employees, and customers.

Think about it this way: Henry Ford could envision what he was going after, but he refused to take into account the needs, desires, and opinions of anyone but his own. His mantra? The Model T car was available, and I quote, in "any color, so long as it's black."

Vlaskovits goes on to say:

> Henry Ford's genius lay not in inventing the assembly line, interchangeable parts, or the automobile—he didn't invent any of them! Instead, his initial advantage came from his creation of a virtuous circle that underpinned his vision for the first durable mass-market automobile. He adapted the moving assembly line process for the manufacture of automobiles, which allowed him to manufacture, market, and sell the Model T at a significantly lower price than his competition, enabling the creation of a new and rapidly growing market.

The car effectively brought an end to horses as a way of transportation in American cities. If you were going to point toward one thing that saved New York City from the Great Manure Crisis, it was Henry Ford. In 1908, the Ford Motor Company manufactured ten thousand cars. In 1915, that number ballooned to 472,350 and took another leap in 1920 to 933,720. Ford was scaling growth and scaling it fast. You could have any car you wanted at an affordable price. So long as it was a Model T. And so long as it was black.

But then things started to go south.

General Motors went to the mattresses, preparing for an all-out market war, with the tagline, "A Car for every Purse and Purpose." Rather than only offering one thing (a new, black Model T), GM started to reflect the needs of a shifting culture. They introduced the possibility of trading in used cars, financing options, innovative models, and upgrades that came out every year. And, get this ... a car that was actually enclosed, so it didn't let in rain or snow (unlike the Model T, which was open and a nightmare to drive in any kind of inclement weather).

Ready or not, culture was changing around Henry Ford. But he refused to budge.

The only modification he made to the Model T was adding windows so the car was enclosed, but apart from that, it remained virtually the same. Why? Because any change would screw up his perfect system. He had a vision in his mind and refused to relinquish it. In 1921, more than 67 percent of all cars purchased in the United States were built by the Ford Motor Company. In 1926, it was down to 33 percent, and by 1927, sales plummeted to 15 percent.

Finally, in 1927, Ford adjusted factories so they could make changes and upgrades to new automobiles, but he largely "borrowed" (and some historians would say "stole") from the innovations of General Motors. Ford's strategy? Observe what GM was doing and copy it.

There was a time when the Model T, and the system that manufactured it, was a wildly innovative concept. But the world around Henry Ford changed, readjusted, kept moving forward, and sadly, Ford refused to move with it. And so he resorted to copying the innovations of others, rather than creating his own.

Despite his incredible initial innovation, Henry Ford began confusing the *vision* (a preferred picture of the future) with the *vehicle* (the actual thing that will move someone toward that preferred picture). Eventually, the vision simply served to prop up and sustain a vehicle (literally!) that no longer resonated with the world in which Ford lived.

Why did this happen? How did one of the iconic innovators of the modern era get so easily thwarted? After decades of beating the odds, why did the odds catch up? It's simple, really. He met the Villain of our story.

6.

In 1965, Gordon Moore, the co-founder of Intel, hypothesized that the number of transistors on a computer chip would double every year. This meant that every year, the computer power of the modern world would see an exponential increase. It's how we've moved from computers the size of warehouses in the 1960s to today's smartphone supercomputers the size of a large business card.

Culture has been changing at a similarly exponential rate. For thousands of years, culture reinvented itself around the rate of each new generation, which is roughly every twenty to thirty years. Sociologist Jane Pilcher wrote that a generation can be defined by "people within a delineated population who experience the same significant events within a given period of time." People now experience the same quantity of significant generational events, that used to occur over a period of thirty years, every *eighteen months*. In other words, whether you're ready or not, the most predictable thing about life today is that our culture will change at a rate that is hard to keep up with, no matter who you are.

If the speed of cultural change is ten times faster than it was ten to fifteen years ago, where does that leave Christian leaders? I think it's fair to say that in the last hundred years, Christians can largely be classified as change averse. In the production of automobiles, Henry Ford didn't seem to be chasing an ever-changing vision of a better life for his customers. He was chasing a vision of *his* perfect vehicle. Once we take a closer look at the history of innovation, we can see it's entirely possible to have a game-changing idea, but be so committed to that *specific* innovation, that it becomes inflexible and eventually, irrelevant. This has happened to all of us, hasn't it? Once the reformers, we become the *reformed*.

The following graph from the Pew Religious Landscape Survey gives us a snapshot of this. It represents a number of surveys conducted by various American organizations, with each line representing the respective results.

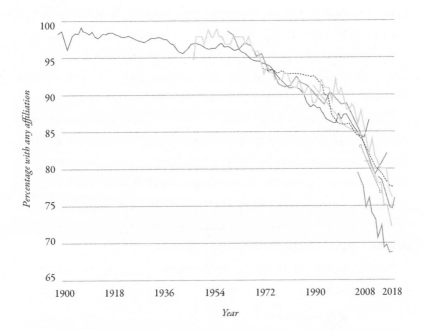

The plummet of religious affiliation between 1960 and 2018 is a stark reminder of the need to let go of our old reforms and step into kingdom innovation.

Pastor, author, and podcaster Carey Nieuwhof said, "Churches who love the method more than the mission will die. It happened in the 1950s, in the 1970s, in the 1990s, and it's happening today. What was effective a decade ago isn't always effective today. Leaders who live in the past end up dying to the future." Ed Stetzer, the missiologist and Chair of the Billy Graham Center, puts it even more succinctly: "If the 1950s came back, many churches are ready. There's nothing wrong with the 1950s, except that we don't live there anymore."

What Stetzer and Nieuwhof are getting at is how our forms of church have become increasingly outmoded. In their book *On the Verge,* Alan Hirsch and Dave Ferguson argue that our current forms of "doing church" can only reach about 40 percent of the population in North America. Shouldn't we be innovating new forms for reaching the remaining 60 percent? It's a while since that book was first published, so I think it's safe to say—and the Pew Survey would confirm this—that today there is an even greater need for churches, businesses, and non-profits to innovate on new models. Chances are, you weren't trained to lead in a culture changing at the speed it's at. But ready or not, this is the brave new world we find ourselves in.

The challenge before us, then, isn't to "catch up" with culture, as if there's a finish line. It's to put something into the water of Christian culture that allows us to instinctually innovate so that the gospel, and the transformation it offers every human and all of society, is always accessible: to *keep reforming*. There won't be one "right model" or "silver bullet." That model you just had to find might work today but may become obsolete in five years' time.

In the following tweet, Scott Erickson paints a picture of the mindset that leaders need to adopt:

Scott Erickson
@scottthepainter

If you love the form, you have everything to lose.

If you love What gives it its form, you're free to receive whatever It is turning into.

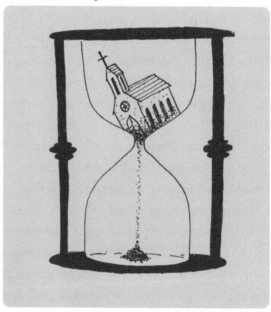

For Ethel Andrus, the innovation started when poverty stared her in the face through the eyes of an aging woman. For me, it was viscerally envisioning what the COVID-19 pandemic might mean for my family, my city, and the Western church.

The question is whether or not we're willing to give up some of our playbooks to see the bigger picture of what God is doing. Will we keep the victories of the past gilded in gold, freezing our forms and models from a bygone era? Or will we let the winds of the Holy Spirit blow off the dust, melt the ice, and join the journey of finding the future, together?

7.

Stumbling into an innovation can feel like catching lightning in a bottle. There is great power and energy found in the initial innovation, but at some point ... poof! It's gone. The world changes and what initially worked so well suddenly ceases to be effective.

In the pages to come, I'm going to unearth, in some rather unusual ways, the five practical phases of kingdom innovation and the accompanying Master Tools I've created and implemented to help others in the process. I've used this pathway for more than a decade, whether working with churches, denominations, networks, or non-profits in the social sector. It's a pathway you can use the next time a wicked problem stares you in the face and you're just not sure what to do.

The structure of the book is broken down into these five phases, with each part going deep on one phase of kingdom innovation. (See the visual summary of the phases at the end of this introduction.)

In some ways, each section of the book is a like a meal in reverse: it starts with the dessert and works its way to the meat and potatoes. While I love thinking and talking about theory or abstract ideas, it always has to get to practical application. In this book you'll see the move from theory into reality, from the abstract into the actionable. As an innovation strategist, it's what I've given my life to.

At the end of each of the five phases, you'll notice the layout change. In the Leader Innovation Lab, I want to get a little technical on the leadership side of things. I'm going to tease out some of the big practical insights for that phase, look at how it fits within the overall picture of the innovation process I use, jumpstart some ideas for your context, explore the implications for leadership, and finally, unearth how the spiritual process is foundational to it all.

Included with this book is a free Case Studies download. I've interviewed hundreds of leaders who are pioneers in kingdom innovation, many of whom I've been able to serve and work with. Their thoughts have greatly influenced this book, and if you go to DougPaul.org/ReadyorNotLab, you can download a curated group of Case Studies, which I'll lightly refer to from time to time.

This book itself is written and stitched together a little differently than most in this genre because I want your mind, heart, and spirit to fire up in some unexpected ways. Just as *Breaking Bad* taught us how to watch a new kind of TV show with its ever-transforming protagonist, or as Bon Iver taught us how to listen to new song structures when it dropped its first album, I'm going to ask a similar thing in the pages to come. Just go with it. I think the payoff is there.

What is "the why" of this book? I believe there is an opportunity to reclaim the ancient heritage staked out almost two millennia ago: The people of God should be the most wildly innovative and pioneering people the world has ever known.

Because when they have lived into this, with the Spirit of God leading them, the world has shifted on its axis.

OVERVIEW OF THE FIVE PHASES OF KINGDOM INNOVATION

1 IDENTIFICATION
We must frame the start of this journey by locating the big idea and framing the problem we're trying to solve.

2 IDEATION
We must generate whole new practices, concepts, and ways of thinking if we're going to solve our innovation challenge.

3 EXPERIMENTATION
We launch, test, adjust, and relaunch the innovation until the prototype we are testing achieves the measured goals set out.

4 MOBILIZATION
Once our prototype has seen breakthrough, we need to know why and how it worked so that we can mobilize many to multiply it.

5 MULTIPLICATION
Make the innovation scalable, removing as many barriers as possible, for as many people as possible, so we can invite them all into a brand new breakthrough.

1

IDENTIFICATION

CHAPTER ONE

Archimedes' Revenge

"HE APPLIED THOSE THEORIES TO HIS ALCOHOLIC
FOLLOWERS WITH THE SYSTEMATIC INTEREST OF A
LABORATORY TECHNICIAN."

1.

In the spring of 1921, an ad was placed in *The New York Times* asking for, "Young men capable of close observation. No particular scholastic requirements." The ad was placed by seventy-three-year-old Thomas Alva Edison, the eccentric founder of General Electric and famous inventor of the light bulb, in the hope of gathering new recruits for an experimental idea.

By train, forty men made their way across the Hudson River to New Jersey, and upon arriving, a designated man picked out twelve of them. The select group filed into a long, brick building that looked like a warehouse and climbed a flight of stairs. Finally, they arrived in a room with tables strewn about and walls lined with sinks, drains, and various lab equipment. Across the room, completely lost in thought and oblivious to the gaggle of men piling into the cloistered space, was the great inventor himself. His clothes were disheveled and stained with chemicals; his face a visual reminder of an experiment with nitric acid gone awry.

Sitting at each table and chair was a stack of papers with exactly 286 questions. The test covered a wide range of topics, all designed to measure an individual's general intelligence. Edison's theory was that the current education methods actually dulled intellect, rather than enhanced it. He was searching for a meritocratic way to measure intelligence; it would cut through race, class, educational background, physical attractiveness, or family experience. His question: What if there was a test that could actually calculate someone's thinking power?

He waited hours and hours as the young men finished their tests, until finally, there was only one person left. This particular individual had started by answering all the questions he knew, and then slowly reworked his way through the paper again, wrestling through the answers. Edison asked if he found the test challenging, and the young man simply responded, "Yes."

Looking over the test, Edison could tell there was something special, perhaps even significant, about the man sitting in front of him. And he was right.

Bill Wilson was a twenty-three-year-old wunderkind who was making a name for himself, quickly learning the ropes of Wall Street. With a "swiss army knife" of abilities and bull-headed persistence, he was also roguishly handsome, lanky, charismatic, and had recently married into a wealthy family. Wilson didn't much care or think about God, but he loved his country and was a World War One Navy hero. Wilson had always been obsessed with the iconic inventor; as a child, he'd read Edison's biography and knew endless details about the old man's life, and had even recreated a number of the experiments Edison pioneered.

Alcohol had struck Wilson's family tree in the past, so he vowed it would never pass his lips—that is, until one night, he found a beer already sitting at every plate at a dinner party. He drank the beverage, engaged in conversation, joined everyone at the piano for a few songs, and then went home.

No harm, no foul. *The first drink.*

A few weeks later, Bill Wilson found himself at another party, and this time cocktails were served. The man who pledged to never drink alcohol stared down the possibility of his second drink. But why not? The beer hadn't done anything to him. So why not be polite and take what was being offered?

It was called a Bronx cocktail.

"It tasted so good that it was gone in what seemed like a moment. The second Bronx cocktail is what really did the trick. Suddenly, the gawky soldier felt completely at home in this fancy crowd."

Over the next few months, Bill Wilson descended into a life of full-blown addiction, coincidentally intersecting with the timing of Edison's test. When months passed, and he heard nothing back about the test, the drinking increased. And increased. And then increased some more. Days blurred into nights and weeks stretched into months, as drinking became his life.

One evening, the doorbell rang, and on the other side was a *New York Times* reporter. Wilson had achieved one of the highest scores on Edison's test and was being offered a job in the inventor's own personal laboratory.

Now think about this for a second: This is the culmination of a dream. A fire that burned within Edison also burned within Wilson, and it was all coming together in a moment of convergence.

And Bill Wilson ... simply never responded.

Now in full descent, he would experience brief periods of sobriety, followed by weeks and months of binge-induced drunkenness. This was all thrust upon his new wife, Lois, who herself was dealing with her own demons as she came to grips with her infertility. In 1922, Bill gave the family Bible to Lois for Christmas, with the following inscription on the inside flap: "For Christmas, I make this promise: No liquor will pass my lips for one year." Within a few days, he was drinking again.

Wilson was not opposed to getting help. Just the opposite. He tried everything to stop drinking. He didn't care how crazy it sounded or what it cost. To fund the treatments, they'd sell their house, live with Lois' parents, borrow money; he'd even throw himself into making money on the stock market. Bill Wilson tried virtually everything and none of it worked.

One night, he made his way down to the Calvary Mission, the inauspicious gathering place of a radical Christian core, the Oxford Group. There was warm coffee waiting, and a shared meal of beans served on a metal plate. A preacher took the stage and asked this group of alcoholics if they wanted to be saved. "Just come to the rail and accept Jesus as your Savior." Bill Wilson jumped up and made his way forward and gave his life to God.

Perhaps this was the cure he had been looking for? That night, he stayed up with his wife, discussing the experience, and the weight lifted from his shoulders. But the next evening, Lois came to the bedroom to find him drunk and passed out on the bed.

A few days later, he readmitted himself to Towns Hospital and sank into a dark depression. Late one night, still not sure if he believed in God or not, he cried out:

> If there be a God, let him show himself! Suddenly, the room blazed with an indescribably white light. I was seized with an ecstasy beyond description. Every joy I had known paled in comparison ... Then, seen in my mind's eye, there was a mountain. I stood upon its summit where a great wind blew. A wind, not of air but of spirit. In great, clean strength it blew right through me. Then came the blazing thought: "You are a free man."

That night, Bill Wilson met God. And he never drank again.

2.

A charismatic alcoholic may seem unlikely a place to begin as any, but Bill Wilson's story challenges our very understanding of how innovation is discovered. Our first phase is *identification: We must frame the start of this journey by locating the big idea and framing the problem we're trying to solve.* But what if we're looking in all the wrong places to locate those ideas?

Many of us equate the innovation process with the story of a warm bath and a naked genius running the streets of Syracuse. Archimedes, the narcissistic, ancient Greek mathematician, and his now famous historical narrative, show us something small but profoundly important for how this process begins (and more accurately, reveal how it *doesn't begin*).

In the third century BC, the notorious mathematician lived in the port city of Syracuse, almost the last bit of land jutting off of the "boot" that is now the country of Italy. A religious festival was approaching, and a golden crown was to be dedicated to the gods. However, the local tyrant, Hiero, was deeply suspicious that his goldsmith was mixing other metals into the gold compound, not only desecrating the religious offering but swindling him in the process. He'd paid for a crown of pure gold, and he was going to make sure he got what he paid for. Hiero called in a favor with Archimedes, asking the scholar, "How can I know if the crown is pure gold, or if it has something else in it?"

Now let's be clear: If it turns out there's anything other than gold in that crown, that goldsmith is not going to survive the night. Tyrants of the time were known for their quick tempers and deathly nature, right? So the heat is on Archimedes. His reputation is on the line, which is no small thing for a man with an ego that claims, "Give me a place to stand, and I will move the earth." The problem? He just can't figure out the solution. It seems like a simple enough question, but he's unable to discover a pathway to the right answer.

One day, he makes his way down to the public baths, dips down into the water, and realizes as he descends into the liquid, that a certain measure of water is displaced by his body, "making the displaced water an exact measurement of his volume." The answer suddenly hits him. "Because gold weighs more than silver," he reasons, "a crown mixed with silver would have to be bulkier to reach the same weight as one composed only of gold; therefore it would displace more water than its pure gold counterpart."

Archimedes leaps from the bath, stark naked, and runs through the streets of Syracuse yelling at the top of his lungs "Eureka! Eureka!" (I've found it! I've found it!)

It's undoubtedly a story you've heard before, or one just like it.

Newton discovered the law of gravity because an apple fell from a tree and hit him on the head. The movie *The Social Network* depicts Mark Zuckerberg starting the "relationship status" feature on Facebook because he wanted to know if a girl was single or not. (It almost certainly didn't happen that way, but it's what we remember.) For Archimedes, it was seeing water displaced when he went for a wash. In each of these innovations something *just happened* out of nowhere.

The pathway to innovation starts with one, big, bright shining moment that provides the winning idea.

Or does it?

3.

Take a closer look and see if you can find anything strange about this story of the naked mathematician. Do you see it? Don't feel bad if you don't, because for thousands of years, historians and scientists didn't see it either.

For right here, at the beginning of our journey in innovation, we must confront the likelihood that the story of Archimedes almost certainly didn't happen.

Our Greek scholar kept notes on the laws of buoyancy, scribbles on finding the radius of a circle with Pi, and wrote the foundations of calculus that no one else would advance for another two thousand years. And yet, there isn't one random scribble in the margins, not one doodle of him running naked, and not one whisper of this account—from a man who loved to project his own grandeur? People still quote his insightful learnings today, but his notes contain nothing even hinting at this story.

So what gives?

The problem-solving principle known as Occam's Razor suggests that the simplest explanation tends to be the correct one. Fast-forward a little over two hundred years from Archimedes, and the historian Vitruvius wrote an introduction to his ninth book on architecture, in which he includes the story of this eureka moment. It's the first time in history this account ever makes its way onto a page. *And it's two hundred years later.* Maybe we should consider this story a little bit like ancient clickbait. Interesting and larger-than-life stories tend to sell a bit more than dry, drab, dusty books on architecture.

Galileo, a significant innovator in his own right, didn't believe this story at all. Why? Because "a scientist of Archimedes' stature could have achieved a far more precise result using his own law of buoyancy and an accurate scale, something far more common in the ancient world than a very precise pycnometer, which is used to measure displacement." Chris Rorres, a self-described "Archimedes groupie" and mathematician at the University of Pennsylvania explains it this way: "The volumetric method works in theory, so it sounds right, but when you actually try it you find that the real world gets in the way."

I know, I know. All this sounds like scientific gibberish. In real talk? The scientific solution the story describes doesn't actually work!

The reasons for the sticking power of this story are probably obvious but worth sharing nonetheless. The myth persists, according to David Biello, because of "the enduring power of the story: a golden crown, a life in the balance, a naked mathematician." In the annals of history, Archimedes is a larger than life character, and this story only reinforces the confirmation bias.

While the story is a myth, it serves as one of the poison pills in the heart of our modern culture, that is: social innovation can happen in the flash of a moment. That there is one big idea, out there, waiting, and once you've found it, everything can and will change.

A cultural myth functions a bit like toxin at the top of a river. Once you put it in there, it flows everywhere and poisons everything. It works its way not just into all of the river, but into all of the streams and underground water supplies. Next thing you know, the plants are all dying, the fish are floating on the surface, and kids are getting exposed to it as they brush their teeth and take showers. One little delivery at the top changes the entire ecosystem.

Think of eureka as a kind of poison pill in our culture.

It seems Archimedes got his revenge for history having him run through the street naked.

4.

Let's consider a little more of what the story of Archimedes suggests about innovation. After all, it isn't that these eureka moments don't ever happen. They do. But there's a subtle suggestion in this tale that inoculates us against innovation, the very thing we're going after. The story implicitly suggests that you've just got to keep waiting and waiting and waiting for that inspiration to strike. Without the inspiration, there's nothing much you can do.

So what do you do if you're poor Archimedes, sitting in the tub, completely uninspired, and the eureka moment never comes? Does it mean the tyrant Hiero is now coming after your head?

In his book *Where Good Ideas Come From*, Steven Johnson unlocks not just where ideas are found but how these ideas evolve over time and eventually make their way into our everyday life. "The trick," he says, "is not to sit around in glorious isolation and try to think big thoughts. The trick is to get more parts on the table." It's not just about seeing what you're doing but about seeing what lots of people are doing. He believes that one of the primary reasons we are experiencing an acceleration in innovation in the modern world is because we have never been more connected to other people's ideas. "As human connectivity has increased throughout history with more and more communication mediums, our innovation has deepened and increased."

Scott Berkun started his career at Microsoft when it was still on the leading edge of all digital breakthrough. He helped pioneer Windows and the groundbreaking internet browser Windows Explorer. (Yes, there was a time when Explorer was groundbreaking!) The point being? He's spent a lot of time thinking about and excavating the grounds of innovation. In Berkun's book, *The Myths of Innovation*, he explains that those epiphany moments really only come after years of hard work. He's saying that these eureka moments are just the final pieces of the innovation jigsaw puzzle.

Until we overcome these myths and barriers, both the ones in our heads and the ones culture has fed us, we will perceive innovation as an impossibility rather than a skill that can be learned. We start in the Identification Phase with the simple fact that there's actually a chunk of time connected to this phase that we rarely consider ... everything that came before in your life! You are constantly absorbing and synthesizing all you've learned from your collective experiences and working to make sense of the world around you. Continually crunching new possibilities. What if there was a way to walk around with eyes wide open to this reality?

"When innovators are asked how they came up with their idea," Berkun goes on, "they say 'it just came to me,' and have some interesting story about how the idea formed in their head. They don't say, 'after thousands of hours of research, the idea became obvious.'" It's not so much that Archimedes discovered the law of buoyancy in one moment. Rather, it's that he was in a *constant mode of discovering*. He found one puzzle piece, then another, then another. Eventually, those pieces formed enough of the picture so that breakthrough was just around the corner.

What Berkun is getting at is the principle of *cultivation*. As time passes, we learn new things, but as we do, new ideas form. And sometimes, those ideas piece together into a *hunch*. It's a guess about something that's based more on intuition or observation than it is about facts. Maybe it's buried deep within you, or maybe you actually say it out loud. But it's this sense that, "If we did _____, I wonder if _____ would happen?"

Steven Johnson builds on this idea with the concept of the "slow hunch." He believes that the bigger the hunch, the more time it takes to develop. "More important ideas take a lot of time to germinate and evolve. Sitting in the background, looking dormant." Sometimes it takes two or three years before there's enough substance to the hunch to allow you to do something with it. Sometimes it can take twenty to thirty years before something genuinely useful emerges.

In the 1980s, Tim Berners-Lee was a computer scientist and engineer working at CERN, the European Particle Physics Laboratory. The principal mission of CERN was no small thing ... to discover the origins of the universe and the moments directly after. They did this by smashing protons together at a velocity greater than the speed of light, simulating the necessary ingredients for matter to come into existence.

But out there on the side, slightly unrelated to the project itself, there was a growing problem: The team at CERN were generating an astronomical amount of data each day, and it was difficult to share it all with the multinational team working in different cities around the world. Berners-Lee needed the team to be connected, and he needed the right data to be in front of them at lightning speed. If he didn't solve this problem, the mission of CERN was never going to happen.

He needed to find a way to transmit tranches of data from one city to another, and a fax machine just wasn't going to cut it. He started with a slow hunch that there was more to this problem; but he had no direct solution or way forward. Slowly, he developed a theory of what could work. That hunch led to another, which led to another theory, which led to another idea and finally, some ten years later, Tim Berners-Lee invented what we now call the World Wide Web. (Sorry, Al Gore, it wasn't you.)

Notice this, though: He didn't start with the World Wide Web in mind. He didn't start the Identification Phase looking to create a decentralized network. He was actually going after a completely different innovation. It just ultimately led him to the start of the journey because he had eyes to see what was going on around him.

He followed the hunches, kept cultivating ideas, put them into action, and finally, it led somewhere. There was no eureka moment. The story, when you actually follow it closely, is kind of a letdown. It certainly doesn't make for a great Hollywood movie.

So what's going on here? Well, let's bring it full circle.

Bill Wilson never had a drink after that night in 1934 when he had a supernatural experience with God. You could be forgiven for thinking it was down to one powerful moment at the Town's Hospital. But the bigger story involves the sovereignty of God and what God did in and through Bill Wilson prior to that night.

What did the last decade of his life look like? Does anything stand out to you?

Remember, he was a man steeped in temperance education, having invested more than fourteen years trying to get sober, desperately trying to break free of the chains of alcohol in his life. He spent all of his money and most of his in-laws' money in this quest. But inside the story of those fourteen years are loads of half-ideas, untested theories, and slow hunches. These ideas were taken from different places and didn't fully intersect with each other: Alcoholism is a disease; dogmatic rules and regulations don't work; meeting in groups is vital; we need simple steps for a way forward; a belief and spiritual experience of the divine is essential. But those ideas weren't laddering up to any sort of cohesive innovation.

These were all things Bill Wilson picked up along the way, not in theory, not on a piece of paper, but in the laboratory of his own life. The Identification Phase can be a little fuzzy because it starts with all of your life and what's already happening as you exist in a constant mode of discovery. As for Wilson, when he found freedom, he was eager to spread the breakthrough, so he started to meet with other alcoholics. As he began to put his theories to the test, standing in the power of his newfound sobriety, he "applied [those theories] to his alcoholic followers with the systematic interest of a laboratory technician."

Now who does that sound like? That's right ... his childhood hero: Thomas Alva Edison. When Edison saw a twenty-three-year-old with a spark of promise and some semblance of himself, he was dead on.

But in spite of Wilson's best efforts, most of the drunks he worked with stayed drunk, a little bit like Edison trying to get the filament in the light bulb to stay on. He was discouraged and downcast, and when he confided in his wife, Lois, she responded in the way only a spouse can: "Your program is working well enough for one alcoholic in particular: You."

You never want to call something the "final puzzle piece," but there was a moment of significance in the spring of 1935, as Wilson was delicately clinging to his own sobriety. He was set to see an alcoholic who needed help, and on his way to that meeting, passed by the bar at the nearby Mayflower Hotel. He resisted the urge to go through the doors, but recognized how close he was to giving into temptation. The man he was meeting was Bob Smith, a surgeon who couldn't stop drinking (even when performing surgeries) and who had asked for Wilson's help to break the addiction. "Armed with the knowledge of his previous failures and the sharp memory of his recent need to drink at the Mayflower Hotel, Bill Wilson told Bob that he wasn't there to help him. He, Bill Wilson, needed help ... and he could only get it from another man with a drinking problem. He hoped *Bob* could help *him*."

It was a core insight that would eventually lead to a working theory. "I knew that I needed this alcoholic as much as he needed me." This relationship between Bill Wilson and Bob Smith was the real-time experiment that evolved into the facets you might be well acquainted with: Twelve Steps, sponsors, group meetings, and a whole list of memorable slogans. This insight, along with the other slow hunches and half-ideas that were pieced together across decades, would prove vital to these two men and the process they formulated as they went on to found Alcoholics Anonymous.

And the rest, as they say, is history. Millions of people would find freedom from the addiction of alcohol and meet God in the process. It would spawn other innovations, such as Celebrate Recovery from Saddleback Church, or the reiteration known as Recovery which sprung out of Village Church.

Perhaps we think of innovation as shiny and glamourous, where the great innovators of our time receive acclamation and praise. But the stark reality is that if it's about *kingdom* innovation, it's going to cost us something. There is death, the cross, letting go of our own bright ideas. Through struggle, pain, back and forth, rejection, real life, real cost, real relationships ... Bill Wilson not only got sober, but God used him to bless millions. It wasn't a simple jump out the bath moment. It was costly.

It's clear, then, that the grand eureka moment is a myth. So what is it that stops us from taking control of this innovation process, rejecting the notion we must wait until the idea just comes to us? It's possibly because for most, it's easier to believe change doesn't begin with me. It happens outside of me. It's easier to put the responsibility *somewhere else* and with *someone else*.

Maybe it's why we don't see more breakthroughs of this size and proportion. Maybe we're the barrier? You see, Alcoholics Anonymous is not only one of the most significant kingdom innovations of the twentieth century, but one of the greatest social innovations in the history of civilization. But a close reading of the story doesn't show one eureka moment. It doesn't even show several moments that when stitched together, somehow produced this kingdom innovation. There wasn't a memorable climax or one big idea that won the day. It was the cultivation of ideas and a piecing together of slow hunches.

If the story of Bill Wilson and Archimedes exposes one of the great innovation myths in our culture today, wait until you hear the second.

CHAPTER TWO

When Experts Stop Asking

"IF THEY CAN PUT A MAN ON THE MOON, WHY CAN'T THEY MAKE A DECENT FOOT?"

1.

The second myth is all about identity and centers around the idea that innovation only comes from a *certain kind of person*. In fact, it might already seem like some of the stories we've looked at only reinforce this myth. After all, when you read about "eureka moments" and "slow hunches" and working the principle of "cultivation," it can feel like we're talking about some kind of super-human mind. It's like those individuals inherited the "innovation gene" in the same way LeBron James inherited the DNA that made him the best basketball player who ever lived. (A controversial statement, I know. But it doesn't make it any less true.)

The underlying message this second myth communicates is this: *Those people have something I don't have.* But like our eureka moment it's a myth, and one we can quickly dispense of, because in the end, kingdom innovation comes from three places, or a combination thereof.

The first, we've already looked at: Innovation driven by a *pioneering mind.* Some people like Henry Ford, by disposition, will simply generate more ideas than others. They see the world slightly differently, ask different questions, make different and interesting connections, and see different opportunities and possibilities.

The second, we've also already explored: Innovation driven by *necessity*. There is a practical need, and only an innovation can bring about a solution. (And often, those solutions come from unexpected places.) Dr. Ethel Percy Andrus wanted to get a woman out of a chicken coop. Bill Wilson needed to stop drinking.

But there is a third place kingdom innovation can come from: Innovation driven by a *holy discontent*. There are times when we can feel the Spirit of God stirring in us, and the gap between "what is" and "what should be" drives us to innovation.

It is clear from reading Scriptures, looking at church history, and many of our experiences, that God uses all three to catalyze change for his purposes.

This idea unlocks a world of possibilities for us, doesn't it? Think of how many places we need innovation right now. We need leaders who can multiply themselves and catapult those in whom they invest to go and do greater things in all the cracks and crevices of society. We need to reimagine what the church will look like here in this place, in this space, in this time. We need cities to flip as justice rolls down and mercy triumphs, breaking the cycle of the rich getting richer and the poor getting poorer. We need worship of the Almighty to become a way of life, not a service we attend. We need the Word of God to permeate and saturate the life of every man, woman, and child who calls Jesus their Lord. We need social media and digital technology to deepen our spiritual experience rather than deteriorate it. We need discipleship processes that transform people into "little Christs" who can then go and do the same for others. We need evangelism practices that help individuals take hold of being sent by God in their everyday lives. We need denominations to experience revitalization and spring back to life. We need churches that reflect the diversity we can expect to see in heaven. The list is endless.

We are not short of possibilities for kingdom innovation, but we need to navigate the pathway to kingdom innovation, exploring and overcoming the prevailing evils of our world.

So what if you could learn to innovate? Whether you're a pioneer, or you find yourself driven by necessity, or you're responding to some holy discontent, this is for *you*. And so it's from here that we turn our eyes to the choppy waves, the blustery winds, and the clear blue water of the Mediterranean.

2.

In Acts 16, Paul is beginning his second missionary journey, and his story becomes quite interesting for the purposes of our innovation treasure hunt.

> Paul and his companions traveled throughout the region of Phrygia and Galatia, having been kept by the Holy Spirit from preaching the word in the province of Asia. When they came to the border of Mysia, they tried to enter Bithynia, but the Spirit of Jesus would not allow them to. So they passed by Mysia and went down to Troas.

The first thing Paul tries to do after checking in with his church plants is to head up to Asia, where Ephesus sits at the gateway to the province, the crown jewel of this half-continent. What we know is that he will finally get there, and we know that through his innovative work, an entire people hear the gospel message (Acts 19:10). But in this text, we see Paul blocked by the Holy Spirit. Ephesus will have to wait.

Kingdom innovation is right there on the horizon ... *and God blocks it.*

One of the key things to understand about kingdom innovation is it can't be done without God. Sure, you can have *innovation* without God. But there is no *kingdom innovation* without the work of the Spirit. This makes all the intuitive sense in the world, yet so many of us live our lives as if we are functional atheists. This is probably most true for those with a pioneering mindset. (You can go ahead and put a "guilty" next to my name.) "If I can do it and it's a good idea, why wouldn't I do it?"

At the very heart of it, kingdom innovation is a spiritual process. We aren't smart enough, charismatic enough, clever enough, intuitive enough, or hard working enough to bring about the transformational promise that only the power of God can bring.

Paul's stuck in Troas, not sure where to go next, but having just been released for a new journey, I'm pretty sure he was itching to get at it. After receiving a vision of a Macedonian man begging for help, Paul immediately leaves and ends up in Philippi, the leading district of Macedonia.

He hops off the boat with a "missional playbook" in hand that's worked everywhere else he's been: Start in the synagogue; when it's his turn as a visitor to share, tell them the long-awaited Messiah has come; his name is Jesus and he's the Son of God ... then see who's interested in hearing more.

But in Philippi, there's no synagogue. He's got a play, but the playbook no longer works, because in order for there to be a synagogue in a town or city, there needs to be a *minyan*—at least ten Jewish men who form the group. Don't have a minyan? Yep, you guessed it. No synagogue.

You can almost picture Paul prayerfully reflecting on this question: If there's no synagogue, how do I find people who might be open to the God of the Jews? Right here, we see that Paul's innovation journey didn't start because he was bored with his previous strategy and was looking to pioneer. It started because there was a need. The *identification* of the idea and framing of the problem didn't start until the need presented itself. And until Paul had eyes to see it.

So let's consider innovation more broadly before we zero in:

Paul had the same *paradigm* he had in other cities where he was breaking up new missional soil: Find where Jesus is already at work in this new city.

Paul had the same *principle* he had in other cities where he was breaking up new missional soil: Start with Persons of Peace (Luke 10) who are open to the God of the Jews and build from there.

But what Paul needed was a new *practice*, a new way of finding and building relationships with people because he no longer had a synagogue to rely on. That's where he needed the innovation breakthrough.

Paul has now engaged with the Identification Phase: He needs to find a new practice that will help him find and connect with people who aren't Jews but are open to the God of the Jews. He's identified the specific innovation, and he's going to fly through the rest of the innovation process (which we'll be breaking down throughout this book).

Having been born and raised outside of the Jewish homeland, Paul almost certainly knew that Gentiles who followed the God of the Jews often performed religious rituals, and these rituals required fresh, running water. And chances are, they'd be doing that on the Sabbath. So, although there might not be a synagogue, there could be a river. And if there's a river, there might be God-fearers performing the religious rituals.

> On the Sabbath we went outside the city gate to the river, where we expected to find a place of prayer. We sat down and began to speak to the women who had gathered there. One of those listening was a woman from the city of Thyatira named Lydia, a dealer in purple cloth. She was a worshiper of God. The Lord opened her heart to respond to Paul's message. When she and the members of her household were baptized, she invited us to her home. "If you consider me a believer in the Lord," she said, "come and stay at my house." And she persuaded us.

Paul meets Lydia, and she and her whole household come to faith.

That new practice Paul did by the river? That right there was a kingdom innovation. Did you catch that? You might have missed it, and it's OK if you did, because we're often accustomed to thinking that *innovation* means *invention*—that it must always be a brand spanking new creation out of nothing. But what Paul does here in Philippi is a slight tweak, just a minor adjustment—like churches going from hymns and pews to guitars and chairs. Not all kingdom innovation is earth shattering. (Let's put a pin in that one now, because we'll return to it later.)

What we might miss about Paul's story is how the "slow hunch" principle is at work. Remember how Tim Berners-Lee knew something was going on as the internet was starting to develop but wasn't sure what it was yet? How those slow hunches and half-ideas led to the invention of the internet? It seems a similar thing happened here with Paul.

And the power of this innovation isn't simply what happened in Philippi but what continues to happen. What starts with a small hunch about how to connect with people outside of the synagogue continues to grow. The learning continues. The half-ideas and slow hunches build, connect, grow, and multiply.

When Paul does finally get to Ephesus, there is unprecedented spiritual breakthrough, as every single person who was of Jewish or Greek descent in the province of Asia hears "the word of the Lord," and dozens of churches are planted. When Jerusalem is destroyed in AD 70, and the church with it, the church at Ephesus becomes one of the most important churches in the world for the next four hundred years.

But if Paul hadn't first seen the innovation breakthrough in Philippi, would the Ephesian church have become this beachhead for the gospel? Probably not. What we see Paul implementing in Ephesus are the things he learned in Philippi, as well as the practices that were built upon that learning. Maybe, just maybe, the Holy Spirit knew what he was doing when he blocked Paul from entering the province of Asia in the first place.

And maybe the Holy Spirit still knows how to lead us into new beachheads here in this brave new world.

3.

This first phase we've been looking at is *identification*, and one of the reasons we get stuck in the status quo is because we're asking the wrong questions from the start. Let me give you two examples that are common with many of the teams I work with.

Recently, I was working with a prominent faith-based non-profit. They had clarity on their mission and vision, but like so many people, they were struggling to activate the clear vision. One thing we knew for sure: It was going to take innovation. We were in discussion around some difficult leadership decisions, one of which involved whether to shut down a particularly beloved program. When I asked if that was a possibility, the room bristled. We continued down the process, and for the life of me, I couldn't figure out why this program existed. It wasn't successful (and never had been). It was a black hole for money, and it wasn't even helping the group of people they were trying to serve. It was completely off mission. I finally asked them, "Real quick, give me the back story of this program. How did it get started?" What emerged was that the two founders, who were no longer with the organization but were still greatly loved by the staff team, had started it mainly as a stop-gap solution for their own kids.

The team was stuck because they were asking the wrong question. They kept asking, "How do we fix this program?" But the bigger (and better!) question they should have been asking was, "Why does this program exist in the first place?"

It's not that they thought the program was essential to their mission; it should have shuttered a few years ago. They couldn't ask the bigger question and make the tough leadership call because they missed the founders, and this program kept their memory alive. This is a group of stellar leaders, and they are leading an incredible, innovative work of God. But something in their thinking was blocking them from moving forward as the failing program was sucking away their cash reserves, as well as their time and energy.

Or take this example: Frequently, churches look at their small group system (or whatever kind of group they have) and think, *these small groups aren't really doing what we'd like them to do*. Maybe they want a higher percentage of overall attendees in groups from their worship service. Maybe their groups won't multiply. Maybe people stay in them for a while, but eventually they stop coming. Maybe people enjoy them, but, overall, aren't experiencing spiritual growth. Maybe they lack outward focus, and there's never any missional engagement beyond the existing members of the group.

"How do I fix this?" leaders ask. But what if that's the wrong question? What if starting with that question means you're almost guaranteed to end up without any innovation?

4.

Simon Sinek, in his book *Start with Why*, looks at a similar phenomenon that happens with many leaders and organizations. The problem, according to Sinek, is that most leaders focus almost exclusively on the *what* and the *how*. "All organizations start with *why*," he says, "but only the great ones keep their *why* clear year after year."

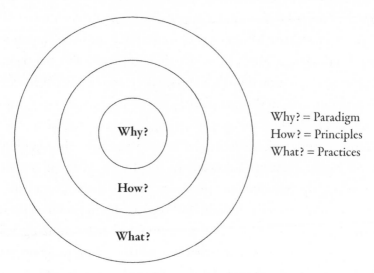

Why? = Paradigm
How? = Principles
What? = Practices

He calls this model the Golden Circle, and it's helpful when thinking about something like our small group problem.

When I'm working with leaders, I'm regularly having them go to the center of the Golden Circle and ask the question, "*Why* are we doing this, and *why are we doing it this way?*" Every leader knows what their organization does. Most know how their organization does it. But very few leaders have the discipline in good times and in difficult times to ask, "But *why* do we do it this way or even do it at all?"

The starting question isn't "How do we fix our small groups?" Perhaps the starting questions are "Why did we start small groups in the first place," and "How do we know when they are working?"

The original question, "How do we fix our small groups?" doesn't go deep enough. The normal starting place is to simply try to retool the method without first examining the mission and vision. But this is the tricky thing: Over time, the survival of the *vehicle* often becomes the prevailing *vision*, and the mission becomes about sustaining the *method*. The original question only allows us to see within the existing box, and it makes some major assumptions about the current method. The alternative starting questions, however, get to the heart of it: "Why did we start small groups in the first place?" "How do we know when they are working?" "What problem/s were small groups trying to solve?" "What mission are they trying to win?" Remember, all of these questions help us get at the key objective of the Identification Phase: Locate and frame the problem we're trying to solve. When we ask these questions, we quickly realize a fundamental principle: It matters *why* you start something.

Think about small groups again for a moment. If we go back and study when and why they started, we realize they came of age during the advent of the seeker-sensitive movement. Churches were attracting new attendees to their worship services, but they weren't necessarily keeping them. They had a "back door" problem. Leaders drew on the maxim, "Big events might attract people, but it's relationships that keep them." And so they started the modern small group strategy, which is something akin to relational flypaper for keeping new visitors and regular attendees in the church family.

Put simply, here is what we discover when examining the *why*: Small groups primarily exist to keep people from leaving.

So what's the point of this cultural flashback? The *why* of small groups, and the results we should expect for small groups, will almost always be in line with why we started them. So actually, for the reasons they were originally started, small groups might be really, really successful. In fact, in my work with thousands of church leaders, I'd anecdotally say when it comes to the purpose of small groups, this is the ranked order of what's most important to churches:

1. Prevent people from leaving the church
2. Community
3. Spiritual growth
4. Mission

So in this hypothetical situation with small groups, we would start the training process with the Identification Phase, to uncover the core innovation we are looking for. Are you looking for better small groups? Or are you solving a different problem? Are you looking for a disciple-making movement? Transformational community? Families on mission? All of the above? When we ask the deeper questions and clearly identify what we're going after, clarity begins to emerge around the innovation we're building toward.

Pastors are often frustrated that their programs, vehicles, or methods aren't producing the outcomes they desire. Perhaps they want small groups that exist as little spiritual families on mission together. But were they designed to do that? In considering how systems produce the required results (or the lack thereof!), W. Edwards Deming, the American engineer, professor, and statistician is credited with saying, "Every system is perfectly designed to get the results that it does." My sneaking suspicion is, if you're reading this book, you're not thrilled about the results you're getting (or, at the very least, you're aware that what "worked" in the past is starting to sunset). The bad news is the systems, structure, and culture you have in place are perfectly designed to get those results, even if that's not your intention.

The good news? It doesn't have to be that way.

Asking a *why* question is something we're less accustomed to. It's a different kind of question; it allows us to move beyond the practices we've become so familiar with and to start examining the paradigms and principles behind them. It's how Paul got off the boat in Philippi, and a continent saw its first church emerge. But it's not always the paradigms that shift. For Paul, what ultimately needed to shift were his practices. The playbook wasn't going to work in Philippi, so he threw it out and stepped into the future.

5.

The tragic (and surprising) story of Van Phillips might help us see how asking deeper and different questions is the ground floor of kingdom innovation.

In 1976, Van Phillips was twenty-one years old and at the peak of health. Warren Berger, in his exquisite book *A More Beautiful Question,* retells the story of Phillips:

> He was water skiing on a lake in Arizona when a small fire broke out on the boat pulling him. In the ensuing confusion, the boat's driver didn't see that a second motorboat, coming around a blind curve in the lake, was headed straight at Phillips.

Waking up in the hospital, coming out of general anesthesia, Phillips was understandably frightened to look under the blanket, but he mustered the courage and pulled back the covers. "There was an empty spot where his left foot should have been. The limb had been severed just below the knee by the other boat's propeller."

Not long after, he was fitted with a prosthetic limb, which consisted of a slab of pink foam attached to an aluminum tube.

This "new best friend" didn't prove all that friendly. In one of his first attempts to walk, he "tripped on a pebble the size of a pea" and hit the ground. His assessment? It was not working. Doctors, parents, friends ... they all told him the same thing: "You've got to get used to this."

Phillips recalls, "I bit my tongue. I knew [they] were right, in a way—I did have to accept that I was an amputee. But I would not accept that I had to wear that pink foot."

A little bit of detective work on his part showed very little innovation in the way of prosthetic limbs.

You can almost hear his inner monologue: *Why can't they make a better foot? Is the mission to just make a replacement foot and call it a day? Or is the mission to innovate a solution that could make the life of an amputee far more inhabitable?*

It's in this moment, Berger recounts, that

> Phillips exhibited one of the telltale signs of an innovative questioner: a refusal to accept the existing reality. As an outsider in that domain of [prosthetic limbs], Phillips was actually in the best position to ask questions. One of the many interesting and appealing things about questioning is that it often has an inverse relationship to expertise— such that, within their own subject areas, experts are apt to be poor questioners. Frank Lloyd Wright put it well when he remarked that an expert is someone who has "stopped thinking because he knows."

Rather than say "they" should make a better foot, Phillips decided to step into the fray. He would take on the responsibility of fixing his problem. (And so must we.) As Berger writes, "In a time when so much of what we know is subject to revision or obsolescence, the comfortable expert must go back to being the restless learner."

Well that's exactly what Van Phillips did. And even though his daily well-being was at stake, he wasn't in a rush. He kept asking questions from different angles, honing it, connecting things together. Polly Labarre, writing for the *Harvard Business Review*, describes the effect of asking these kinds of questions as, "fundamentally subversive, disruptive and playful and seem[ing] to switch people into the mode required to create anything new."

In his book *5Q*, Alan Hirsch introduces the concept of *soft eyes*. It's unclear where the phrase originated, but it seems to have become popularized on the television series *The Wire*, in which one of the detectives explains how to examine a crime scene. Hirsch recounts the salient point of the metaphor:

> If you have hard, cynical eyes, you're going to miss the details necessary to solve the crime. Hard eyes have already reached a conclusion before really seeing the scene. Most of us aren't homicide detectives, of course, but we all require soft eyes at numerous critical junctures of life. A doctor needs soft eyes in diagnosing a complex medical syndrome; a mechanic when repairing the electrics of a motor vehicle; a political analyst in anticipating global trends; the economist tracking the invisible hand of the market; the scientist doing breakthrough research; a scriptwriter in a successful TV series; a computer programmer in developing the killer app; the business entrepreneur in seeking to exploit unanticipated gaps in the market; and so on. In fact, hard eyes—the unwillingness to look deeper in order to accurately diagnose the real situation—in any of these situations would likely prove to be disastrous.

What Van Phillips had were soft eyes. He kept looking deeper, and as he did, honed his core question to something with an innovative punch: "If they can put a man on the moon, why can't they make a decent foot?"

> The more Phillips learned, the more questions he had: About the materials being used (Why wood, when there are so many better alternatives?); about the shape (Why did a prosthetic foot have to be shaped like a bulky human foot? Does that even make sense?); about the primary purpose of the replacement foot (Why was there so much emphasis on trying to match the look of a human foot? Wasn't performance the most important part?).

You see how these are all *why* questions? In the Identification Phase, we bring these questions to the forefront, allowing them to disrupt, confront, and ultimately frame the challenge at hand. Not every question has to begin with the word *Why*, but it's always digging at a deeper understanding of the core problem, insight, or idea. "A journey of inquiry," Berger comments, "is bound to lead you into the unknown (as it should), but if you have a sense of the kinds of questions to ask at various stages along the way, you've at least got some road markers."

Perhaps that's why Albert Einstein said, "We can't solve problems by using the same kind of thinking we used when we created them." That's what asking deeper and different questions in the Identification Phase does for us. It challenges our own thinking about the problem itself. The Jewish theologian Abraham Joshua Heschel frames it in a similar way: "Our sight is suffused with knowing, instead of feeling painfully the lack of knowing what we see. The principle to be kept in mind is to know what we see *rather* than to see what we know."

The way to start the innovation process, therefore, is by asking different questions.

In their excellent book *Future Church*, Will Mancini and Cory Hartman put it like this:

> When you consider retooling [the organized church for mission], it is natural to ask, "How can we make our worship, connection, and service programs facilitate practice better?" Yet that is the incremental question. The more radical question is 'If there were many disciple-making disciples in this community and no publicly visible churches, why would they create one? What would it do?"

In my experience of working with churches, denominations, and networks, the ability to ask these kinds of powerful questions poses one of the greatest challenges. Not because, as some might assume, these leaders don't want to question anything. Rather, guiding people in an innovation process with these kinds of questions is a skill set in and of itself. There have been many times when I've felt the underlying tension rumbling around inside of leaders who know they need to go after something fresh and new, but they don't know the right questions or process to get them there. It's not just about courage; it's about skill. It's a sense that they're on the cusp of something, but it just won't reveal itself.

Central to innovation is the idea of disruption. Disruptive innovation seeks to interrupt the status quo, bringing fresh eyes, thinking, and practices to places that feel tired or stuck. Van Phillips wasn't looking to disrupt the prosthetics market; he wanted to interrupt the status quo of the foam foot. But we've all been there, haven't we? We've been the friends and family telling Van Phillips to adjust, and we've also been those leaders in the room who know something more is needed, but feeling powerless to produce it.

What made Van Philipps unique was his ability to ask questions outside of his relative area of expertise. He didn't make prosthetics for a living; he was just asking common sense questions. He wasn't a pioneer, and he didn't have a holy discontent; he just had a practical need that was driving the innovation. Some of the most impactful kingdom innovations don't come from anything other than God multiplying something that was a breakthrough in the life of one person. But almost always, that person has soft eyes to ask different kinds of questions.

Hirsch, again in *5Q*, puts it this way:

Christian leaders will need soft eyes if they are to negotiate the increasing complexities of the world in which they are responsible to lead. Our human craving for easy answers, ready-made formulas, quick fixes, stability, and order have made our eyes hard and have predisposed us to simply repeating what we already know. But as a result, we have been blinded to the deeper patterns, concepts, and potentialities that God has built into human life, the church, and in his cosmos. Soft eyes are therefore necessary to see beyond what has become overfamiliar and habitual.

And that's exactly what happened with Phillips. The questions he was asking, the notes he was scribbling down, and the ideas he was tinkering around with started to connect to some unlikely memories. When he was growing up, his dad had a unique C-shaped Chinese sword, which was part of his antique collection. It spurred an idea in his mind: "Instead of a traditional L-shaped lower leg and foot, what if he dispensed with the heel and created a limb that was one smooth, continuous curve, from leg to toe?"

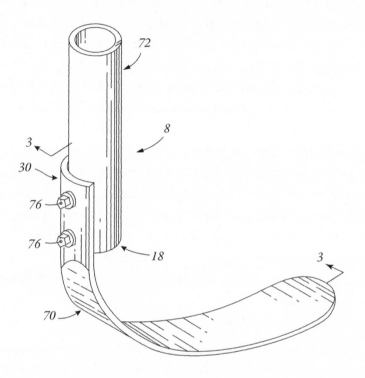

Phillips started developing the Flex-Foot prosthetic in the early 1980s and it revolutionized the industry. He later sold the company in 2000. There were different models, but perhaps the most well-known is the prototype known as the Cheetah. As Bergen writes in his analysis:

> Using Phillips' creation, an amputee climbed Mount Everest; the runner Aimee Mullins became the first double amputee to compete in the NCAA track and field for Georgetown University; and most famously (and now notoriously), the South African runner Oscar Pistorius ran on two Cheetahs as he competed in the Olympics. As

for Phillips himself, [it] enabled him to return to one of his deepest passions in life: He now runs every day on the beach near his home in Mendocino, California.

For Phillips, the mission wasn't to find a foot that *looked like* a real foot; the mission was to get the *performance* of a real foot.

There's a universe of difference between those two objectives.

What does the story of Van Phillips tell us?

If you're a socialpreneur, your vision isn't simply to make money: You want to help transform the world for the common good. If you're running a non-profit, your mission isn't about beating last year's fundraising tally: You need money to fund the vision, but it's only worth it if lives are changing. If you're a pastor, the mission of your church probably isn't to get people to show up and then hopefully stick around long enough to get nicer over time and throw some money in the offering plate. No, you want something much bigger for them, don't you? You want them to have a life utterly transformed by the power of God. A life so transformed that God then uses them to transform other lives, businesses, cities, culture, and beyond.

Can you import solutions, models, and ideas from other places? Absolutely. We always want to learn from others. For every church, common good business, or non-profit, it will probably look different because of your vision, values, theology, and convictions. But we don't have to reinvent the wheel every time, and it's arrogant to assume we need to. But sometimes ... sometimes ... your church doesn't need Andy Stanley's small group system or whatever the newest famous business leader came up with.

What you need is to innovate, develop, and run on your own Flex-Foot Cheetah.

LEADER INNOVATION LAB

KEY PRINCIPLES FROM PHASE 1: IDENTIFICATION

Goal: We must frame the start of this journey by locating the big idea and framing the problem we're trying to solve.

Two Foundational Innovation Myths
- Innovation starts with a big eureka moment.
- Some people can innovate, others can't.

Overcoming the Poison Pill
- What are the myths we believe when it comes to locating the big idea?
- What barriers do we need to overcome?

Kingdom Innovation Comes from Three Different Places
- A pioneering mind
- Necessity
- Holy discontent

Cultivation
In order to synthesize what we're learning, we need to explore, hone, research, and connect our emerging ideas to other ideas.

Slow Hunches and Half-ideas
This is what we are cultivating. An idea doesn't go from nothing to formed in 3.2 seconds. We develop hunches and unformed ideas that evolve over time.

Ask the Why Questions
Why are we doing this and *why are we doing it this way?*

The 3 Ps We Need Alignment on

Examine the *paradigms* and the *principles* that support all of our current *practices* to begin with.

Soft Eyes

The ability to see and experience the world optimistically, with possibility, and without the belief that we already know all of the answers. The ability to see "deeper patterns, concepts, and potentialities that God has built into human life."

The Master Tool for the Identification Phase: The What's Your Why? Tool

As an innovation strategist regularly working with Christian leaders, I developed the five phases of kingdom innovation as a way to not only help teams navigate around the constraints and brick walls they were facing, but to pivot and springboard off of them. For each phase, there is a particular Master Tool that will help you navigate that part of the process.

PHASE 1:
IDENTIFICATION

WHAT'S YOUR
WHY? TOOL

Watch the training video for the What's Your Why? Master Tool at DougPaul.org/ReadyorNotLab

Nuts-and-Bolts Leader Coaching

In this section, at the conclusion of each phase, I'll give one or two pieces of practical coaching to help implement a few of the ideas in your life and leadership. For more practical insights, including some free training, you can visit: DougPaul.org/ReadyorNotLab .

As we've explored in this phase, innovation doesn't happen because a light bulb, seemingly out of nowhere, simply "lit up." No one finds a magic "innovation faucet" and innovation juice just starts flowing out. No, innovation happens when half-ideas and slow hunches are cultivated over a long period of time.

Steven Johnson shares this practical piece of advice: "So part of the secret hunch of cultivation is simple: write everything down." I've certainly found this to be the case, as have a number of people I work with. Personally, I use the Evernote app, and half of my life is probably in there. But I have a number of different folders. For instance, one folder is called "Teaching Metaphors," where I'm able to capture pictures, videos, stories for future sermons, content illustrations, or book fodder when I run across it. Another is called "Innovation Pathways," where I capture new intel on what other practitioners are doing. I've got one called "Articles Worth Saving," which is a simple way of cutting and pasting links of articles I thought were significant, profound, or helpful, and why I thought so at the time. And I also have a folder called "Big Ideas," which is a place where I simply capture random ideas or hunches.

All we're doing is tracking and cultivating ideas *as we have them*. Rather than designating, "this is the time for new ideas," we've baptized all of life into this space. The radar is up all of the time.

At least once a month, I open up my "Big Ideas" folder and read through everything in there, jotting down new hunches or learning, or connecting dots to other things as I go. It probably takes twenty to thirty minutes and then I move on. I also regularly make time to do this with my team, or will send random texts with questions to people I'd love feedback from. Personally, I set aside time and space when I do this to listen to what God is saying and stirring in me. Is this a yes, no, not you, or not yet? Or maybe it's still unclear.

If there's clarity on what God is saying, then we can move.

Core Question Idea Starters

Included in these practical application sections will be some idea starters around six core components of Christian life I want to explore: Discipleship, Leadership, Mission, Worship, Reconciliation, and the Operating System of the church, business, or organization. These aren't exhaustive, nor are the idea starters inherently "right." They are meant to illustrate a key insight from the chapter and start you down the road of discovery.

The first set of questions are going to focus on the paradigm shift that can often happen as we journey through kingdom innovation. For this phase, we'll explore questions related to the church. In future phases, we'll broaden it to include non-profits, socialpreneurs, and businesses.

Discipleship

Current Question	The *Why* Question	The *New* Question
How do we get more people into groups?	Why does Jesus' plan in the Great Commission rest on making disciples?	How do we catalyze a reproducible movement of disciple-making that forms people like the people we see in the New Testament?

Leadership

Current Question	The *Why* Question	The *New* Question
How do we find more leaders to run the programs we have?	Why has God set aside "good works" for each leader to do?	How do we create a self-generating leadership pipeline that develops people into the leaders God created them to be in every place and space they inhabit?

Mission

Current Question	The *Why* Question	The *New* Question
How do we get more people to come to our worship service and/or programs?	Why don't we see more people leading their friends and family to faith?	How do we equip and mobilize our church family to go into the places they live, work, and play with the good news of Jesus?

Worship

Current Question	The *Why* Question	The *New* Question
How do we make sure our worship music and preaching are relevant?	Why aren't more of our people worshippers outside of weekend worship services?	How do we use the worship service to shape people to be worshippers in all 168 hours of a week?

Reconciliation

Current Question	The *Why* Question	The *New* Question
How do we get a more diverse church?	Why do we want to be a diverse church?	How do we live out our calling into the "ministry of reconciliation" while living in such a racialized culture?

Operating System

Current Question	The *Why* Question	The *New* Question
How do we grow our church?	Why is the overall % of lostness of our city increasing even when we grow numerically?	How do we go after gospel saturation of a place in collaboration with other churches in our city?

This is a Spiritual Process

Probably the most important thing to hear, and I'll return to it often, is that kingdom innovation is an inherently spiritual process. Paul ends up in Philippi and not in Ephesus because of the work of the Spirit. It would be easy to ever-so-subtly believe that this was true with Paul, but not so with us.

What I'm suggesting is that if we want to find the future, kingdom innovation cannot be done apart from the leading and sustaining of the Holy Spirit.

Chances are there are many problems you're looking to solve. How do you know which innovation to chase, which idea is right, and which ones might be the result of a taco night gone bad? Well, we have the Word of God, the body of Christ, and the Holy Spirit working through all of those different possibilities. In the same way that Paul was sensitive to what the Spirit was up to, so must we be. Just because we think something is a good idea, doesn't mean we should move on it. Just because there's a need, doesn't mean we're meant to move toward finding an immediate solution. Just because there's a prophetic stirring, doesn't mean I have enough to go on. It takes the ongoing work of the Holy Spirit.

The challenge, however, is not simply to get the "green light" from the Holy Spirit and move on from there. The Holy Spirit is not just the one who initiates the innovation process, but the active force for driving it forward and achieving breakthrough. Just because I have the word to "go" doesn't mean I know "how" the Spirit wants to drive it. The Holy Spirit isn't interested in inspiring the idea and then handing the baton to us. Most of us would never say that, but that's how we functionally lead. We need the Holy Spirit to initiate and sustain this process, and part of that process will be owning exactly where God has placed you, what he is calling you to, and finally, that it's going to cost you something. Because make no mistake, there will be a death to self and a cost involved. The only way to come through that tunnel of spiritual chaos is to have a Spirit-saturated life and process. As Paul said, "Since we live by the Spirit, let us keep in step with the Spirit."

In the downloadable Case Studies for the Identification Phase, you'll notice it's no coincidence that we're seeing transformational innovation through the work of Rob Wegner, Bryan Phipps, and Todd Milby. Being around Todd Milby in the morning is a powerful thing, because you never quite know where it's going to go. For decades, he's gotten up, read his Bible, spent time in prayer and worship, taken a walk, and for the first few hours of the day, most conversations start with the "fresh bread" God has given him that morning, which becomes his nourishment for the day. It doesn't matter who he's with or what the purpose of the meeting is. Chances are, the meeting will start with what God is stirring in him through the Scriptures and his time in prayer. There is no substitute or shortcut for this within the process of kingdom innovation.

Bryan Phipps, who catalyzed a disciple-making movement in Kansas City, says his spiritual life is "like breadcrumbs leading from one place to the other; it's just regular dependence. My favorite times are walks in the morning after my daily devotions. It's a process of working out that big idea I picked out in the Scriptures, and the action stuff that goes with it. I pray for this, go through that, list new ideas, pray some more."

Again from the Case Studies, as Rob Wegner considers what God has accomplished through his innovative work: "I probably stayed two years too long [in one ministry] because I wasn't listening to the

Spirit. And it really hurt my soul. It harmed my marriage. So you have to be walking in the Spirit enough so that when the Spirit highlights something, you can respond. It's almost always out of the corner of my eye. It's not directly in front of me. It's off in the margins, so the innovation is happening on the edges."

Dr. Ethel Percy Andrus felt something stir in her soul when she saw a destitute teacher, and Bill Wilson met God after fourteen years of searching for a cure.

These are the kinds of brave leaders we need if we are to find the future of the church together.

As you get a sense of the specific thing unfolding before you that God is inviting you to innovate with him, start to ask the big, beautiful *why* questions. But as you do, be continually aware of what the Holy Spirit is up to. As Jesus says in John 5:19: "he can do only what he sees his Father doing." This must also be our call.

2

IDEATION

CHAPTER THREE

The Curse Comes Calling

"ONCE WE KNOW SOMETHING, WE FIND IT HARD TO
IMAGINE WHAT IT WAS LIKE NOT TO KNOW IT."

1.

Opportunity knocked for twenty-three-year-old Richard Warren
Sears one day at the rail station in North Redwood, Minnesota. The
year? 1886.

Serving as a station agent for the St. Louis Railway Co., he regularly
witnessed a very particular scam, and this day, oh yes, this day would
produce a very different outcome. The scam went something like this:
Wholesalers would ship their goods to retailers and ask for payment for
the order, at a price that was steep for the goods-on-hand. The retailer,
having never ordered the product in the first place, would refuse to pay.
The wholesaler, pretending the whole thing was a mistake, would hem
and haw about the expense of shipping and losing their shirt in the
process. Finally, they'd ask the retailer if they would take the products
at a ridiculously discounted rate. The retailer, thinking they're getting
the steal of the century, agrees to the "bargain price." In the end, the
wholesaler makes above what they were expecting in the first place and
the retailer barely breaks even.

On this particular day in 1886, however, the scam backfires. The
hustlers try to play a local jeweler by the name of Edward Stegerson,
but he isn't biting on a shipment of gold watches. He'd seen the scam
before and flatly turns down the offer. Well, now it was the wholesaler

who was stuck. Shipping was expensive, and they had sunk up-front capital into the production of these watches, which were now just sitting on a railway station platform.

At this point, Richard Sears, who's had his eye on the whole state of affairs, steps in and gets the wholesalers to agree to a different kind of arrangement: He'll buy the watches for $12 from the wholesaler, but whatever amount he makes on top of that, he gets to keep. Furthermore, they'll have to take back any watches he doesn't sell. He has them over a barrel.

Sears buys the watches and sells them up and down the railway line to the other station agents. They sell like hotcakes on a cold winter morning, and within six months he makes $5,000 (which in today's dollars, would be worth about $126,000). Sears quickly incorporates his company in Minneapolis, and, within a year, moves to Chicago. He reinvests his money, expands operations, and scales up.

Flyers start showing up in mailboxes in the towns and cities dotting the path of the railway. He places ads in farming magazines and writes copy that everyday people can understand. The first Sears catalogue is mailed in 1893, and it only carries watches. Shortly thereafter it expands to other jewelry. Then men's and women's clothes. It keeps growing in size and scope—from seed to plows, silverware to bicycles, and everything in-between.

The magazine was the first of its kind, and it popped. Two years in, Sears, Roebuck & Co. was mailing three hundred thousand catalogues of more than five hundred pages each. They catered to neglected and forgotten rural communities. No longer would farmers and those living in remote areas suffer from understocked general stores and overpriced merchandise—with a few orders from the Sears catalogue, the life of the ordinary farmer and their family was transformed.

As they scaled up their raw production and mailing numbers, the company became a well-oiled machine. But, in a way we've already explored, the culture shifted beneath their feet. The innovation of the car wasn't just a game changer for the urban manure crisis; it changed the way Americans interacted in many aspects of ordinary life. Suddenly, it no longer took most of a working day to get to a physical store, and chain stores became far more appealing. So what did Sears do? They got into the bricks-and-mortar retail business. By 1931, Sears made more money through its stores than through its catalogues.

Sears started to produce its own offshoot brands: Kenmore, Allstate, Craftsman, Dean Witter, and many more. By 1969, it was the largest retailer in the world and one of the most profitable and respected businesses of the twentieth century. Four years later, they opened the Sears Tower in their home city as a monument to their success. Surpassing the height of the World Trade Center in New York City, the skyscraper (now renamed Willis Tower) was a visible reminder of their innovative approach and their ability to pivot as culture changed.

And within forty short years of building this monument, the company would be all but dead.

2.

In the pages of this book so far, we've seen that extraordinary innovation is less about big moments or the DNA of pioneering minds and more about cultivating slow hunches, half-ideas, and asking different (and better) questions.

In this chapter, we'll dig deeper into why we so rarely see original ideas, and in doing so, I want to introduce you to the Villain of our story. For years, we've held assumptions about what it means to have experience and expertise, but what if we've been making a critical error in these assumptions? Bill Wilson went to the professionals and didn't find what he needed. Henry Ford was the expert, and yet in the 1920s he ran Ford into the ground. There was no one better in the business at selling home goods than Sears, and then they filed for bankruptcy.

Not far from the long shadow of the Sears Tower is a very different Chicago.

The southside of the city is renowned in the same way Compton is: More about notoriety than fame. Both neighborhoods are known for extreme poverty, broken systems, and regular moments of touch-and-go violence. They are also known for producing some of the most urgent and inspired modern art and compelling stories of the last thirty years. Perhaps you've even heard Chance the Rapper's song "Dear Chicago Summer," in which he compares his Chicagoland neighborhood to East Compton.

Unfortunately, you've probably heard the overused cliché a thousand times: People born into these neighborhoods rarely "get out."

Jonathan Brooks was one of the many kids born on the southside of Chicago in the late 1970s and 1980s, specifically into a neighborhood called Englewood. Raised by a single mom who believed education was the shortest train out of poverty and a culture of violence, Jonathan was given opportunities that other kids in Englewood would almost certainly miss. His mother got him into the right schools, found magnet programs and did whatever it took, so that one day he could "get out."

As with many kids growing up at this time in predominantly black neighborhoods, going to church wasn't optional—it was as intertwined with life as blockbuster movies are to summers, or Big Macs are to special sauce. As a child, Brooks loved the unique culture of the black church. But as he moved into his teenage years, three different things hit at the same time: 1) A love for hip-hop music and hip-hop culture. 2) Attendance at mostly affluent white middle and high schools with little interest (or even awareness) of black culture. 3) A growing disillusionment with the church and how it intersected with the rest of his life.

For a kid growing up in Englewood, Jonathan Brooks beat the odds and ended up with his pick of colleges. But something was stirring deep within him: Questions about identity and blackness, questions that others would also give voice to, including writers such as

Ta-Nehisi Coates, Bryan Stevenson, and Eugene Robinson: *Who am I as a black man in America?*

Brooks chose Tuskegee University, Alabama, one of the most distinguished colleges in the United States, and one of the standard bearers for Historical Black Colleges and Universities (HBCUs). There, he was free to explore what it meant to be black, while walking in the same hallowed halls as Booker T. Washington, Winston C. Hackett, Ralph Ellison, Roscoe Simmons, General Oliver Dillard ... among many other greats. But his choice also delivered one essential ingredient: It was far away from Englewood and far away from his home church.

The funny thing about Alabama, though, is it had a vibrant church—particularly the black church! Over time, Brooks found himself back inside the sanctuary of a church building. But this time, it wasn't because he had to; it was by choice. Faith was taking root and blooming in new and unexpected ways.

Not long after graduating college, Brooks received a heartbreaking phone call: His mom had suffered a serious stroke while teaching her pre-K class, and there was no one to look after her or Brooks' adopted brother. It didn't seem like much of a choice: Jonathan had to move back to Chicago. As he wrote in his memoir, *Church Forsaken*:

> I felt a deep pit in my stomach, wondering how I ended up back here ... I knew it was the right decision to come back to Chicago after graduating from Tuskegee University, but that feeling did not remove the frustration of finally making it out of the inner city just to find myself back again.

Brooks had received an architecture degree and found a job in Chicago—but he hated it. So he quit and found a new opportunity right in front of him, serving as the youth pastor of the church his mom now attended: Canaan Missionary Baptist Church (later referred to as Canaan Community Church). "I was offered the position for two reasons. First, I already had an existing relationship with the teens at the church ... they already knew me as 'Jay.' Second, to be honest, no one wanted the job."

The years to come would prove fruitful: Marriage, a master's degree in education, children. The youth group that started with seven to eight kids was now bursting at the seams and was intersecting Jesus, family, hip-hop, and neighborhood life. Then, out of nowhere, the senior pastor announced he'd accepted a position from his hometown in North Carolina and gave Brooks a thinly veiled ultimatum: "I am offering you the position today, and if you take it, we will announce next week that you're going to be pastor. If you decide not to take the position, then we will make the congregation aware that the doors of the church will be closing, and they should find a new church home."

As you might have guessed, the following Sunday it was announced to a bewildered and slightly shocked congregation that Jonathan Brooks was their new pastor. Or at least to serve as the interim pastor until they could find a suitable replacement.

Seemingly forced into a position he hadn't asked for, Brooks began on one of the biggest days of the year on the black church calendar: Mother's Day.

Leaving his seat, he stepped into the pulpit, and after welcoming everyone and praying, he started his sermon.

"I could see a young man from the neighborhood walk inside the sanctuary and motion to another young man in the back row to come outside," Brooks recounts. "Now, I knew both of them ... Just as I was about to name the passage of Scripture, [one of them] stepped onto the front steps of the church, and a large group of guys rushed at him and began to beat him violently."

Brooks yelled for help, frantically pointing to the back of the sanctuary, but he was the only one who could see what was happening. Finally, people started to turn around and look in disbelief at the full-on melee that had broken out on the front steps of the church on Mother's Day morning.

Bang! Bang!

Two shots rang out.

3.

In 1990, a famous study was conducted at Stanford University by a student named Elizabeth Newton. She gathered a group of people together and divided them into two sets: "tappers" and "listeners."

Here's how the study worked: A tapper was partnered with a listener, and each was given a list of twenty-five popular songs like "Happy Birthday" or "The Star-Spangled Banner." The tapper secretly selected a song and tapped the rhythm of the song by knocking on a table in front of them. The listener, having twenty-five songs to choose from, was to name the song the tapper was knocking out on the table.

Newton conducted the experiment 120 times. Any guess on how many times the listener correctly named the song being tapped out?

Three.

Three out of 120. That's 2.5 percent.

But this is where it gets really interesting. After the tapper knocked out the rhythm of the song, but before the listener gave their guess, Newton asked the tapper to guess the chances the listener would get it right.

Where'd they place the odds?

50 percent.

The results would in fact yield not 50 percent correct guesses—but just over 2 in 100.

If you do this a few times with friends or family, you start to see the same kind of response Newton was seeing in the tappers. They were increasingly frustrated and irritated. Here's what researchers say is happening: When you tap the rhythm out of the song, you've got the song playing in your head. You can almost hear it. *You can't not hear it.* But at the same time you're tapping out the tune, the listener isn't hearing anything in their head. They just have a list of random songs to pick from and something resembling the sound of unidentifiable Morse code coming straight at them.

What it produced in the tappers was an emotional reaction that went something like this: *How could you be so stupid? How can you not hear it? It's so freaking obvious!*

In the introduction of this book, we examined how Henry Ford, one of the greatest pioneers of the twentieth century, never really got over the Model T. Why? Because he was wrestling with the same Villain at work with the tappers and the listeners. One of the biggest Villains in our great journey toward kingdom innovation is known as the *Curse of Knowledge*. In *Made to Stick*, Dan and Chip Heath write that, "Once we know something, we find it hard to imagine what it was like not to know it." In a sense, our knowledge has "cursed" us.

The second phase of the process of kingdom innovation is *ideation: We must generate whole new practices, concepts, and ways of thinking if we're going to solve our innovation challenge.* Simply put, ideation is the act of forming new ideas. But the Curse of Knowledge? Our Villain? It's the thing that blocks our capacity to generate these new ideas. It's like we can't see beyond our suddenly limited vantage point of how to do something quite differently.

As organizational psychologist and Wharton business school professor Adam Grant writes in his book *Originals*, "The more expertise and experience people gain, the more entrenched they become in a particular way of viewing the world. ... As we gain knowledge about a domain, we become prisoners of our prototypes."

The funny thing is, the Curse of Knowledge impacts us and our leadership in all kinds of ways.

Consider what ultimately led to the downfall of Sears.

The company was killing it in the early 1980s. They were one of the most respected retailers in the world, and were by no means newbies when it came to digital technology. In some ways, they were right on the bleeding edge of early tech innovation. They had money to invest, but for some reason, even as the internet morphed into everyday life in the late 1990s, they couldn't see past their own bricks-

and-mortar stores. By 2004, the retail game had swung Walmart's way, and a buyout occurred, with Sears and Kmart merging forces; two fading retailers coming under one holding company.

There is a great irony in this situation. Sears viewed Walmart as their greatest competitor. By conventional wisdom, Walmart should have perceived Target, with its "cheap chic" aesthetic, to be their prime market challenger. But Walmart was able to see what neither Target nor Sears could see. Their biggest competitor wasn't another bricks-and-mortar retailer.

It was Amazon.

As Walmart started to pour money into revolutionizing their online platform and marrying together digital and bricks-and-mortar services, Sears double-downed on stores and essentially pressed pause on digital innovation. Their subsidiary Kmart was losing money hand over fist, and the revenue from Sears needed to be diverted into shoring up the drowning company.

In 2006, the combined profits of Sears and Kmart was $1.5 billion. By 2010, it was almost zero (you read that correct). Between 2011 and 2016, Sears Holding Co. hemorrhaged money, losing $10.4 billion, and finally, filed for Chapter 11 bankruptcy.

So exactly how did that happen? Think back to the tappers and the listeners. The tappers couldn't unhear the song playing in their heads in the same way Sears executives couldn't unhear the unparalleled success of their bricks-and-mortar stores. Their expertise was the song in their heads. It was the Curse of Knowledge.

One of the markers of the "curse" is expertise and experience clouding our ability to hear or see what's going on around us. There's an ever-increasing gap between "experts" and the rest of the world.

Think about Henry Ford and the Model T. He was an expert in efficiency and brought together several inventions to form one great innovation to make our lives permanently more efficient. But all around him, people were starting to ask for something different, and it wasn't something Ford was terribly interested in pursuing.

The same was true of Sears. There was a window of time when they could have branched into something new and innovative; after all, the invention of the internet brought huge potential for all areas of business. But Sears were experts in bricks-and-mortar retail and were slow to budge from their ivory tower. Eventually, that ivory tower of expertise became a prison, and they couldn't find the way out.

The expertise that had made Sears so successful ultimately became the thing that killed it. Success created walls that made it increasingly difficult to see new and different ways of doing things. It's the Curse of Knowledge. As humans, we start to self-protect what we know how to do.

Could that help explain why some of the brightest and most creative leaders and organizations, having tasted success with a winning innovation, proceed to hit a giant brick wall?

4.

Let's take the Curse of Knowledge idea one step further.

We return to Jonathan Brooks, because the rest of the story is going to show us the left hook of the "curse."

For Brooks, the good news is that those two gunshots didn't come from the fight happening outside of the church building, but rather, from Mark Yelverton, an off-duty police officer whose gun was pointed straight to the sky. Those involved in the brawl stopped, looked straight at the gun, and ran off across Garfield Boulevard.

Police cars, ambulances, and fire trucks quickly screamed down the street to the church, and Brooks returned to the sanctuary, locking the door behind him. "I saw the mothers, wives, and daughters distraughtly hugging their sons, husbands, and fathers," Brooks recalls. "Some [were] gently wiping blood from their lips and brows. ... I remembered I was a pastor and everyone was looking for me to provide an answer. Walking down that aisle was one of the longest and most excruciatingly intimidating walks of my life."

When Jonathan hit the pulpit, a sentence burst through his lips, a play on the words of the church tagline, *where love makes a difference*: "Welcome to Canaan Community Church, where *guns* make a difference!"

The congregation erupted in laughter.

That day, something was planted in Brooks: He had an emerging insight about Englewood, and a hunch about how the church needed to innovate. Something was crystallizing.

Often, in neglected and under-resourced neighborhoods, there isn't a shortage of churches. But many churches have a history like Canaan Community Church, where the majority of the residents left the neighborhood long ago, desperate to escape the cascading effects of poverty. Even when a new church is planted and tries to reach the residents of the neighborhood, leaders and members usually choose to live outside the geographical area. In both cases, the church is telegraphing a message that Brooks received his entire life: *You need to "get out."* Like 90 percent of the church congregation, the Brooks family didn't live in Englewood. He, his pregnant wife, and daughter lived on the South Shore of Chicago in an apartment building facing Lake Michigan, a fifteen to twenty-minute drive from the neighborhood. Chicago is a city of seventy-seven very distinct neighborhoods, and even this short drive felt like a million miles away from Englewood.

"Babe," Brooks said to his wife, "I think God is telling me to move back to Englewood."

This isn't what Miche'al wanted to hear. And it's not what Brooks wanted to hear either, quite honestly. But soon after, the family of four moved to Englewood, setting off a chain of events that would change not only their life and the church's life, but the whole neighborhood itself.

Jonathan Brooks received a holy deposit into his spirit and saw the neighborhood not as the city saw it, or even as the residents saw it, but as God saw it. And that's an important point for us to log in our process of kingdom innovation: We need to develop a keen sense of what God is up to and what he is saying in the moment and have the spiritual capacity to wait until his revelation comes.

Think back to Paul at the beginning of his second journey, stuck in modern-day Turkey, not knowing where to go, only knowing where *not to go*. The Spirit kept blocking his path and Paul yielded to the Spirit's work. Ultimately, Paul received a prophetic message in a dream, a man from Macedonia saying, "Come ... help us."

Jonathan Brooks similarly received a prophetic revelation. People saw something to escape, but God saw a place he sent his only Son for. People saw the blights and brokenness, but God saw hope and healing. It was worth investing in and sacrificing for. The neighborhood was *good*.

If you spend five minutes in conversation with Brooks, you're bound to hear a quote from Jon Fuller, the former director of Overseas Missionary Fellowship: "There are no God-forsaken places, just church-forsaken places." Maybe you can see how the half-ideas and slow hunches were starting to connect for Brooks: What if the neighborhood was the way it was because the church had forsaken it? What if Canaan Community Church could live into the paradigm that the neighborhood was *already* good, but it needed Christians living and investing there? What if it wasn't something to escape but something to embrace as home?

This was it. The sun was rising in the east, and the day of dawning was coming. The innovation was within grasp.

Not long after, Jonathan Brooks strode up the steps into the pulpit, into the same sanctuary as the Mother's Day Melee, and said, "If you're not from Englewood, either move into the neighborhood and own the responsibility for it, or leave this church."

He almost didn't make it out of the sanctuary alive.

5.

For Jonathan Brooks, the Curse of Knowledge hit in a similar way to the tappers and the listeners. In the same way the tappers were hearing "Happy Birthday" play in their heads, Jonathan Brooks was hearing his revelation about the neighborhood of Englewood: *God loves this neighborhood. And a church made up of people in this neighborhood could change everything.*

The problem, of course, is that no one else had yet had this revelation. And that is the left hook of the Curse of Knowledge: Being able to see something, but struggling to communicate it to those who haven't been on the same journey.

Just because Brooks conveyed the idea to his congregation didn't mean it would take root for them. He himself only received the "good neighborhood" revelation after *years* of experiences, filled with half-ideas and slow hunches, along with an insight from the Holy Spirit. So, in some ways, it was inevitable that standing up one Sunday and calling his congregation to move to the neighborhood was never going to cut it. This was too big a leap for everyone, even if it was a seemingly logical plan. What seemed like one step forward for Brooks felt like a jump the size of the Grand Canyon for everyone else. They couldn't see what he could see. All they could see was a neighborhood that was run down, violent, drug ridden, and quite frankly, dangerous.

Brooks was staring the Curse of Knowledge square in the face. He'd cast the vision for folks to move back into the neighborhood, and no one was biting. This revelation had put a melody in his head that no one else could hear and a vision no one else could see. I imagine his inner monologue perpetually returned to the same thought: *Why can't they see what I see?*

But before we cast judgment, let's remember we're not so different from him, are we? As leaders, how many times have we thought something similar: *How can everyone else not see this? Why don't they understand? Why are they so hardheaded? How can they not get it? Don't they know that if they just do this one thing, everything will change?*

Like a great villain in an epic story, the Curse of Knowledge is one of the key reasons why substantive kingdom innovation rarely happens. Recall back to what we said about Phase 1. If Phase 1 is about identification and framing the required innovation, Jonathan Brooks had successfully identified the problem: He needed a way to transform the neighborhood, so it reflected more of heaven itself. If in heaven there is no poverty or violence or homelessness, that's what he wanted to see in Englewood. But what the story of Brooks shows us is that even with the crystal-clear identification of where we need breakthrough, we are so often captive to our own expertise or the "tapper rhythms" only we can hear. The thing we know most deeply can quickly become a cage to creative thinking and miraculous problem solving.

Even our own success starts to work against us. How can we break through the prison of our own experiences and expertise to get new and fresh ideas? And how can our success, expertise, and experience come into play in a way that's helpful rather than a hindrance?

If we want to understand how we can leverage our strengths, how to beat back the Curse of Knowledge, and understand how God is breaking through, we need to learn a little about something called *the Moonshot.*

CHAPTER FOUR

The Moonshot Rule

"IT WASN'T UNTIL WE TRIED A MOBILE VERSION THAT
WE NOTICED A DIFFERENCE IN PEOPLE, INCLUDING
OURSELVES."

1.

In September 1962, on grainy, black-and-white tube televisions all
across the United States, John F. Kennedy threw down a challenge,
ending his speech to forty thousand people at Rice Stadium in
Houston, Texas on a surprising and awe-inspiring note:

> We choose to go to the Moon in this decade and do the other things,
> not because they are easy, but because they are hard.

As twenty-first-century readers, it's hard for us to grasp just how
outrageous these words would have sounded to their original listeners.
But make no mistake, this was earth-shattering, and Kennedy's speech
coined the word "Moonshot"—an undertaking of something so
ambitious, so out of the realm of possibility, that it seems halfway crazy.

In many ways, the Moonshot gives us the key to overcoming the
Curse of Knowledge: something so audacious, so unlikely, it breaks
us out of the cage of our creative thinking.

The Moonshot defeats the Curse of Knowledge. How? By slaying
the foundational belief that you can do it.

Why is this important? Because it breaks the glass ceiling that's
been holding back our capacity for ideation, our ability to see beyond

our own experience and expertise. The point is our current capacity and skills can't accomplish the Moonshot. So we're going to have to think, see, and respond differently.

This is essential for kingdom innovation, because this very spiritual process only becomes possible when we start to remove our pride and self-belief from the equation. *You* can't make kingdom innovation happen. No, really. You can't. I don't care how clever or competent you believe yourself to be. Only Jesus can make it happen. In John 15, Jesus says, "apart from me you can do nothing." Moonshot thinking puts a hypothetical goal out there that's so big, so outlandish, that we know there is no way it happens without the work of the Holy Spirit. The whole process has to be saturated with his presence and submitted to his will. It takes us into the deep waters where we can't touch the bottom, and we can't see land.

And really? There's no better place to be. It's why Paul says,

> But he said to me, "My grace is sufficient for you, for my power is made perfect in weakness." Therefore I will boast all the more gladly about my weaknesses, so that Christ's power may rest on me. That is why, for Christ's sake, I delight in weaknesses, in insults, in hardships, in persecutions, in difficulties. For when I am weak, then I am strong.

When you realize you can't do it, when you see that you aren't enough, it changes the questions you ask. It changes the people you involve in the process. It opens up the possibilities, tears down the walls built by the Curse of Knowledge, and leads to different theories of how to get to the Moon.

Moonshot thinking is foundational to ideation, the second phase of kingdom innovation. It forces us to come up with new practices, concepts, and ways of thinking that go beyond what we already bring to the table.

Notice I'm not using the word "brainstorm" at this point, because brainstorming doesn't mean what most people think it means. Ideation is about walking through a very specific process, in which we uncover and discover new ideas that can get us from Cape

Canaveral to the Moon. Today, whenever leaders feel stuck with their team, they pile drive into a conference room, find a whiteboard and say, "Alright! Let's brainstorm! We're not leaving the room until we figure this thing out." Ideation, however, helps us come up with new ideas and practices we want to test out and experiment, but with the assumption that what I bring in my head isn't enough. We need people with different experiences and different ways of thinking who aren't all suffering from the Curse of Knowledge.

There is an art and science to effective ideation because it is a genuinely creative process ... the whiteboard brainstorm really isn't what it looks like. But the good news is that you can learn. And if you're going to defeat the Curse of Knowledge (thus slaying the great Villain of our story), then you must.

2.

We could be forgiven for assuming that creative problem-solving means absolute blue-sky thinking, with no hindrances, fences, or obstacles to hold your mind back. "That whiteboard is blank and anything could go on it!" But in reality, that's rarely helpful. One particularly useful concept in helping us learn the skills required for ideation is the concept of *constraint*.

Though we may not always perceive it as such, constraint is a gift because it forces us to focus and see things in new ways. Often, as we lead the specific things God has called us to, we lament the areas of constraint forced upon us:

- We don't have the right team.
- People aren't committed enough.
- We don't have enough money.
- Our facilities aren't right.
- The neighborhood has changed around us.
- We can't keep our best leaders.

All these reasons might prevent us reaching the Moonshot, and allow the Curse of Knowledge to win the day. But we can use those restraints to force us to think differently.

Wasn't the 2020 pandemic one big proof point of how constraint can actually drive innovation? If you could only leave your house for basic essentials and nothing else, how would you do church? Lead a non-profit? Run a business? The constraint itself wasn't chosen, but placed upon all of us. And what happened as a result? *Innovation.*

We can also choose to use *hypothetical constraints* to aid us in the Ideation Phase, helping us to focus and see new ways of thinking. As Adam Morgan and Mark Barden write in their book *A Beautiful Constraint,* constraints can be "fertile, enabling, desirable ... catalytic forces that stimulate exciting new approaches and possibilities."

Take your local church, for instance: If it was illegal for Christians to own or rent property, how would your church still live out the Great Commission? If your staff budget was cut in half, how would you grow your church by 100 percent in attendance? If, within ten years, all the leaders of the church had to be twenty-eight years old or younger, what would you do? If people didn't have access to a written or audio form of the Bible, how would you disciple people toward spiritual maturity? If you had to successfully plant a church every year or shut down, how would you ensure an annual church plant? If national borders didn't exist, what would you do with refugee people groups? If the church could only happen online, how would you reach people far from God? If you had to ask 90 percent of your church congregation to leave, who would you choose, why, and what would you build with the remaining 10 percent? For those leading in the COVID-19 pandemic, some of these hypothetical constraints came close to being their reality.

Or take your non-profit: If you had to decrease your budget by 50 percent but increase your programming scope by 100 percent, how would you do it? If each person you were serving had to receive prayer once a day, what would you do?

Or perhaps your business: If you couldn't sell any of your current products in eighteen months, but had to sustain the same level of revenue, what would you sell instead? And how would you get there? If you had to take your exact same product and expand into a new market aimed at kids, what would you do?

Just imagine how many innovative ideas those conversations would foster in your leadership team. Learning the skill of ideation, knowing how to generate new ideas that might work, is key in this second phase of kingdom innovation. And pressing into hypothetical constraint is an enormously helpful place to start.

If an amputee with no medical training can invent a way to run, two alcoholics can start a movement of sobriety, and a group of pastors can conquer an online video platform like Zoom, why can't God use you, right where you are, for such a time as this?

3.

If you're reading this book, I'm guessing there is a 97.2 percent chance you have the YouVersion app on your phone. And chances are you're probably a lot like me and Bobby Gruenewald, the CEO of YouVersion. We believe in the centrality of the Word of God and want people to engage with the Bible each and every day.

The difference between Bobby and myself, of course, is that I'm not responsible for creating a revolutionary and free Bible app with more than four hundred million users.

But here's the Phase 1 innovation problem Bobby faced early on: While the average American household has something like four Bibles, less than 20 percent of Americans read it at least four times a week. And the younger the person, the more likely they are to be less engaged with the Bible, and the more distracted they are by digital technology and the endless supply of apps and social media options.

As church leaders, we might say something like, "We want individuals to read the Bible every day, but we can barely get people to come to a worship service twice a month, much less put down Twitter, Facebook, or Snapchat for ten seconds." This is a natural constraint of the digital age, right?

But what if the constraint was actually a gift? What if the constraint allows us to put together all of the slow hunches and half-ideas that were leading to a working hypothesis?

The innovation success of YouVersion is so noteworthy, it was turned into a case study in Nir Eyal's book *Hooked*. Eyal quotes Gruenewald describing the challenge he faced: "Unlike other companies when we started, we were not building a Bible reader for seminary students. YouVersion was designed to be used by everyone, every day." Gruenewald attributes much of the Bible app's success to a relentless focus on creating habitual Bible readers. "We originally started as a desktop website, but that really didn't engage people in the Bible. It wasn't until we tried a mobile version that we noticed a difference in people, including ourselves, turning to the Bible more because it was on a device they always had with them."

For us, the big lesson here is that YouVersion is predicated on a beautiful constraint. One viewpoint might say, "People won't ever put down their phones long enough to engage the Bible." Another perspective might instead pose a hypothesis, invert the constraint, and turn it into something positive: "I bet we could create an app on a phone that gets people hooked on reading the Bible." They took the drawback of the constraint and turned it into a strength: We can use the phone to create the habit of daily Bible usage.

How was Bobby Gruenewald able to do that? *Soft eyes.*

A few friends on Twitter similarly had soft eyes when what started as a hashtag became a movement involving over three million women. The innovation? #shereadstruth. As Kate Shellnutt, an associate editor for *Christianity Today* writes, #shereadstruth "turned into the fastest growing Bible-reading community on the internet."

Started by Amanda Bible Williams (yes, that's her real middle name) and Raechel Myers, this kingdom innovation centered around a few key observations: A younger generation is living their life in an age of social media and digital sharing; most Bible resources don't have an aesthetic that appeals to younger women; and, in general, most women don't feel equipped to understand what they're reading in the Bible.

In his book *Understanding Media*, Marshall McLuhan famously wrote "the medium is the message." Remember what amputee Van Phillips taught us to do: Ask different (and better!) questions. So what is the intrinsic message of a book whose medium, even with the smallest typography and the thinnest pages, is a thousand pages long? I imagine these were the kinds of questions Myers and Williams were asking. And in the end, these questions highlight the inherent *constraint* around the perceived challenge of regularly reading the Bible: "It's long, dull, and I don't understand it," many might say.

At the end of the day, every innovation starts with a simple hypothesis. Merriam-Webster defines a hypothesis as "a tentative assumption made in order to draw out and test its logical or empirical consequences." Remember, it goes like this: If we do _____, then we think _____ could happen.

For Myers and Williams, the hypothesis seemed to be this:

If we
design beautiful resources for daily Bible reading,

then we think
more women will find it easier to engage with the Word of God every day and spur and encourage other women on to do the same by sharing it online.

So that's just what they did. They created an app, downloadable Bible studies, a Bible reading plan, daily emails, and a host of other things that are affordable and always straight-up beautiful. And behind all of it, there is a vibrant, passionate tribe of women who constantly share what they are reading, processing, and hearing from God.

Let's go back to our 3 Ps, that we discovered in chapter two, and see how this growing movement found a core insight in the Ideation Phase of this process.

The *paradigm*: Every page, from cover to cover, is given that we might know God.

The *principle*: Women in the Word of God every day.

The *practice*: An online community, stylized reading plans, and beautifully designed shareable content that's tailored to women.

For Bobby Gruenewald, soft eyes allowed him to see the possibilities of an interactive Bible app rather than simply seeing the *constraints* of digital technology. For #shereadstruth, it was the ability to see how injecting beauty could mobilize a movement despite the perceived *constraint* of the Bible being stale, boring, and hard to understand.

In the end, the innovation came out of the constraint.

4.

Jonathan Brooks found himself experiencing a similar pressure of an unwanted constraint: Canaan Community Church was located in a neighborhood that everyone was trying to escape, and 90 percent of his congregation didn't live there anymore. But when he tried to address the issue head-on, it didn't work. People didn't see what he saw. They saw a neighborhood too dangerous to live in.

Think about our 3 Ps again, but this time in relation to the conundrum he found himself in:

The *paradigm* was simple: Englewood is a good neighborhood but in need of transformation.

The *principle* was locked in: In order to transform the neighborhood, we need to live here, investing our time, talent, and treasure into the collective common good of this place.

But the *practice* for getting people to move there was still up in the air.

The problem was that Brooks and the congregation weren't even aligned on the paradigm and the principle, so of course the people of Canaan Community Church weren't going to say yes to the practice of moving into the neighborhood.

A shift had to come for the congregation, but in order for that to happen, the real shift needed to start with Brooks. Over the course of the next few years, Brooks adjusted his leadership from being the *source* of the ideas to *stewarding* the process for finding the right ideas. Through listening parties, surveys, ad hoc conversations, and community events, they created intentional space to listen to the residents of the neighborhood themselves. This time around, ideas didn't make it off a whiteboard unless it made sense to the rest of the neighborhood.

Over time, they learned something about themselves and something the wider neighborhood valued: They had a special grace for investing in young people. In a church in a neglected neighborhood with very few financial resources, their people were their greatest asset. This led to more conversations, more listening, more dreaming. They were beating down the Curse of Knowledge with every conversation they had, adding more perspectives, experiences, and thinking to the mix. But now the church family weren't only hearing *Brooks'* voice; they were hearing the voices of the neighborhood. And as they did, their own perspectives and paradigms started to change.

A new hypothesis began to emerge for Brooks and his team, one that would be tried and tested, and ultimately, proved true:

If
the people who've "made it" choose to stay,

then we think
that not only could we change the narrative, but with enough time and with the power of the Holy Spirit, these leaders could transform the whole of Englewood.

The *paradigm* was still: Englewood is a good neighborhood.

The *principle* remained: In order to transform the neighborhood, we need to live here, investing our time, talent, and treasure into the collective common good of this place.

But, with this new hypothesis, a *practice* was coming together: They would start a scholarship for graduating high schoolers, and if the student accepted the funds, upon graduating college, they would come back and live in Englewood. That was the condition of the scholarship fund: Rather than getting out of the neighborhood, they'd return.

The church who'd responded so poorly to the idea of simply moving into Englewood rallied around this innovation. They didn't have a lot of money, but they came together anyway. There were raffles, fundraisers, and initiatives for non-profits to earn money at Chicago's Soldier Field stadium. All of the proceeds went to what the church named the Edward T. Dunn Scholarship.

Once the scholarship was up and running, the community started to host an annual celebration where all of the alumni of the program return to celebrate. The whole church, heck, the whole neighborhood comes out and marks what's happening. *And to date, every recipient who's graduated is currently living in Englewood.*

When Brooks stood behind the pulpit and told everyone to move into the neighborhood or leave the church, he was telling them to shift their paradigm when they couldn't yet see or understand what he could. What he needed was a catalyzing initiative that people could get around so that, given enough time and by the power of the Holy Spirit, people would *experience* a paradigm shift.

Today, Canaan Community Church has completely flipped: More than 90 percent of the congregation not only live in the neighborhood, but are now living out the truth that Englewood is already a good place. And the narrative about the neighborhood is changing along with it. Heaven is visiting earth; the future is touching the present.

5.

Sometimes small innovations have huge reverberations. A Bible app on your phone. A beautifully designed Bible Study. A five-hundred-page catalogue delivered by mail.

A local scholarship fund with a stipulation that college graduates return back to their home neighborhood may not sound like a Moonshot to you. After all, this was only going to get a few more people to live in Englewood. But to this church ... in this neighborhood ... it *absolutely* was. Raising the required cash seemed impossible. Convincing kids to return to a neighborhood where the narrative is "get out" would be like trying to persuade a Red Sox fan to pull for the Yankees. We can't overestimate how strong that cultural conditioning was.

One thing we learn from the story of Jonathan Brooks is that the journey from idea to innovation is a difficult one. And particularly in the Ideation Phase, we can be all over the place. We enter into the process, but who knows if we're ever going to get anything useful out of it. You see, I think somewhere along the way we picked up the notion that generating new and actionable ideas is easy, or a skill we're either born with or we're not. Sound familiar? Well it should, because it's all part of the poison pill—the myth that some people have that unique innovation gene and others don't. Ideation is easy for the special people, but only if you have the special DNA. So when teams gather to step into the Ideation Phase, people can quickly become frustrated and deflated, feeling they've wasted time. A lot of nothing that's going nowhere. And it only seems to confirm the myth that a few people have the innovation juice and the rest of us don't.

There are certainly ups and downs to the Ideation Phase, but there is a trajectory to the process. Tom Kelley, the founder of IDEO and one of the foremost thinkers on innovation, puts it this way in the organization's book, *The Field Guide to Human-Centered Design*:

> You'll find yourself frequently shifting gears through the process, and as you work through it, you'll swiftly move from concrete observations to highly abstract thinking, and then right back again into the nuts-and-bolts ... By going really big and broad during the ideation phase, we dream up all kinds of possible solutions.

One of the main myths leaders need to bust in this phase is that the first idea is the right idea, and if it's their idea to begin with ... all the better! If I could challenge almost any myth around innovation, it's this one: Rarely is the first idea the right idea, and rarely does it come from just one person.

Clayton Christensen is a legend in the field of innovation. I mean *a legend* (insert British accent). In 1997, he wrote a book called *The Innovator's Dilemma,* which is widely considered the most important business book of the last thirty years. Christensen was a professor at Harvard Business School, and about nine months before he died, I was able to spend some time with him, conversing around some of the core ideas in this book. In Walter Isaacson's seminal biography on Apple founder, Steve Jobs, the mercurial innovator cited *The Innovator's Dilemma* as having a profound impact on his thinking. In it (and we'll come back to this in the next chapter), Christensen points out that of the new businesses that succeed (and most fail from the outset), 90 percent of the successful ones ultimately won with a different idea than the one they started with.

Just think about that for a moment: *The idea you started with is probably the wrong one.* And if that's not enough, statistically speaking, the idea that will ultimately prevail will almost certainly not come from you. This was a paradigm-shifting moment for me as a leader, and I imagine it will be for many of you as well.

Ideation is about moving from a place of scarcity (there aren't enough good ideas) to abundance (there will always be more ideas). That's one of the key distinctives of this phase. We want to generate as many ideas as possible, killing almost all of them, until we not only land on a truly great idea, but a working hypothesis that gets us the Moonshot. We're looking for something we can put into action, something that gives us a window into how we get from Cape Canaveral to the Moon—we're not going to get that with the first idea we think of.

Psychologist Dean Simonton has spent his career studying creative productivity. His final analysis? "The odds of producing an influential or successful idea [are a] positive function of the total number of ideas generated." Put succinctly: If you want to increase your chances of success, spend more time generating ideas and less time believing you had the right idea to start with.

Ideation is also about gathering ideas as a collective. As Brooks discovered, the role of the leader in this phase is to shift from being the source of the ideas to stewarding the process for finding the right ideas.

This kind of communal process is happening in Paul's first letter to the Corinthians, where he's giving instructions on church life in the fourteenth chapter. When someone feels they receive a revelation from God, they give it to others, who then have the responsibility to "weigh carefully what is said." In other words, just because you think you heard something from God doesn't mean others don't have the spiritual responsibility to speak into that. Who knows, you might have just had a bad slice of pizza last night? With kingdom innovation, we don't just want a load of *good* ideas. We want *God* ideas. Those are the only ideas that get us to *kingdom innovation*, because they are inspired by the Holy Spirit. And those need to be confirmed within a trusted and mature spiritual community.

We need to hear from people who are wildly different than us, who aren't having to slay the Curse of Knowledge. They need to be in all the rooms of this phase. We need people who have different experiences, gifts, backgrounds, and ideas. We need to look at how other people are dealing with similar situations. We need an honest assessment of what's working, or not working, in our current context. We need to have those blue-sky-thinking sessions, including times of beautiful constraint. We want to factor in our organization's core DNA (mission, values, theology, strategy, etc.) as well as the truth of the gospel. We want to spend time in prayer and in the Word, by ourselves and with others, hearing from God and discerning together what he is up to.

Maybe the emerging hypothesis for kingdom innovation originates from you. Then again, maybe it doesn't. The sooner we give up the need to act on the first idea and surrender the desperate desire for the idea to originate from ourselves, the sooner we'll begin to see kingdom innovation.

In the years before its bankruptcy, Sears was actively funding projects that would lead to the establishment of the internet. So surely someone in that organization was savvy enough to see the future of business and the internet? My suspicion? Someone higher up the food chain killed the idea because it wasn't theirs, or it didn't line up with their experience.

And just like that, one of the titans of commerce was snuffed out. But they didn't need to be.

6.

Whirlpool refuses to go the way of Sears. In a 2009 article in *Bloomberg,* it was reported that Whirlpool's system of generating new concepts each year produces thousands of ideas. *Thousands.* The Whirlpool company calls it "green housing," and the ideas don't just come from the "idea people;" *anyone* in the company can submit an idea. Why is this so important? Because innovation rarely comes in one sudden epiphany, but through the cultivation of creativity, driven by constant idea generation.

The company have created a system to evaluate each idea, with a scorecard and a fifteen-member panel that decides which ideas to fund. It's a meritocracy that doesn't simply reward "The Leader" for coming up with the idea. Nope. The best idea wins. And not surprisingly, it pays off: They expect to have $4 billion in sales from their new innovations arising from this kind of idea generation.

Whirlpool doesn't simply want to sit in the success of the past. They refuse to rely on experts only. They refuse to believe there's only one good idea. They refuse to believe the best ideas come from only the select few. In other words? They've figured out how to take out our Villain from the culture of their company.

What do you and Whirlpool have in common? You're both looking for the exact same thing: *a working hypothesis* (an idea you can test) to believe in. It's almost a statement of faith—of what we believe God is leading us to and is already at work in ahead of us.

Bill Wilson wondered if he could help other people stay sober if they had a sponsor to walk with them on the journey. Dr. Ethel Percy Andrus believed the way to help people age with dignity was to create a movement with serious lobbying power. Myers and Williams thought that if the Bible was visually beautiful, more women would read it more often; and Jonathan Brooks was convinced Christians living in and investing in Englewood could change the whole neighborhood.

The hypothesis you bring to the table, along with the other intel you and your team gather in the Ideation Phase, helps you locate what you're going after. And once you have that, you're able to construct a working prototype to test the innovation. We're not looking for something elaborate or perfect. In fact, just the opposite. We're looking for the simplest, most stripped-down version of it, so we can begin experimenting as quickly as possible. You're looking for something basic and testable. In the process we run for churches, non-profits and other organizations, we call this prototype the *Minimum Viable Process* (the MVP).

Think about how more and more restaurants open today. They don't jump from idea to a bricks-and-mortar space with high overheads and small margins. Many start with a pop-up: Rent a space for one night, get the word out, cook one meal, see what people think. Right there, that's the MVP for a restaurant. Now, if that one night works—great. Rent the space again, this time for the whole weekend and maybe expand the menu just a bit. Still working? What if you got a food truck and road tested the menu and the concept for six months to really see if it works. Then, if all that confirms the hypothesis, start to think about opening a restaurant.

The point is that when you leave the Ideation Phase, your MVP serves as the most minimal version of a prototype to test your ideas. #shereadstruth didn't need a whole Bible commentary written out to test the hypothesis. An MVP could have looked like a one-day study of Habakkuk 3 that was simply written and beautifully designed. Richard Sears didn't need to start out with a five-hundred-page catalogue delivered to hundreds of thousands of households; his MVP probably could have been a thirty-page catalogue delivered to one town. If you're starting a new non-profit that's going to sell positive-message clothing for teenagers, don't go straight to mass market. Print twenty-five t-shirts, try them in five different high schools, and see what people think. If you're a pastor, don't scale a whole new system for small groups or a new program for the whole church. Grab a few people, try out the new kind of group you've designed for three months, and see if it works the way you think it will.

In the Ideation Phase, all roads ultimately lead us to the MVP. It's the beta form of the kingdom innovation we're hoping and praying will ultimately multiply far beyond what you can hope, dream, or imagine. But before we get to multiplication, we have to know it works and doesn't just look good on a piece of paper.

So let's kick this up from third gear to fifth gear and get really practical.

This working hypothesis we've created sheds light on the *kind* of kingdom innovation we're looking for. After all, there are different kinds, and they require different types of work and experimentation. One of the great barriers to innovation is the belief that there are extra spiritual gold stars for inventing something like the YouVersion Bible app. Sometimes the most necessary innovation is a small adjustment, or a simple shift from being people who *talk* about the things of Jesus, to being people who faithfully *do* the things of Jesus!

Remember, the point isn't innovation. The point of the innovation is the kingdom and the mission of Jesus. *That's the point.* There aren't extra points because it was a specific kind of innovation. We're just trying to be faithful, rejecting the temptation to make something more important than Jesus.

I once heard that we form idols any time we make a *good* thing a *great* thing. We are not attempting to make innovation the great thing. It's only a good thing meant to serve the great thing: Jesus Christ and his mission.

Maybe you don't need to *invent* something. Maybe you just need to *tweak* something to get to the breakthrough you've been praying into and going after. In the Ideation Phase, we're identifying within our MVP the kind of innovation we think we need.

Below is a matrix I've created to look at the four different kinds of kingdom innovation, each one tailored to help leaders meet the moment (I've adapted some of these ideas from Will Mancini's book *Innovating Discipleship*):

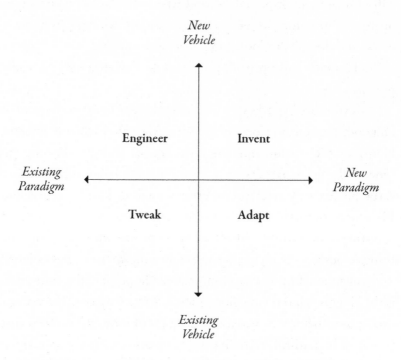

For the sake of illustrating these four kinds of kingdom innovation, I'll use examples from leaders I've worked with in the last twelve months:

Tweak: *Existing* **paradigm and** *existing* **vehicle**
Example of a faith-based non-profit involved in tutoring kids after school: Adding a meal and discussion time to an existing Bible study to promote deeper relationships both inside and outside of the organized meeting time.

Adapt: *New* **paradigm and** *existing* **vehicle**
Example of a business seeking the common good: Creating a clothing line for teenage girls of color that sows seeds of grace, truth, and possibility.

Engineer: *Existing* **paradigm and** *new* **vehicle**
Example of a leader serving in a juvenile detention center: Moving from a typical chapel service, to teenagers leading a gospel and hip-hop choir for the entire detention center.

Invent: *New* **paradigm and** *new* **vehicle**
Example of a local church: Moving from small groups created to build community for people already attending the same church, to creating a homegrown and decentralized missional vehicle built on both discipleship and mission.

So as we think about our hypothesis and the innovation task we've identified in Phase 1, we ask: Does it require a paradigm shift? What's the core principle involved? What new practices do I want to test? Does it require a different kind of vehicle, or multiple vehicles?

As you start to sketch out your MVP, the prototype you want to test and experiment with, it's incredibly important you design with the end in mind. What I mean is this: If you want the breakthrough to multiply and spread, you need to bake that into your prototype. If you design something that only a few people can access because of location, price, the intellect required to participate, or a million other factors, from the very beginning, you're limiting the number of people you can impact. It's the difference between an Alcoholics Anonymous (AA) meeting and a rehab center. They both do incredible work, but they are doing different things. An AA meeting is lightweight and low maintenance. That makes it easy to multiply. A rehab center is heavyweight and high maintenance, making it much harder to go from one center to two. This isn't to say that one is better than the other; rather, you need to know what you're going after and design your prototype accordingly.

As you'll remember from the Identification Phase, the bigger the innovation idea, the more time it takes to test. It took Bill Wilson fourteen years to get sober, and several more years before he and

Bob Smith figured out the practical components that would allow the scalability we'd ultimately see from AA. So as we think about expectations, there are some practical implications for us.

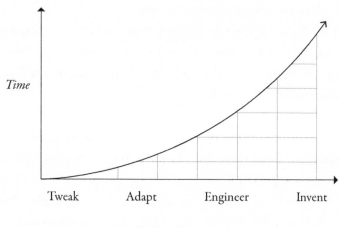

Difficulty of Innovation

When I stood up from my third night of praying at 3 a.m., I had a strong sense of the kingdom innovation we needed to push out. I called a few people, texted a few others, and set a time to share what I'd been processing in my time with the Lord. It wasn't a "revolutionary" kingdom innovation. In fact, using the matrix above, it was a simple *adaptation*. But that meant it would take significantly less time to launch and scale. I proposed we start a few coaching groups to help pastors walk through creating their church response to the pandemic and then activate that plan in a community of other pastors. We'd have a simple framework, a repeatable template for the groups, utilizing live troubleshooting, best practices, and large doses of peer learning.

But I had a strong sense it should be a collaborative effort. This should be the body of Christ coming together, for such a time as this.

As a group of leaders representing different organizations, networks, and tribes of churches, we talked, submitted our thoughts to each other, prayed, and concluded that it seemed good to the Holy Spirit and to us to move forward together.

Not long after those meetings, I was talking to Daniel Yang, the director of the Send Institute, and one of the key leaders alongside me in all we did with these groups. I'd been working with him and a few others to get some early information out for church response. "Any idea on your expectations?" he asked me. "How many churches do you think will jump in one of these coaching groups?"

"I don't know," I said. "I have zero idea. If we had fifty? If we had fifty, I'd feel like it would be such an incredible investment. But I really don't know."

And I was right. I had zero idea how many we'd be serving and how fast it would all happen.

LEADER INNOVATION LAB

KEY PRINCIPLES FROM PHASE 2: IDEATION

Goal: We must generate whole new practices, concepts, and ways of thinking if we're going to solve our innovation challenge.

Ideation
Rather than believing you have the right idea from the start, discipline yourself and your team to come up with as many ideas as possible before jumping into experimentation.

The Curse of Knowledge
When we already know something, not only can it be challenging to see a different way of doing things, it can also be hard to communicate a concept to others who don't yet see or know what we do.

The Moonshot
The God-sized goal we're going after that can drive creative thinking and practice.

Constraint
A limitation that's placed on you that you wouldn't choose, or a hypothetical restraint to help drive the creative process.

Hypothesis
If we do _____ , then we think _____ could happen.

The Minimum Viable Process (MVP)
The most minimal version of a practical prototype to test whether ideas work as stated in the hypothesis.

Design with the End in Mind

Whatever you want the fully scaled version of your innovation to do, design your prototype with that potential. If you want it to multiply easily, make sure your prototype will support that.

The Master Tool for the Ideation Phase: The MVP Tool

PHASE 2:
IDEATION

MVP TOOL

Watch the training video for the MVP Master Tool at DougPaul.org/ReadyorNotLab

Nuts-and-Bolts Leader Coaching

I've spent a lot of time talking about the Curse of Knowledge in this phase. There are two specific ways it hurts us as leaders.

1. The more expertise or specialization we have, the harder it is for us to see another way. It creates boxes that are hard to break out of.
2. What is plain and clear to us can feel like a completely different language to the people we are leading.

Let me give an example of how you can lead through this.

When I'm working in our Innovation Lab, we're often working with church leaders who want an expression of "church family" that mirrors Acts 2–4. But for many of the people they are trying to lead, it's incredibly difficult for them to see past the church vehicles they've experienced (Bible study, small group, Sunday school, etc.). Things can get really tense, really fast!

Sometimes, you'll arrive at a point in the Ideation Phase where a new idea or hypothesis is emerging, and there's something about it that feels very right. And if you're the leader, it might hit you first. But what you don't want to happen is to announce a hypothesis that people aren't ready to see yet. Your intuition says it could be right, but most people are concrete thinkers, not abstract thinkers. If this is the case, it's very important that before you continue down that path, you make sure everyone sees what you're seeing. What I use is something called a *touchstone*. It's a way of talking about something new by connecting it to something emotionally positive from the past.

Here's an example of how I use this principle as we're constructing a new vehicle for spiritual family that combines both discipleship *and* mission (rather than either/or). The touchstone I use in this scenario that helps ground something new to an emotionally positive place is Thanksgiving Day.

Step 1

I get everyone together, and I pose this question: *When Thanksgiving works well, why does it work well?*

We then fill up a whiteboard with all kinds of answers. I've done this dozens and dozens of times, and it always produces the same kinds of responses:

- Everyone is bringing food to the table.
- The family has some time together, some time spread around the house. It doesn't feel like we all have to be in the same room together the whole time.
- There are people you haven't seen in forever, but they still feel like family.
- There are people you're closer to than others, and that's OK.

- Sometimes there isn't quite enough room and people are squished together or sitting on the floor, but that's actually a good thing.
- People are sharing stories and laughing and catching people up on what's going on in their life.
- Often, as the day goes on, we'll watch football together or play a game outside.

Step 2

Then I pose this question: *"What are the pieces of Thanksgiving that we'd like to be more "normal" for spiritual family?* We then have a good conversation around that.

Step 3

We read Acts 2:42–47 together and have a discussion around the intersection points of this text and our Thanksgiving conversation. What can we learn?

All in, this exercise takes probably forty-five minutes. But what it does is creates a touchstone of common experience that we can regularly refer back to. It provides a resting place for both positive emotions and common imagination as we look to pioneer the future. But finally, it opens people up to a whole host of new possibilities because Thanksgiving and that Acts passage aren't representative of most church vehicles. It means there could be other solutions that we already have strong positive feelings about and are still biblically based.

Creating Your Own Touchstone

The example above creates a "this is that" experience. What you're trying to do is say "this new thing we're talking about is emotionally like that thing you're connected to from the past." So you start with the thing from the past and engage in a conversation or exercise about why it worked, why it was meaningful, why people look forward to it. Then you ask people to identify some core principles working in it. After all, Thanksgiving isn't the only place people can experience family, so what are the principles at work? Then we pivot to the new thing: How can this new thing we're developing keep those principles at work?

Beautiful Constraint Questions

My advice: Many of us learned to innovate under immediate constraint with the 2020 pandemic, but I believe we should continue to grow our muscles here, so test out my theory about *beautiful constraint*. Grab three to four people, pick a question, and see what ideas you come up with in sixty minutes or less.

Discipleship

If you only had two years to disciple five people who were fairly new Christians, but you knew in two years they were each going off to another country to disciple people in an unreached people group as a co-vocational business leader, what would you do?

Leadership

Your organization is now situated on a military base, and after five years, all of your leaders and volunteers are redeployed. How would you replace them without skipping a beat?

Mission

In one year, your church's goal is to pray for a member of every household in your city, live and in person. How would you do it?

Worship

For a six-month period, every Christian in your city, including you, has gone deaf. How would you create a worship experience that is just as meaningful and connects people to the heart of God?

Reconciliation

The demographics of your church have suddenly flipped. Whatever percentage of people who were black, are now white, and vice versa.

(Or whatever racial demographics best encapsulate the makeup of your church.) What things would you need to change in the next thirty days?

Operating System

A new pandemic has hit, and everyone is under quarantine. No one will be allowed to gather in groups larger than fifty. Your organization has the same mission as it did before the pandemic. How would you accomplish the mission?

This is a Spiritual Process

The challenge of kingdom innovation is that it's not just about the competency of the leader; it's also about the character. We mythologize people like Steve Jobs, but it's unlikely he had the character necessary for *kingdom* innovation.

Through this process, leaders are often confronted with the desires of their heart that are not based on Jesus and his mission. Many leaders in the Ideation Phase have an almost desperate need for the idea to be theirs in order to advance through the process (which is about their need to be right), and for the idea to come from them (which is about their need to be the center of the story). Not only is this going to short-circuit the innovation itself (because the idea will almost certainly be the wrong idea), it ultimately will short-circuit the life and leadership of the leader, as it's revealing who they believe is the hero of the story.

What we're talking about is Christlike humility, which is a by-product of the Spirit's work in a leader's life. There's no other way that fruit comes about.

At the end of the day, humility is not thinking less of myself than I am, or more of myself than I am. It's knowing exactly who I am in relation to Jesus. The irony is that the humblest leaders are also the most secure, because they have nothing to lose. They aren't trying to preserve anything or prop something up.

That's often what's at play here in our need to be the one who comes up with the winning idea or to be the savior of the organization. My friends Steve Cockram and Jeremie Kubicek talk about what it looks like for leaders to break through this wall of self-preservation. There are three questions they ask that I've found profoundly helpful to reflect on with the Lord during the Ideation Phase.

- What are you afraid of losing?
- What are you trying to hide?
- What are you trying to prove?

It never ceases to amaze me how one of those questions will reach up and smack me in the mouth, as the Holy Spirit brings conviction in this phase. Not because God is somehow out to get me, but because they reveal my own struggle, sin, and brokenness, and my ongoing need for the gospel to outwork in my life. It's the Lord's kindness that is leading me to repentance.

My advice? Invite the Holy Spirit into all of this process, into all of the cracks and crevices, including your own heart as a leader. The innovation process is wild and extraordinary, but it also reveals things about who we are at a fundamental level. At the end of the day, there is room for only one hero of any kingdom innovation. And that's Jesus. The true center of the story.

3

EXPERIMENTATION

CHAPTER FIVE

The Genius of Burl Cain

"WHEN I SEE THE HANDS OF MEN RAISED IN WORSHIP, I
KNOW THESE ARE THE SAME HANDS THAT HELD A RAPE
VICTIM, THE SAME HANDS THAT HELD STOLEN GOODS, THE
SAME HANDS THAT HELD THE MURDEROUS GUN."

1.

Sitting on about eighteen thousand acres and bordering the
Mississippi River outside Baton Rouge, Louisiana, is a former slave
plantation. The slave breeder who owned the plantation believed
the "best slaves came from [the country of] Angola." He specifically
looked for male "studs," descended from those who survived the
brutal sea journey from Angola, after being kidnapped and beaten
into submission. Until the state intervened in 1901, thirty-six years
after the end of the Civil War and thirty-eight years after Lincoln's
Emancipation Proclamation, the plantation continued to operate a
form of slavery.

This is a place of historical demonic activity, a place where
unspeakable evil was exercised on a group of people who had done
nothing wrong but be born on the wrong continent, in the wrong
country, at the wrong time in history. Sitting on the former slave
plantation today is Louisiana State Penitentiary, also known as
Angola Prison, the largest maximum security prison in the United
States, with the vast majority of its inmates serving time for violent
crimes. Half the prisoners are incarcerated on the charge of murder.

In the 1970s it was one of the most violent prisons in the United States, and earned the reputation of being one of the bloodiest prisons in the world.

In Louisiana, a life sentence comes with no chance of parole. In this state, if you're sentenced to death row or a life sentence, you have a 100 percent chance of ending up in Angola, with only two ways out: A pardon from the governor or president, or death. And 89 percent of convicts will die behind the walls. For years, it was common for inmates to serve as prison guards, and a culture of inmate-on-inmate assault was not only perpetuated but encouraged. Special treatment was given to inmates who killed escaping prisoners. The men often wore layers of newspaper or magazines under their shirts at night, to defend against a possible assault from inmates looking to take them out with shivs while they slept.

And yet ... *a revival took place in Angola Prison.*

This is a story of hope, healing, and heaven coming to earth. And for the curious mind, it raises the question: *How did this happen?*

2.

What was the Moonshot for iconoclastic sports journalist Bill Simmons?

Create a digital *Rolling Stone* for a new generation.

It's been a while since *Rolling Stone* magazine was considered groundbreaking, but back in the 1960s and 1970s, it was the be-all and end-all of youth pop culture. It covered music, movies, politics, and social movements, and at a time in Western history when there was a monumental shift in youth culture, *Rolling Stone* was right smack in the middle of it.

In the twenty years running up to 2010, Simmons had broken every cultural norm in sports journalism; he'd reinvented the entire industry in his image.

In the early 1990s, as a Boston sports fan, Simmons took his newly minted master's degree, his fan-oriented writing style, outsized personality, and acerbic wit to the *Boston Herald*, a flagship paper for Boston sports. "He grew almost immediately impatient with the hierarchy of the business, and the time required to get ahead," wrote journalist Lacey Rose, offering a world of insight into the sometimes mercurial superstar writer. Soon after, Simmons quit writing and tended a bar, trying to figure out what was next.

Quitting writing didn't exactly "take."

A new communication medium was opening up, of which no one really knew the full possibilities: the World Wide Web. Simmons started writing for the Boston page on AOL, turning sports fandom and pop-culture savvy into an art form. In those days, this was an about-face to the rest of the sports writing world, which never allowed writers to be fans; it required they remain neutral and objective. Sports journalists were *journalists*, which meant they couldn't display their own leanings or any of the almost obsessive quirkiness of sports fans the world over (yes, I'm talking to you, English "futbol" fans). Furthermore, Simmons blended multiple worlds together in his writing: sports, movies, wrestling, music, politics, stand-up, play-by-play analysis, interviews, family observations, ridiculous fan rankings, and all kinds of crazy conspiracy theories. In his mind, it all belonged together. The world wasn't neatly segmented into categories; conversations with his dad and his friends didn't occur that way, so why should his writing?

He wrote like a maniac fan possessed, but more importantly, his strength as a writer was on full display. Unorthodox? Sure. But people loved what he wrote. Before long, Bill Simmons had his own nationally syndicated column on ESPN.com, at the exact same time the internet was coming into its own and Boston sports hit its apex (the Patriots, Celtics, Red Sox, and Bruins all won scads of titles in the fifteen years that followed). Backed by a multi-billion-dollar company with an emerging web platform, Bill Simmons became a household sports name.

But in the midst of the sometimes biting, searing, and hilarious sports commentary, there was always a very real beating heart. He wrote adoringly about his dad, clearly one of the heroes in his life. His random collection of high school and college friends made their way into his articles, and even some of his pets; one in particular, a golden retriever named Daisy, who the Simmons family inexplicably nicknamed "The Dooze." In one of his finer pieces, writing to fanatics clamoring for his take on sports, he didn't write about sports at all. *He wrote about the death of his dog.* It might just be one of the most passed around articles of the first ten years of this millennium. Not just of sports articles, but of any article.

The last paragraph? Man, it'll kill you:

> The day after The Dooze left us, our little boy woke up and my wife carried him downstairs to feed him like she always does. I was still half asleep and could hear her footsteps. Then I heard this: "Day-zee. Day-zee." That part didn't make me sad. The part that made me sad happened three mornings later ... when my wife was carrying him downstairs again and he didn't say anything.

Before Bill Simmons, sports journalism did not exhibit that kind of writing. He invented a genre, in the same way Hunter S. Thompson invented gonzo journalism during his time working at *Rolling Stone*.

By 2010, Simmons was on an unprecedented run. He was the most popular sports writer in the country, with a *New York Times* bestseller and a Twitter following a mile long. But "writing" had never fully defined what he brought to the table. Simmons loved to chase down ideas and turn them into something. He was an early adopter of podcasting, with one of the most downloaded podcasts of any genre. The wildly successful *30 for 30* film series he produced on ESPN was not only his brainchild, but earned him an Emmy award in the process.

Not long after the success of *30 for 30*, ESPN approached him with a new opportunity, which in essence was this: Create *Rolling Stone* for a new generation.

Naturally, he accepted. In 2011, Bill Simmons and his team launched Grantland, an online platform for sports and pop culture.

He had an uncanny knack of spotting undiscovered talent; he would give them a platform, mentor and coach them, and next thing you knew, they'd be everyone's favorite content creator on whatever subject they were specializing in: Mallory Rubin, Zach Lowe, Wesley Morris, Chris Ryan, Katie Baker, Rembert Browne, Shea Serrano, Andy Greenwald, Bill Barnwell ... the list goes on and on.

In considering Grantland's impact, *The New Republic* commented, "Almost nothing Grantland published could have appeared in print. The pieces were either too long, too weird, too obsessive, too silly, or, ideally, all of the above."

Ultimately, Grantland became known as a mecca for long-form journalism. Critically adored and the recipient of prestigious awards, it never got the most eyeballs on its content, but became a tastemaker platform. Those who passionately loved sports and culture, to an obsessive degree, always seemed to end up there. As *Chicago Tribune* writer Stephen Carter put it, "This is sports writing for grownups." Even the president of the United States wanted to appear on the Grantland podcast.

With Grantland, Simmons had shot for the Moon. And by all accounts it might appear as if he'd hit it. The problem? He'd missed it by a mile. *Rolling Stone* magazine was the youth obsession for a generation. Grantland was cool, hip, smart, nuanced, thoughtful, long-form, and a magnet for creative people ... and "for grownups."

Do you know what youth culture doesn't want to do?

Grow up.

You see, you can be seemingly "successful" in what you're doing and still fail in your mission. You can make a lot of money in your business, but if a key aim of your business is to seek the common good, money isn't the only metric. Your non-profit could be working with hundreds or thousands of people, but if you're not seeing lives changed for the reasons the venture was started in the first place, what's the point? Your church could be the "it church" everyone wants to go to right now, hitting double-digit percentage growth numbers. But if people aren't living on mission and discipling people as they go … aren't we failing to live into Jesus' plan to change the world?

Bill Simmons was wildly successful.

He just hadn't started the new *Rolling Stone* magazine.

3.

It began with a phone call in the late1960s.

Henry Blackaby was living in Southern California with his young and growing family, and was facing a very uncertain future. Born Canadian, he'd felt called to overseas missions early on and had been preliminarily approved by the Southern Baptist Convention's International Missions Board to teach at a seminary in Africa. At the same time, his son, Richard, began having inexplicable fainting spells, believed by doctors to be caused by a tumor. Richard was put on heavy and expensive medication, and the family were advised against moving to a remote part of the world where access to medical treatment was limited.

All global missionary plans were put on indefinite hold.

When the phone rang that day, Blackaby could never have imagined what lay ahead. The call was from a church in a small town in Saskatchewan, Canada, which was on the brink of closing, having dwindled to ten members. Blackaby was informed that the church would die if he didn't come. They had no salary or benefits to offer him—just a ramshackle parsonage.

It clearly wasn't the most appealing offer, but Henry Blackaby had one, overriding spiritual conviction that determined the direction of his entire life: *God is at work. Join him in what he's already doing.*

After a time of prayer, Blackaby discerned that God was at work in the call from this church and set course for this new beginning. He raised funds for his own salary, as well as for a worship pastor, and a group of twelve people made their way up to the small town in Saskatchewan, to a church they'd more than double just by their arrival. Reflecting on this time, his son Richard mused, "I couldn't believe this dumpy broken-down church building, 'This is what you were talking about?!' But Dad was such an optimist. He could see what could be. It was the dumpiest church in the entire city partnered with the dumpiest parsonage."

But Blackaby believed God was already at work there. They were simply joining him in what he was already doing. They'd only just arrived when five guys who had driven ninety miles, jumped out of their car and asked if Henry could be their pastor. Just out of nowhere.

For the next two years, Blackaby drove that ninety miles twice a week to pastor the young church plant. It was their first mission of many to come. When Blackaby's church grew to about sixty people, he brought on another full-time staff member to oversee new missions work in the area. The new role was simply this: Drive up and down that ninety-mile stretch of highway and discern where God was already at work. Once they'd determined the place, they'd start the next church plant, or "mission," as they often referred to it.

Henry had always had a passion for college ministry, but there was just one problem: There weren't any college students at the church. "So we prayed for a university ministry. The first two people we baptized were a university professor and a student." Over time, the church transformed into a vibrant university congregation.

The thing about Christian students is they are constantly asking one central question: *How do I know God's will for my life*? So Henry Blackaby taught these college students to discern God's will for their life but also how to experience the reality of a life spent with God. He took his core spiritual conviction that God was already at work and made it practical. He developed sticky, useable content, and year after year, invested what he knew about a life fully following God.

All the while, as he worked with this group of college students serving as guinea pigs, Henry Blackaby was *experimenting*: testing, honing, and adjusting his prototype over and over again to best equip students in their walk with God. *This experimentation process took years.*

"He never had the same notes," Richard explained, "so every talk was a little different than the last, with new illustrations." In the midst of this, he was regularly counseling students, using the family living room as the primary place of ministry—from helping individuals process huge life decisions to walking couples through premarital counseling. But he didn't just teach them content—he helped people live it out. Over a hundred students went into ministry from this one little church in Canada.

"I think part of Dad's genius," Richard continued, "is that his material was constantly field tested. It wasn't written in an ivory tower. It was forged through years of doing it—he was fifty-five years old when his book came out. He'd gone through lean and difficult years—just him and God making [life] work. Everything was stripped away; but he just kept going deeper."

Now did you catch that phrase in there? It's easy to miss. Richard uses the phrase *field tested,* and continues later by saying the process "was forged through years of doing it."

Field testing gets at the very nature of experimentation itself. Before something is scalable, it needs to be tested. Is it actually doing the things we want it to do?

The third phase of kingdom innovation is *experimentation: We launch, test, adjust, and relaunch the innovation until the prototype we are testing achieves the measured goals set out.*

Richard goes on, "In the 1970s, people were very much wanting to get in touch with themselves, but my dad tried to focus them on God. People had it backwards. They'd go to God and say, 'Here are my plans—will you bless them?'" For Henry Blackaby, and the students he was training, the revolutionary truth was that God was at work all around them. And they began to see him at work all over the place. Their life in Canada was certainly different than they'd expected, but it was filled with abundance. They had planted thirty-eight churches from this little Saskatchewan church and saw the power of Jesus transforming lives. In other words, *the field tests were working.*

4.

Word started to get out. Soon, Henry Blackaby found himself on the university conference circuit, teaching and training at retreat weekends and gatherings of university students in Canada and the United States. Year after year, for more than a decade, he kept doing what came so naturally to him with the college ministry in Canada: train, counsel, morph, adapt. He continued to look for a better process and sharper content to equip people to experience God. For Blackaby, this was never simply a theoretical or conceptual process— it happened in the laboratory of his life, in his actual living room, with real people, whose lives were noticeably changed as a result. Undoubtedly, there were small missteps or failures along the way, but Henry Blackaby kept tweaking and adapting, and eventually, it laddered up to something extraordinary.

Richard Blackaby tells an endearing story about this period in time:

> In 1988, I was in seminary in Texas, and I taught a Sunday school class for thirty to forty single adults. My dad was coming to town, so I asked him if he'd teach my Sunday school class for me. When the other seven teachers heard he was coming and the content he was speaking on, they all showed up, even though they had no idea who he was. So there's this big room filled with all the single adults. He gets up, this soft spoken Canadian, and I know what's going to happen. It starts with people politely listening because he's my dad, and they're being nice to me. Then, a few minutes in, they start grabbing things to write with. They are taking pages and pages of notes. One guy photocopied all of his notes, and they got passed all over the place. My dad doesn't look like a rock star or anything. He's just this Canadian guy.

What Richard is describing is not just someone with killer content, but someone who actually embodied that core message and its convictions. But maybe most of all? He knew how to equip people to do what he was talking about. After all, he'd spent more than a decade honing it in his life, his family's life, and the life of the students who poured into this small Canadian church year after year. He taught them that the Christian life wasn't so much knowing *about* God, but *knowing* and *experiencing* God.

Eventually Avery Willis from Lifeway publishing heard him speak and asked Henry for some time one-on-one to help flesh out some of his material. By the end of their conversation, Willis said, "OK. We've got to get this in writing."

Blackaby wasn't terribly interested in publishing what he was doing. Plus, he didn't exactly have the time between the Bible college he was serving at, the church he was leading, all the university and church conferences, retreats and trainings, and new church plants. He agreed in principle to getting his content and training on paper, but the publisher could never really nail him down.

Let's just pause for a moment, because it's here we can learn about a key characteristic that is vital for kingdom innovation: *obedience*. Up until this point, Blackaby had been serving in a very small town in rural Canada. The primary focus of the church was on college students, and while they had multiplied the church many times over, Blackaby continued to spend most of his time with these young adults. If he had been looking to intentionally spark a worldwide movement, he probably wouldn't have started by living in a rural town, working with college students and young adults. It's likely if Blackaby was doing the same work today, he wouldn't be invited to teach at all the hip conferences, with all the accompanying prestige and acclaim. (Leadership influence in the Western church is not generally directed toward college students and young adults, is it?) But Blackaby wasn't searching for influence and praise. He was looking to be obedient. He wasn't trying to be a phenomenon; he was devoting himself to what God was doing.

If success in the kingdom is actually about *obedience*, then Blackaby was perfectly postured to partner with God.

If we're going to go after kingdom innovation, we have to remember *who* we're going after it for. We're looking for where God is moving and how we can obediently join him in his kingdom work. The Experimentation Phase involves a faithful pursuit of this and is always in obedience to him, rather than the pursuit of our own version of success.

Given Blackaby's reticence to put time and energy into writing, Lifeway publishing enlisted Claude King to follow him around and capture what he was doing. Claude went to two different conferences and recorded everything Henry said. Claude observed live audiences experiencing Blackaby's words and demeanor, and his interaction with those listening—somewhat like a laboratory environment filled with experimentation.

In 1990, *Experiencing God* was published. It contains Bible content, but it's not exactly a Bible study. There's a workbook, but it's not a Mad Libs tour of fill-in-the-blanks. Is it a study guide *and* workbook? Yes, but not quite that either. Perhaps it's best described as a simple, but revolutionary way to equip people to learn the process of experiencing God in a group setting, without Blackaby sitting right there with you.

Lifeway started with a print run of five thousand copies, a standard run for a new kind of study from an unknown author. With virtually no marketing dollars behind, they started flying off the shelves. People couldn't buy the book fast enough. They sold 100,000 ... 200,000 ... 300,000 copies. As soon as it appeared to be reaching its apex, it would cross into a new denomination or group of people.

You see, *Experiencing God* invited people into a process to not just learn about the Bible or about God or about his will ... but to experience an electric, live-wire relationship with God. The hypothesis seemed to be that if people could learn how to be with God and not just know about him, the power of God would change them. What Blackaby was experimenting with for decades was the practical handles that delivered on that hypothesis. And that hypothesis didn't just look good on paper. It worked in real life.

This is crucial to our understanding of kingdom innovation. We want the innovation to actually work. Remember the definition of kingdom innovation? *It's new, it works, and it brings glory to Jesus.*

That's not to say that "if it works, we should do this." This isn't pragmatic Christianity with a sprinkle of Jesus thrown on top. But the posture of our heart should be, "If this is from God, I want it to actually work." Part of our faithfulness to the ideas God places in us is to adapt, tweak, iterate, and experiment with them as we go. Imagine if Peter, Paul, and Priscilla hadn't learnt as they went. Blackaby was committed to the *Experiencing God* process working because he wanted people to ... wait for it ... experience God! He didn't believe he had the perfect process from the get-go. So he kept experimenting and honing. That's what faithfulness looked like for him. As Eugene Peterson said, it was "a long obedience in the same direction."

To date, the original *Experiencing God* process has more than ten million copies in print, with countless more having experienced the transformation of coming to know Jesus at this deep, relational level. I personally can still recall my parents gathered around a kitchen table with their friends, going through the book. I remember hearing their conversations. *I remember the way our house changed.*

5.

In the 1970s, Angola Prison was known as one of the bloodiest prisons in the world. As you walked through its gates, it still had the ethos and appearance of a plantation. Prisoners worked each day on a sprawling farm within the walls of the prison itself. Because it was a plantation during the Civil War, it is highly likely, both then and now, that some of the prisoners were or are descendants of those slaves. In the prison, many of the complexities of generational sin were on full display: white supremacy, demonic activity, institutional racism, broken homes, what's known as "the new Jim Crow" of mass incarceration, and the tidal wave of violent culture—*all colliding in one place.*

If ever there was a God-forsaken place where hope should be flickering out, this was it.

In 1995, Burl Cain became the prison warden of Angola Prison.

A stout man with a lilting Louisiana drawl, Cain is an unlikely character to usher in a revival of God through an out-of-the-box prison reform. But he'd had a profoundly personal spiritual experience as he walked through Henry Blackaby's process for learning how to know God. The idea that God was at work all around brought the revelation to Cain that God also had to be at work in Angola. One day, while overseeing an execution, Burl felt God say, *Did you ever tell that man about me? You just sent a man into eternity.* Immediately, Cain felt defensive. (I mean ... *who wouldn't?!*) But God was inviting him to see something ... something Jesus was already up to. Burl shifted his perspective—instead of seeing these men first as murderers, he saw them as people without hope.

Soon thereafter, Cain started leading an *Experiencing God* class in Angola Prison.

Eighty inmates showed up.

It went well enough, but if you've made it this far in the chapter, you probably have an idea of what Cain went on to do: Learn, tweak, adjust, iterate. The next time around, two hundred inmates came. You see, the thing about experiencing good news is you want to *tell people.* Every time they did a class, numbers swelled.

Burl Cain had walked through *Experiencing God*, and he knew how to use what I refer to as the "Grooves of Grace" principle: Find what God is doing and join him in it. There was something happening with the prisoners, so he kept experimenting and iterating. In 1999, Cain brokered a partnership with New Orleans Baptist Seminary to open an extension center in the prison. Men who had put people into the grave had found Jesus and were being trained in gospel ministry. You can see how this innovative leadership pipeline started to develop. People came to faith in Jesus, and then some of them were trained to lead in the prison as pastors. So when Hurricane Katrina and Rita hit, it was graduates of the program who were offering pastoral care in other maximum security prisons.

What's key to see is that Cain didn't fully know what would happen when he started. He was experimenting with the course, experimenting with jobs programs and theological education, but he didn't have it all right out of the gate. He discovered what worked by tweaking and adjusting as he went.

Thousands of inmates made new professions of faith in Jesus Christ. A Bible college was started inside the prison along with a re-entry jobs program. Acts of violence were down 74 percent. Convicted rapists and murderers who would never see outside the prison walls were ordained as pastors and began starting congregations within the prison itself. Some ordained inmates requested transfers and were sent to other maximum security prisons, serving as missionaries, starting new congregations, and bringing the hope of the gospel to some of the darkest places in the United States. (Think, for a moment, how this parallels the story of the Apostle Paul. A man guilty of murder who gives his life to Jesus and becomes an imprisoned apostle of Jesus Christ. If that doesn't get your heart racing, I don't know what does!)

The turnaround at Angola Prison was so unprecedented, so extraordinary, that everyone took notice. *The Atlantic* not only ran a feature article, but after seeing it live and in person, sent a documentary film crew to capture it. A journalistic entity, usually known for being at least slightly antagonistic to American Christianity, *The Atlantic* reported, "Today, hundreds of inmate-ministers are turning thousands of their incarcerated brethren to Jesus."

One prisoner, who'd been there for more than three decades said Angola had "changed from night to day." Because of the strict sentencing laws that make it almost impossible to get out of Angola Prison, there is a much greater incentive for keeping peace within this penitentiary than there might be within other prisons. With the practices of *Experiencing God* at the center, Cain began to introduce the prisoners to a new reality of Christianity and the gospel. Worship services happened every day. A group of inmates started something called *Malachi Dads,* through which they train other incarcerated fathers how to be good dads to their kids living outside the prison. Hundreds of inmates have been trained as ministers of the gospel.

The good news of Jesus, the promise of abundant life today, actually means that people *can change.* That places of generational sin *can change.* That places of slavery and racism and violence and hatred *can change.*

"When I see the hands of men raised in worship, I know these are the same hands that held a rape victim," one inmate says. "The same hands that held stolen goods, the same hands that held the murderous gun."

The genius of Burl Cain is this: His kingdom innovation gave prisoners access to the only thing that can change the centuries of brokenness we see at work on the land of Angola Prison—King Jesus and the unfolding of his now-and-not-yet kingdom.

CHAPTER SIX

Apollo Burns

"EVERYONE'S GOT A PLAN UNTIL THEY GET PUNCHED IN
THE MOUTH."

1.

In September 2014, Bill Simmons was suspended by ESPN for three weeks.

Roger Goodell, the commissioner of the NFL, was navigating a domestic abuse scandal, and, candidly, he was doing a really poor job. A video had surfaced of one of the NFL's best players violently abusing his girlfriend. The video of the attack ran endlessly on the news and social media ... and the commissioner was bungling his response. Bill Simmons called him out. Simmons believed Goodell was a liar and that he knew what was on the tape long before it was leaked to the public.

After the official report on the situation was released, Simmons was interviewed in 2015 on *The Dan Patrick Show*, where he continued with his scathing comments of Goodell: "He knows the results before the report is released to the public, and yet he doesn't have the *testicular fortitude* to do anything until he gauges public reaction."

Now think about this for a moment: ESPN pays *billions* of dollars just for the rights to the NFL's crown jewel, *Monday Night Football*. And here was one of ESPN's employees calling out the commissioner, labeling him a liar, and challenging his testicular fortitude. Needless to say, ESPN wasn't about to play around with a television rights

107

contract which brought in significant revenue. They chose not to renew Simmons' contract (the equivalent of firing him). In a comedy of errors that says everything you need to know about our digital age and the icy relationship Simmons had with then-ESPN president, John Skipper, Simmons discovered he was fired via Twitter. The sports analyst refused to get in line with the corporation, and just like that, it was over.

Suddenly, Bill Simmons found himself living in Southern California, thousands of miles away from his native Boston, unemployed, and searching for answers. He took a couple of months and said ... literally nothing. He planned, he plotted, he revised, he schemed, and he mulled. Rather than pack it in or hedge his bets inside a preexisting network or company, Simmons decided to push all of his chips to the middle of the table. He waited a little while, relaunched his personal podcast under a new umbrella, and started talking about something new.

On June 1, 2016, The Ringer launched.

To call it a website is to really misunderstand the adjustments Simmons and his team made from Grantland to this new iteration. "This site had a pretty different direction," Simmons said. "We were leaning much more heavily right away on multimedia, especially the podcast network. We knew from our Grantland experimentation it was going to be a big part of what we did; video, social, all the different opportunities we had."

Most people who are Millennials or younger are considered to be digital natives—they don't see a separation between real life and digital life. It's just *life*. In the same vein, when interacting with a brand and their content, they aren't thinking about a website; but rather the full digital experience of the brand across all platforms. This was the insight that Grantland didn't seem to have but The Ringer carried in spades.

What did that mean practically? Yes, there'd be a website, but it would link to their YouTube channel, which crossed into their live Twitter shows, which pushed toward an HBO special, which circled back to all of these interesting podcasts. It was all one digital landscape that would seamlessly lead from one thing to the next ... to the next and cross-pollinate together.

Even more so, The Ringer carried the belief that finding young talent was on the front burner. "This time around," Simmons said, "we were betting on a lot of younger people." You can't build the next *Rolling Stone* if it's not built with young people, can you?

Truth be told, a lot of it didn't go well. Simmons referred to Grantland as a time of experimentation, but *everything* in The Ringer was treated like an experiment: Throw it against the wall and see what sticks. He tried a weekly HBO show talking about sports and pop culture. It didn't take, barely making it through one season and was cancelled after only seventeen episodes. You could see what he was going for, but it just didn't quite work.

The Ringer tried live shows with Periscope, Twitter, and Facebook Live. They were all over Instagram, Snapchat, and a whole host of other platforms. Some of it worked, but a lot of it was just a swing and a miss. They debuted a second show on HBO. The show was OK at best, and failed to renew for a second season. So they adjusted some things and tried a different version of the show on Twitter.

This time it took off.

"You just never know what's going to happen," Simmons said, reflecting on this period. "You hire someone to do one thing, and they turn out to be better at something else. You try something and it turns out to be way bigger than you thought. You try something else and it doesn't work. The key is to keep trying."

So they kept trying. Launching new ideas, measuring, learning, adapting, launching again. If Phase 3 is about experimentation, this is textbook.

Iteration is the process of doing something again and again and again, but doing it a little differently, with changes, new learning, and adjustments each time around. As Eric Ries says in *The Lean Startup*, "The faster you can move through your iteration process, the faster you will win."

As we saw with Jonathan Brooks, trying to get every church member to move into the neighborhood was as successful as selling snow cones to Eskimos. But after several rounds of iterations, he discovered a scholarship fund would do the trick. Henry Blackaby spent the better part of his forties and fifties tweaking, honing, and adapting his content and process for *Experiencing God*. Some things worked, some things didn't. Launch, learn, adapt, relaunch. Rinse. Repeat. What all these individuals were living into was one of the key principles we'll explore in the Experimentation Phase: Fail fast so you can succeed sooner.

This is one of the most fundamental principles in innovation. Why? Because ... *Perfect is the enemy of great.* (A little spin on Voltaire's short idiom.) We'll never construct something perfect, and if that's what you're going for, you'll never get it on the road for a test ride. It is widely believed the iPhone 5 most closely resembles the picture Steve Jobs had in his head when they started developing the iPhone. Jobs was a notorious perfectionist, to an almost pathological degree. But he released four iterations of the iPhone to the public *before* he got to one that mirrored the idea conceived in his mind.

The sooner you start experimenting, the sooner it *won't* work. The sooner you can learn from it, the sooner you can get to a place where you've had enough iterations where it *could* work.

The Ringer had a lot of misses. But they weren't done yet.

2.

What we see in the stories of Henry Blackaby and Burl Cain are innovations that are the embodiment of the third phase of our innovation process: Experimentation.

Mike Tyson was once asked whether he was worried about his upcoming fight with Evander Holyfield. His response? "Everyone's got a plan until they get punched in the mouth." (Clearly Tyson wasn't worried.)

As you go after kingdom innovation, there is no question you will get punched in the mouth. The Curse of Knowledge will punch you in the mouth. Making wrong assumptions will punch you in the mouth. A hypothesis that didn't work out or a Minimum Viable Process (MVP) that wobbles and falls could punch you in the mouth. Your own sin patterns and pride will punch you in the mouth. And undoubtedly, our enemy, the evil prince of this world, will throw everything (including the kitchen sink) at you.

It's not about the plan and whether it's right. It's about whether your plan factors in that you *will* get punched in the mouth.

In each tale of innovation success, there was a litany of failures along the way. Why? Because things that start on paper rarely work that way in real life! In *The Ten Faces of Innovation*, Tom Kelley writes about a principle we have highlighted already: "Fail often to succeed sooner." He goes on to say, "Experimenters delight in how fast they can take a concept from words, to sketch, to model, and yes, to a less than polished prototype."

It's not whether the MVP plan and the prototype you launch works the first time. *It almost definitely won't.*

Coming out of Phase 2 of our process, we have an MVP; a prototype to test. But we don't know if it works yet! As Ash Maurya writes in *Running Lean*, "In the initial stage of validating an idea, everything is just a guess. Nothing is certainty."

Bill Wilson didn't have a picture of hundreds of millions of people finding freedom in sobriety; he just kept using the laboratory of his own life to find freedom from addiction. Henry Blackaby didn't know *Experiencing God* was going to become a worldwide phenomenon; he just wanted to keep getting better at teaching college kids to know the will of God for their lives. For Bill Simmons, he didn't know which platform idea would catch for The Ringer; he just knew if they kept trying, kept iterating, eventually they'd figure it out.

3.

Doug Dietz is an innovation architect for GE Healthcare who helped design a state-of-the-art Magnetic Resonance Imaging (MRI) scanner. One day, he visited a hospital using his machine and spent time with the technician who operated the device he helped design. The technician had all kinds of wonderful things to say about the machine, and he also gave some constructive feedback on some minor improvements that could be made. All in all, I imagine Doug Dietz was feeling pretty good about himself.

But that feeling would soon change. Just a few minutes later, Dietz watched a family with a sick little girl come into the room. The little girl *freaked out* when she saw the large, imposing machine before her. There was no way she was going into that scary machine, regardless of how important the data would be to her prognosis. Eventually, the hospital staff had to sedate her, and only then could the machine be used.

Did the machine work? Yes. But is this really how Dietz wanted the experience of the machine to go? Of course not.

He did some research and found that up to 80 percent of small children needed anesthesia before being scanned. What he'd witnessed with the little girl wasn't an isolated experience ... it kept happening, and he hated that his machine was having this effect on kids. So he put together a team with a host of different people: designers, technicians, social workers, employees from a children's museum, and kids. Using the power of experimentation, they went back to the drawing board with a clearer sense of what was needed for the innovation:

> Instead of machines that looked like "giant car crushers," they designed machines that looked like pirate ships, space crafts and canoes. Now at hospitals with Doug's new machines, kids are almost never sedated before a scan. In fact, they often ask if they can come back again for another.

Did the original machine work? Yes. Would it have been a good thing if that machine prototype had been mass-produced and put in every hospital with a radiology department? Absolutely not. And yet, that's what so many leaders do when we have a new idea we want to put into action. We make the same mistake again and again: If it looks good on paper, it'll not only work in reality, but it must be scalable *immediately*. We go from zero to sixty and launch it to the entire church, business, or organization in one fell swoop.

Peter Drucker, author of *Innovation and Entrepreneurship*, writes, "Effective innovations start small. Do one specific thing and then adapt." And yet, it's almost impossible to overstate how contrary this is to our thinking and decision-making as Christian leaders. If given the choice, why not "start big?" Our leadership instincts around this specific topic are hardwired the exact wrong way. We go after the glory. We go after the quick fix. We go after instant gratification. We go after short-term results, setting the stage for long-term decline. And often, we leave a trail of relational wreckage in our wake.

What we need is a period of experimentation, where we can learn what works, what doesn't, and continue to hone and develop the prototype we're testing. Tim Brown, CEO of IDEO says, "Rarely do we get it right on our first try. ... Failure is an incredibly powerful tool for learning. As we seek to solve big problems, we're bound to fail. But if we adopt the right mindset, we'll inevitably learn something from that failure."

Tom Kelley, IDEO's founder, also emphasizes this in an unusual story of a baseball team looking for a turnaround. Not only did the team have a losing record year after year, they had a losing culture. Rather than learning from failure, it crushed them time and time again. You see, in baseball, failure is built into the game. A batter who hits one out of every three balls is one of the best hitters in the game. But that's a 66 percent failure rate! The key is *to embrace failure as normal*, learn from what happens, and then move on. Finally, the coach decided to break the cycle and instill a new expectation, and with it, a new culture. The coach created a "mistake ritual." If a player struck out, hit into a double play or had any other kind of morale-zapping failure, they'd come back to the dugout and literally "flush away" the mistake with a palm sized, realistic looking (and sounding) toilet. Failure and mistakes are normal, so they created an artifact and ritual to constantly reinforce this point. Maybe you guessed it: They went on to win a national championship. Now what's the point of this silly baseball story? Simple. We need to normalize the expectation of failure in our personal leadership and in our culture. After all, if we're not failing, we're either not risking anything or we're not being honest.

Rather than hoping we don't fail, why don't we create a process where we expect failure to happen, reward people for taking smart risks, and then build the learning and adaptation right into it?

Kennedy said they were going to put a man on the Moon by the end of the decade. There were all kinds of experiments and iterations that went into making that mission a reality. Apollo 11 was the spacecraft that ultimately landed two men on the Moon, but there were ten essential missions that went *before* that one, each providing critical information for a successful Apollo 11 mission (including the first one, Apollo 1, which tragically ended in a flash fire, killing three astronauts). Within each individual mission there were many micro-missions. Did NASA want to get a man on the Moon in the first Apollo mission? I'm sure they did.

But that's rarely how innovation works.

4.

As we now know, innovation works best when we fail fast and iterate as we go. And what we can learn through the examples of Henry Blackaby, Burl Cain, and others, is that the process of experimentation is part of a spiritual discipline: obedience to pursue God's call. Our pursuit of success in kingdom innovation is about God's power, through the Holy Spirit at work in us, not our own efforts. It's said that as Christian leaders, we overestimate what we can do in one year and underestimate what God can do in five. (Truth be told, I have no idea where that quote originated from. I just know I didn't come up with it.) True kingdom innovation takes time, it takes patience, it takes discipline, it takes iteration, and it takes the power of the Holy Spirit. And lastly? We don't know if it will "hit." We can't control those outcomes. The only thing we can control? Our faithfulness through obedience to what God has asked us to do.

Coming into Phase 3, you'll have a prototype sketched out that you're going to experiment with. But it's still an open question, isn't it? You have a hypothesis, but it could still be wrong. The church leadership gathers the right group of people to pilot the prototype for a set period of time, and you go through an iterative process. You already know what you're looking for, having identified exactly what you're going to measure as "success." In other words, you need to know if your innovation is actually solving the problem you've identified.

In our Innovation Lab, I often work with churches who create a homegrown vehicle for discipleship and mission. These churches have a sense that rather than import or copy-and-paste someone else's vehicle (like small groups, Discovery Bible studies, Fight Clubs, missional communities, etc.), they need something that is completely true to their DNA.

I recently worked with a church who came into the Experimentation Phase with the following hypothesis:

If we
gather in groups of 20–40 people (the size of an extended family) and pattern our practices after the life of Jesus,

then we think
this will create a relational ecosystem that sees individuals come to faith, disciples people, and ultimately, multiplies in number.

Together, we discussed and developed ideas around the shape and rhythm of the group, how relational discipleship and mission would practically take place using their DNA and values, and then created a scalable leadership pipeline. Their first iteration was over a three-month time period, and the overarching goal was to create a Jesus-centered spiritual family of twenty to forty people with the DNA of that specific church. Here are some of the "testing questions" we used to evaluate each iteration:

- Did the group grow in the number of people who weren't Christians?
- Did the Christians in the group grow spiritually? If so, in what ways?
- Did the leaders successfully apprentice at least one future leader?
- How often did people from the group spend time together outside of the "organized" group time?
- Did participants and leaders both feel the group was lightweight and low maintenance?

So the iterative process began.

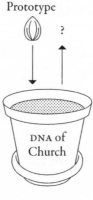

Iteration 1

We put the prototype into the soil of the DNA of the church with the group of people we tested it with, and we asked the question,

"OK, what will grow?" After that period of time was over, we looked at what happened. What grew? Where did it go as we thought it would? Where was it different? Where did it miss? What mistakes did we make? What do we need to adjust? What was surprising?

We tweaked, adapted, adjusted, and we iterated again.

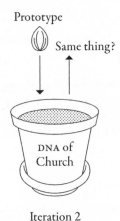

Iteration 2

In this second iteration, we took the learning we discovered from the testing questions, and using our missteps and the things that worked, we honed it even more, tailoring it to the outcomes we hoped and prayed to see and multiply. As it grew, we asked, "OK, did the same thing grow, and did it grow stronger?"

We paid attention to whether it was growing in a way that carried the essential DNA of the wider church. Does it look, smell, feel, and sound like our DNA? If it achieved that in the first iteration, did it the second time around? If it was missing something critical the first time around, did it grow the second time?

In his book *Canoeing the Mountains*, Tod Bolsinger puts it this way: "I encourage leaders to escape the expert expectation by becoming an expert experimenter, an expert question asker instead of answer giver." So in thinking about this advice, we press into asking different (and better!) questions about what we've practically seen.

Here are some practical roadblocks that various churches I've worked with have run into, expressed through the questions they're asking:

- Why was the vehicle so good at discipling people for spiritual growth, but ineffective at getting people on mission?
- Why did it lose all momentum the first time we talked about multiplication?
- Why are people growing spiritually, but don't have a vision for leading?
- Why are people coming to faith in Jesus, but not choosing to step into the calling of making disciples?

Well, the good news is there are more iterations to come!

Iteration 3

By this third iteration, the prototype we were experimenting with was not only growing strong, but growing in a way *that embodied the DNA of the church.* (Notice how this third image shows a large, strong plant.) They were still asking the testing questions, making adjustments, and tweaking things as they went, but at this point, the innovation had taken root and proven viable. It wasn't perfect, but we were never going for perfect.

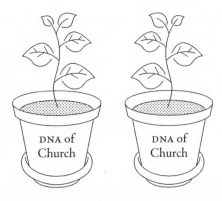

Iteration 4

Finally, in this last iteration, we looked to see if we were able to get a kingdom return on investment, for as Alan Hirsch and Dave Ferguson write in *On the Verge,* "In every seed is the potential for a tree, and in every tree is the potential for a forest. But the potential is all contained in the initial seed." Can this new expression of kingdom innovation, this thing that we wrote down as our Moonshot, started as an MVP, and iterated on several times with the prototype ... can it multiply?

That's the final stage of iteration. Can it multiply? Can something that started with one ... become two? And then three? And then six? And then twelve? (And far beyond?)

When Burl Cain started his first *Experiencing God* class, he didn't know where it would end up; he was just throwing mud up against the wall. When Bill Simmons started his first podcast, he didn't know he was stumbling on the next great wave of social content. Myers and Williams were just trying to encourage a few friends to read the Bible and started experimenting with hashtags and beautiful layout.

They all experimented with open hands.

5.

From the outside, it looked like The Ringer was throwing everything against the wall to see what would stick.

But they also had something important, something they knew already worked: podcasts. They'd gotten into the market space early and had put a stake in the ground. The success of one idea was allowing them a lot of freedom and flexibility to experiment with others.

But as we've already learned, The Ringer didn't view all of these experiments as failures, but as necessary stepping-stones to ensuring the long-term success of achieving the mission. Remember what Clayton Christensen said in *The Innovator's Dilemma?* More than 90 percent of successful start-ups use a different strategy than the one they first started out with. Simmons and The Ringer had a whole host of things they were trying. One of the first steps out of the gate was a public failure (the HBO show *Any Given Wednesday*). But if you expect failures to happen, if you know that's a very normal part of the process, it doesn't feel like a death blow. Simmons noted that they had an "advantage" with The Ringer, because of their experience with Grantland:

> Especially me. I was there from minute one. You're not always going to have wins. How do you deal with something that doesn't work? How do you fix it? How do you take something that you thought was going to work, and it bombed? How do you take heat for something and how do people react? Do they stick together, or maybe you have some crisis behind the scenes. All that stuff, how you handle it collectively, is really important.

In his podcast in June of 2020, Simmons discussed the civil unrest and racial tension across the United States. But his response was tone-deaf, ill-informed, and in some ways, hurtful. It was not one of his finest moments. Twitter exploded (as you might expect). But Simmons opened the next podcast with a thoughtful apology, acknowledging his mishandling of the situation, what he had learned, and how he would do things differently moving forward. Believe it or not, the response on Twitter was mainly gracious. Simmons' willingness to reflect on what didn't go well and to apologize was the same impulse that kept him experimenting with The Ringer, expecting it to be messy along the way.

It doesn't always happen this way, but in this case, the Moonshot actually hit the Moon. Currently, there are *one hundred million downloads* from their podcast network each month (it started with one single podcast, and now they have more than thirty). Read that number again. It's an astonishing number. Between their articles, podcasts, social media videos, GIFs, Twitter personalities, YouTube channel, and a whole host of other things, they embody how young people engage with content in this digital age. In February 2020, Spotify purchased The Ringer for somewhere around $200 million.

Now is The Ringer successful because it sold for a lot of money? Financially, sure, it's successful. But was that the mission, or was the mission the Moonshot? When you look at their staff, a large percentage of those producing content are people in their twenties. The content and the mediums epitomize "youth culture." Which isn't to say it looks anything like *Rolling Stone* magazine. Rather, it looks and feels like what Rolling Stone would feel like if it launched today.

Consider this story for a moment. The Ringer hit the Moon because they were willing to adapt and adjust when something failed, and they had confident leaders embodying that culture. They were open to people and projects working in different ways than expected. They weren't married to one idea as the winning idea. They were able to spot and retain talent, even talent that was raw and in need of development.

What if we took a leaf out of The Ringer's book? What if we became open to trying almost anything? To be willing to adapt and adjust when something failed? To be open to people and projects working in different ways than we expected? What if we became brave leaders willing to live in the ever-present-now and to step into the possibility of mistakes, missteps, and miscues, so we can fail faster and find the future?

Why?

Because we want to see the kingdom of heaven come.

6.

In some ways, Jonathan Brooks *stumbled* into the innovation he was looking for. He wanted the people in his church to physically live in the neighborhood and invest their time, energy, and resources there. Starting the scholarship fund wasn't an accident, but who would've predicted that a scholarship fund would work out the way it did? But God was at work, and the grace was there. Brooks spotted what God was up to and adjusted the innovation accordingly.

When iterating, you start to pay attention to the Grooves of Grace. As Henry Blackaby said, *our task is to find where God is moving and join him in that place.* This is essentially an articulation of the principle in John 5:19, where Jesus says he can only do what he sees his Father doing. That is one way of thinking about a Groove of Grace in the Experimentation Phase. We need eyes to see what God is doing; where there is a supernatural ease, a pathway for kingdom breakthrough that exceeds the effort we're putting in.

Normally when we think about making tweaks and adjustments to something we're iterating, we think of it in terms of what's going wrong or not measuring up. But what if we flipped it and asked, "Where are the Grooves of Grace? What's going well, and the only explanation for the success is that God is at work?" We can spend an enormous amount of time, energy, people-power, money, and resources on all the things that aren't working. But instead, as we're experimenting, perhaps we should be paying more attention to where the fire of the Holy Spirit is at work and throw more gasoline on it! Look for the Grooves of Grace. Remember, there is no kingdom innovation without the ongoing power, presence, work, and leading of the Holy Spirit.

The story of Alpha, one of the most widespread evangelistic innovations of the last twenty-five years, contains all of the essential elements of the innovation pathway. Originally started in 1977 by Charles Marnham at Holy Trinity Brompton, it was designed to help Christians dust-up on their core doctrine, or for believers who were new to the faith. When Nicky Gumbel took over the course in 1990, he saw the potential for something different, if for no other reason than he wasn't like most church leaders. He'd grown up in an agnostic and very secular household, went to all the best schools England had to offer, and ultimately became a Christian in university at Trinity College, Cambridge (later getting a theology degree at Wycliffe Hall, Oxford). When Nicky looked at Alpha, he didn't look through the Curse of Knowledge, but through the eyes of his own unique experience. He was asking different (and better!) questions: *What if the Alpha course was more suitable for people who weren't yet Christians but wanted to explore the Christian faith?* And so the grand experiment began.

The mechanics of Alpha are pretty simple. Individuals interested in exploring the big questions of life and Christianity are invited by friends and family to engage in a ten-week journey. Each week involves a meal, centers on a big question which is explored in a short talk, and engages in well-facilitated discussion. It's low pressure, warm, and very relational. Some of the topics covered include: Who is Jesus? Why did Jesus die? Why and how should I read the Bible? How can I resist evil? Does God heal today? Towards the end of the ten weeks, there's a short retreat weekend where participants get away together for a deeper dive into the faith, and is often affectionately dubbed the "Holy Spirit weekend," as the Holy Spirit is the main topic of discussion, and it's a time when many have their first meaningful encounter with God.

As of today, twenty-six million people have gone through the Alpha course. God has undeniably used this kingdom innovation to lead *millions* of sons and daughters into his family. But let's think about this story for a second, asking a specific question: Why has Alpha been so successful?

There are, undoubtedly, many answers to this question, but what most caught my attention is how Alpha combines two elements that aren't always common bedfellows: rationalist thought and charismatic expression. And these two things clearly come together in the life of Nicky Gumbel himself. He quite literally attended one of the best universities in the world, surrounded by some of the sharpest minds alive, where he earned his law degree before becoming a pastor. I think it's reasonable to assume that Gumbel really knew how to think things through, systematically and logically. But in the 1980s, the late, great John Wimber visited Holy Trinity Brompton, intersecting with Nicky and greatly impacting him. One of Wimber's lasting legacies, and in the UK in particular, is bringing a strong dose of Holy Spirit activity to a people who often describe themselves as *reserved.*

As Rob Warner observes in *Reinventing English Evangelicalism,* "Alpha can be summed up as rationalistic conservatism combined with Wimberist charismatic expressivism ... this is a highly unusual, even paradoxical hybrid." As you can imagine, for those who are Cessationists or unfamiliar with this kind of charismatic experience, there is a natural wariness of the Alpha course. But wherever you land, theologically or pragmatically, this is one of the principle reasons it works: The head, the heart, and the hands come together in one Spirit-saturated experience.

Wimber had a way with words, regularly using clever turns of phrases, sticky sayings, sometimes referred to as *Wimberisms.* One of his most popular Wimberisms echoes both the concept of Grooves of Grace and Blackaby's key insight: "Find where God is, and get behind what he's doing. He always wins."

So here is Nicky Gumbel, one of the sharpest Christians minds of his generation, but also someone apprenticed in joining Jesus in what he's up to. Gumbel sees the Grooves of Grace and pivots Alpha from being a class that taught basic doctrine to believers, to something that became an evangelistic phenomenon.

How did Nicky Gumbel find out Alpha worked with people who weren't Christians? He experimented with people who weren't Christians!

One of the barriers to kingdom innovation is that we design things *for* people, rather than design *with* them. My overwhelming experience again and again in kingdom innovation is that people are inherently curious, and if something is posed as an experiment and with an end date, they are incredibly gracious.

If you're looking for a breakthrough in evangelism, involve people who aren't Christians to help you (no seriously, it really works!). If you're looking to figure out disciple-making, find people who've never been discipled before. If you're starting a new business, experiment with people who are most likely to purchase your product. If you're in the non-profit space, get feedback from the people you're wanting to serve.

Launch your MVP.

Start small with your prototype.

Expect to get punched in the mouth.

Iterate.

Use the laboratory of your own life.

Find the Grooves of Grace.

Join Jesus in what he's already doing.

LEADER INNOVATION LAB

KEY PRINCIPLES FROM PHASE 3: EXPERIMENTATION

Goal: We launch, test, adjust, and relaunch the innovation until the prototype we are testing achieves the measured goals set out.

Iteration

As you experiment, pay attention to what's working and what's not working. Make adjustments, adapt, and tweak as you go.

Scalable

We want to design with the end in mind, and the end that we want is something that can spread and rapidly reproduce.

Fail Fast. Succeed Sooner

The sooner you start experimenting, the sooner it won't work. The sooner you can learn from it, the sooner you can get to a place where you've had enough iterations that it could work.

The Laboratory of Your Life

One of the patterns we see in the Scriptures and in history is people using their personal lives as a laboratory for God to do something in and through them.

Grooves of Grace

When you're experimenting, ask God to give you eyes to see where he's at work. Where is something supernaturally easy or bringing more kingdom fruit than you expected that can only be explained by God's work?

The Master Tool for the Experimentation Phase: The Make the Mark Tool

PHASE 3:
EXPERIMENTATION

MAKE THE
MARK TOOL

 Watch the training video for the Make the Mark Master Tool at DougPaul.org/ReadyorNotLab

Nuts-and-Bolts Leader Coaching

Whatever you're launching with your MVP, you'll want to pay close attention to the team you're inviting to lead and participate, as you push your prototype out to sea.

In *Making Ideas Happen*, Scott Belsky outlines the need for putting together a team with different skills and points of view that will all complement what you're designing with your prototype. When putting a team together, you're wanting to find the alchemy of the following.

Big Picture Pioneers

These are people who can see the big picture and feel the innovation in their gut. They are often dreamers, highly intuitive pioneers, and abstract thinkers who can connect unlikely dots together.

Pragmatic Doers

These are people who may not lead with pioneering, but they don't mind being guinea pigs! But what they bring to the table is a nuts-and-bolts know-how of the way to run things in the real world, and have a keen sense of what will work and not work for "normal people."

Need-the-Breakthrough

These are people who need the breakthrough themselves. They will love that you're trying to figure this thing out, will be incredibly forgiving, and give important feedback to what they are experiencing.

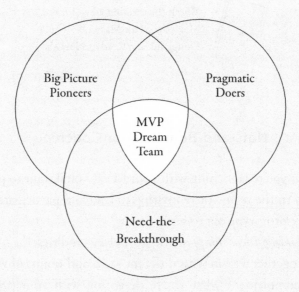

Remember the story of Doug Dietz and the scary machine? This is exactly the alchemy he created when he put his team together: designers, technicians, social workers, employees from a children's museum, and kids. "Instead of machines that looked like 'giant car crushers,' they designed machines that looked like pirate ships, space crafts and canoes. Now ... kids are almost never sedated before a scan. In fact, they often ask if they can come back again for another."

Questions to Sharpen Your Iteration Skills

Discipleship

Who are the people in your church that have seen extraordinary spiritual growth through your church family? What happened? Where are there Grooves of Grace in their story?

Leadership

When have there been times in your life where you've pivoted your leadership after making a leadership mistake? How can you multiply that learning into your leadership development culture?

Mission

When was the last time you saw a whole "household" (either biological family or a network of relationships) come to faith in your current church setting? How did it happen? What can you learn from the Grooves of Grace in that situation?

Worship

Evaluate the last three years of ministry life in your church. When were the times that people were most open and available to God? What was happening in their life or in the life of the church? What was God up to?

Reconciliation

Where are there unlikely friendships in your life or in the life of your church? How were those friendships formed? What keeps them strong?

Operating System

When was the last time you or your church attempted a significant "change" in the central DNA of your church, either because of DNA clarification or because of a call from the Lord to repentance? What things went well? What things didn't go well? What would you do differently?

This is a Spiritual Process

When you're in the Experimentation Phase, you're confronted with the possibility of failure. And when that possibility comes to the surface, it reveals all the motivations of your heart, doesn't it? At the end of the day, when it comes to motivations, we are all a mixed bag. There are the pure reasons we started the journey, but pretty quickly, a lot of "us" gets mixed in. Our desire for success, attention, accolades, rewards. Many of us have a savior complex. All of the trappings are right there.

Mark Sayers, in his book *Facing Leviathan*, puts it like this:

> Christian leadership is a strange beast. In its truest form it runs counter to almost everything the world has taught us: To create ourselves by accumulating riches, experiences, and relationships, and, most importantly, to broadcast them to the audience that will mirror back to us the messages we wish to hear. The gospel asks us to do the opposite of this. Out of Jesus' mouth is uttered the strange, jarring commandment: "Whoever wants to be my disciple must deny themselves and take up their cross daily and follow me."

The question is whether we take our great fear of failure and mixed bag of motivations to the cross. Will we choose to die to these things? Will we let Jesus lovingly ring those things out of us, like oil from a dirty rag? In real time, that is what the process of sanctification does for us.

But understand how this spiritual process works out practically:

- Without failure, there is no innovation.
- Until I choose to die to self, I'll never regularly choose failure as a normal part of my life.
- So am I willing to choose to die to self?

It is often in the Experimentation Phase when we see our own humanity in a new way and our continued ability to turn the good things into the supreme. We see how we can make idols out of anything. We are, after all, a crafty bunch. We can make an idol of innovation itself. But we can do the same thing with perfect theology and doctrine, success, safety, or significance. Put anything in our hands, and we can make it into an idol.

For me personally, I have to keep dying to the timing of the experimentation process. I'm what could be generously described as a control freak, and as we are iterating with outcomes that can only work if God is in it, I come face-to-face with my need to control outcomes and timetables. But when we lose control, we're not actually losing it. We're losing the *illusion* of it. And honestly? Left to my own devices, I kind of like that illusion. On some days I really like to think I'm in control of my own destiny.

I was recently working with a church, and they got to a place in this phase where it became really obvious that unless God did a work in their hearts and minds, the only place they were going was backward. They weren't going to get the innovation; they were going to get a souped-up version of what they were already doing. But there was nothing I could do but pray and intercede. As the book of James says, God needed to intervene and reveal the wisdom that only comes from heaven. When that revelation came, they needed to respond to this grace by walking in the grooves he was creating. There was no other way forward. But fortunately, as the song says, he's a *Way Maker.*

In this phase, for me, one of the great spiritual speed bumps is facing my own fear of failure. According to Clotaire Rapaille, this isn't that big a surprise. In his book *The Culture Code*, he contends there is a code written into the very DNA of a country's culture, and one core piece of American culture seems to be the need to succeed. For many of us who are North American, that means our root fear is the fear of failure. In some ways, whether you have "the need to succeed" or not, we're all swimming in those cultural waters.

But here's what that ultimately does inside of me. It helps me surrender more completely to what God wants to do, and to surrender to his perfect will in my life.

Success in the kingdom means obedience and abiding in Jesus. There is no better place to be.

4

MOBILIZATION

The Secret Trick to Hacking a Hit

"THE ONLY TIME I COULD WRITE SONGS WAS WHEN MY
FROZEN DINNER WAS IN THE MICROWAVE. THE REST OF THE
TIME I WAS DOING HOMEWORK."

1.

Hannah More was born into humble circumstances in 1745 in Fishponds, England, a small town just northeast of Bristol. Her father, Jacob More, taught at the local free school, which provided education to underprivileged kids through charitable giving. Jacob believed girls should receive an equal education to boys, and so after he'd finished teaching each day, he returned home to teach his five daughters all of the foundations of education, including Latin and mathematics. Theirs was a close, Christian family, and the Mores instilled Christian virtues and sensibilities into their daughters.

At the age of eighteen, Hannah wrote her first play. Entitled *The Search After Happiness*, it was a virtue-based drama encompassing the wisdom and wit More would eventually become known for.

When More was twenty-eight, she moved to London where she seemed to find a Groove of Grace, as door after door opened for her. She met the legendary actor David Garrick, who also managed the Theatre Royal, and was one of the most important figures in London theater society. She had forwarded him a draft of a play she was working on, and he loved it.

At thirty-two years old, More wrote a play called *Percy*, a tragedy that debuted at the Covent Garden Theatre. It was a huge success and became the most renowned play of that generation. The printing presses couldn't keep up, as productions and sales of the screenplay spread from England to France to Austria.

More continued to churn out plays, poems, essays, and pamphlets at an unparalleled rate, almost all of them literary in nature. As Eric Metaxas points out in his book *Seven Women*:

> That an unmarried woman via her own talents and efforts could rise from humble circumstances to eventual fame and great wealth was an idea far ahead of its time. Social mobility of any kind was not the norm in the late eighteenth and early nineteenth centuries, so a poor school-master's daughter mixing it up with London's elites was remarkable. Perhaps more remarkable yet is her acceptance as an equal by many of the most prominent men of her era.

We don't have a true grid for understanding More's popularity, but it would be something akin to that of J. K. Rowling, the English author of the *Harry Potter* series.

As More rose to fame, the Christian understanding she had been raised with began to deepen into a profoundly personal faith. She'd read *Cardiphonia,* written by John Newton, the former-slave-trader-turned-minister who also wrote the hymn "Amazing Grace." Captivated by his experience and his insights on faith, they began a spiritual friendship through exchanging letters, in which Hannah regularly asked him questions about life.

After a few years of corresponding with Newton, More finally met him in person, and in that same fateful year, she also met a young politician by the name of William Wilberforce, who would become her closest ally in winning the great fight of her life: the abolition of the slave trade.

In the span of a few years, the slave trade moved from being a largely abstract reality in the British consciousness to being at the forefront of its politics. During that time, More, Wilberforce, and other members of what became known as the Clapham Sect threw everything against the wall to see what would stick. Through years of persistent innovative effort, the campaigners successfully mobilized public support, eventually leading to the enactment of a law that banned slavery from the British Empire.

As we will soon discover, it was poems, posters, and pamphlets that eventually mobilized much of the nation to campaign and petition for the abolition of slavery.

But what we want to uncover with Hannah More and the abolitionists is one big question: *Why* did it work?

2.

Toward the end of 1995, Rivers Cuomo enrolled at Harvard University to study classical composition.

There were two factors that separated Cuomo from the rest of his classmates. First, he'd recently undergone the Ilizarov procedure. When he was born, his left leg was two inches shorter than his right leg, and the painful medical procedure involved breaking the bones, attaching an external steel brace, and months of stretching and physiotherapy. The second differentiator? As the frontman of the band Weezer, he was one of the most famous new rock stars on the planet. *The Blue Album* had just certified platinum (selling more than one million copies), and included iconic tracks such as "Undone—The Sweater Song," "My Name is Jonas," and "Say it Ain't So."

In the end, classical composition didn't stick. "The only time I could write songs," Cuomo later commented on his time at Harvard, "was when my frozen dinner was in the microwave. The rest of the time I was doing homework." He dropped out two semesters before graduating, citing a hatred for modern classical composition and a wistful longing for a Weezer reunion reunion. (He eventually finished his degree in 2006, earning a BA in English.)

But one thing *did stick* from his time at Harvard, and not something you'd expect for someone who'd later write inane lyrics for songs such as "Pork and Beans" or "Beverly Hills."

Coding.

Cuomo started to obsessively code, using the programming language Python, to study music and then generate new music ideas.

As Gab Ginsberg wrote in her article for *Billboard* magazine,

> The Weezer frontman has long used algorithms to optimize his songwriting, funneling creativity by way of laptop applications just like the programming language Python. Cuomo is known to carefully dismantle a hit song, examining each element to find out exactly what works, and apply that knowledge to his own writing process.

In other words, Cuomo wanted to take the mystery out of why some music works and other music doesn't. *Why does a song become a hit?*

Over time, his acumen grew, and so did his legendary spreadsheets. In describing the writing of a recent Weezer album, Cuomo commented,

> I wrote a program to get all the information from Spotify's API, and used the songs that have been hottest [since] 1994 ... about 200 songs within the report. So we picked the highest ones and began studying them.

But he didn't just study them. He used them to generate tempos, chord progressions, and *hooks* (the catchiest part of a song that gets stuck in your head). Talking about Weezer's 2017 release, *Pacific Daydream*, journalist Dan Hyman of *Rolling Stone* wrote,

> Cuomo estimates he drew on thousands of riffs, chord progressions, and beats stored on his home computer for the album, and even wrote a custom formula in Google Sheets to pair up musical ideas—some dating back to 2000—based on their key and tempo.

People assume that what makes some songs successful is a mystery. But Rivers Cuomo turned it into an algorithm on Python.

Here in our fourth phase of kingdom innovation, we move to *mobilization*: *Once our prototype has seen breakthrough, we need to know why and how it worked so that we can mobilize many to multiply it.*

Weezer has released thirteen albums. According to Nielsen (a music sales tracking system), they have 1.4 *billion* on-demand streams. The ridiculous song "Beverly Hills"? At the time of writing, it's been watched fifty-two million times on YouTube. Weezer songs are generally stupid, shallow, and inane. But they are also wickedly catchy, and they've been writing hits (and cashing those royalty checks!) for more than twenty-five years.

Rivers Cuomo literally created an algorithm to crack the code of "Why and how do these songs work?" And if we can similarly figure out how to answer the "why" and "how" questions, we might just get an innovation that can reach the many.

3.

In Roger Martin's groundbreaking book *The Design of Business,* he describes a process that is fundamental for understanding mobilization—what he refers to as *the knowledge funnel.* It's the movement from something being a mystery to becoming something we can repeatedly and predictably put into action. It's the same process Rivers Cuomo underwent by reverse engineering successful songs in order to write *new* successful songs. After all, why stick with one hit song when you could have twelve?

Here's how Martin starts to explain the knowledge funnel:

> Over the course of time, phenomena enter our collective consciousness as mysteries—things that we observe, but don't really understand. For instance, the mystery of gravity once confounded our forefathers: when they looked around the world, they saw that many things, like rocks, seemed to fall to the ground almost immediately; but others didn't— like birds, and some seemed to take forever, like leaves.

In response to these things, Martin says that we bring questions to the table around things that seem mysterious or complex. It could be something as big as the mystery of gravity or as concrete as "What makes a hit song a hit?" We take on the role of the detective and enter into the process of unwinding a mystery.

The Knowledge Funnel

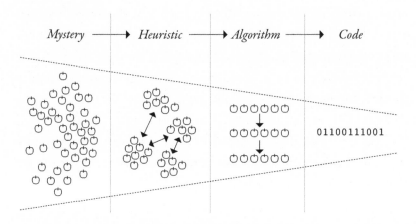

As we ask questions and get under-the-hood of the mystery, we start to see the way things connect and even repeat. Patterns start to emerge. We develop what Martin calls *heuristics*. "Heuristics," Martin says, "are rules of thumb or sets of guidelines for solving a mystery by organized exploration of the possibilities. So why do things fall down? We develop a notion of a universal force called 'gravity' that tends to pull things down."

Once we have a general rule of thumb and some principles to work with, Martin says the next step is to develop an *algorithm*: a repeatable, practical formula for doing something. There was a breakthrough, but it's a mystery why it happened. Maybe it felt like a blind squirrel finding a nut. After spending time working on the heuristic, you're able to start to understand why it happened and create some general principles for not only why it happened, but how it could happen again. With an algorithm, we're systematizing the innovation.

Finally, there's *code*:

In the modern era, a fourth important step has been added to the sequence of mystery to heuristic to algorithm. Eventually, some algorithms now get coded into software. This means reducing the algorithm—the strict set of rules—into a series of 0's and 1's—binary code—that enables a computer to produce a result.

For our purposes, we're not too concerned about diving into software development but rather what coding can mean for us as it relates to kingdom innovation—the concrete practices we can repeat over and over again that make the innovation sustainable. After all, perhaps the only thing more frustrating than being stuck and in need of an innovation is experiencing it once and not knowing how to repeat it.

What Martin is describing on a conceptual level is what we're uncovering on a practical level in this book. We're trying to understand a codified process for how kingdom innovation happens so we can repeat it. I believe this is one of the most important skills for any Christian leader to develop. It's the difference between stumbling into something and not being able to repeat it, versus creating a virtuous cycle of kingdom innovation because you've developed that specific leadership muscle.

Here's how Martin articulates that critical difference between seeing innovation once and seeing it repeatedly:

> The difference between them is the difference between one-hit-wonder Don McLean, author of "American Pie", and Bruce Springsteen, composer of scores of hit songs. For McLean, the mystery remained just that: he came up with a single inspiration that created one random event—one of the biggest pop song hits of all time. Yet he failed to produce another hit of any consequence in his entire musical career. In contrast, Springsteen developed a heuristic—a way of understanding the world and the people in it—that enables him to write songs that have great meaning to people and are immensely popular. His mastery of heuristics has allowed him to generate a steady stream of hit albums over a 30-year period.

To a certain degree, there's a reason some songs become hits and others don't. Springsteen went about it in a different way, but he figured out what Rivers Cuomo figured out. They both *codified* the process.

Now, perhaps you might be persuaded to tenaciously learn the skills of kingdom innovation by asking yourself this question: Do I want my leadership track record to look more like Don McLean or Bruce Springsteen?

Let me bring it big picture for you: In the third phase of kingdom innovation, you launch your Minimum Viable Process (MVP), and you keep iterating on that MVP until it hits the marks you set. You want to know it works. Once that innovation starts really humming, the mobilization question is: *Why is it working?*

When I was growing up, there was a lay leader in our church, and everywhere he went, he discipled people. He did that for more than thirty years, and all these years later, there are hundreds of people who've been discipled into spiritual maturity. His patience, faithfulness, and persistence over many decades was remarkable. The problem? It never went beyond him. People never understood how he did it—*why it was working*—and as a result, very few people repeated for others what he did for them. Discipleship therefore stopped at one generation. Imagine if he had codified his process and taught it to everyone he discipled? What if everyone he discipled then went and discipled others in the same way?

When we know *why* something is working, we move from mystery in the Identification Phase, to heuristic in the Ideation and Experimentation Phases, to algorithm and code in the Mobilization Phase.

If you know why something is working, and drill it down to best practices that are easily transferable, the innovation that starts with a few can spread to the many.

Codification is what happens when the blind squirrel goes from simply being lucky to finding the nut over and over again. When Rivers Cuomo started tinkering with algorithms and spreadsheets, he was able to decode the mystery of a great song hook, ultimately leading to dozens of singles reaching millions of fans. It was enough for Bill Wilson's wife that he was sober, but Wilson wanted other people to experience freedom from addiction. The only way he could do that was by walking through the knowledge funnel. It started with mystery and a giant *why* question: *Why* can't I stay sober? By asking *how* questions, he was able to add general principles from the patterns he observed (addicts need people to walk alongside them, and every day must be viewed as a battle to conquer) and by asking *what* questions, he discovered practices that were not only simple and wildly effective, but highly reproducible (sponsors, Twelve Steps, and sticky language).

Stitching it all together, can you begin to see how the intersection of the Golden Circle and our three Ps align with Martin's work?

Big Question	3 Ps	Knowledge Funnel	Bill Wilson
Why?	Paradigm	Mystery	Why can't I stay sober?
How?	Principle	Heuristic	Every day is a battle to conquer; addicts need people to walk alongside them
What?	Practice	Algorithm & Code	Sponsors, Twelve Steps, sticky language, etc.

Codification is the key. By pushing through the mystery, into the heuristic, and finally getting to the algorithm and code, Wilson went from one sober person to one hundred million sober people.

From one hit song to dozens. From a few abolitionists to a movement of them. Codification is where mobilization begins.

4.

"Why did it work?"

That's the question we asked earlier of Hannah More and the abolition of the slave trade. If mobilization is the process of discovering why something worked so it can spread to the many, then we must consider what actually mobilizes people into action.

Undoubtedly, the abolition of the slave trade is one of the most significant breakthroughs we'll explore in the pages of this book, and what they uncovered is instrumental to our understanding of how to mobilize others.

When William Wilberforce met More, she was wealthy, famous, and the voice of a generation. Shortly after first meeting, More approached Wilberforce, along with a small group of other leaders, and asked him to take on abolition as one of his only political issues; to commit to it until it became the law of the land. After a time of reflection and prayer, Wilberforce agreed.

The strategy was simple, yet sophisticated: Wilberforce would lead the political operation of abolition in Parliament, while Hannah More led out the cultural populist arm. Very early on they recognized that if they were to change the law, they needed to win the hearts and the political will of the people. It would take both More *and* Wilberforce, and it would take them working together.

When Wilberforce worked with Sir William Dolben to pass the Slave Trade Act of 1788, Hannah More published her poem *Slavery*, which was specifically written to help the average person engage with a topic they knew very little about. Knowing she had a captive audience, she gave the general public a first glimpse of the horrors of slavery.

"Most of Hannah's readers," Eric Metaxas writes, "had never seen an African and thought of slavery as an abstract economic necessity." More coordinated with artist Josiah Wedgwood, who mass-produced the now-famous poster and medallion of a slave in chains, with the question emblazoned beneath, "Am I not a man and a brother?" Posters were created to show how tightly slaves were packed into ships. At the exact moment the bill was introduced, the posters and the poem were *everywhere*.

More, Wilberforce, and Wedgwood all knew and understood the great evil of slavery. They knew *how* they got this revelation themselves, so they were almost certainly looking to recreate the conditions for others. It started with a move of heart and a paradigm shift for the few. If they could codify their own transformation for other people, moving from mystery to code, they could try to replicate the same process for the many.

Most other people were largely unaware of the implications of slavery. And so introducing a bill without first explaining the plight would be like giving an answer to people who don't yet know the question.

While there was now a populist surge behind the bill in Parliament, the bill that was passed only slightly altered the conditions of slave ships. The posters and the poem were wonderfully innovative, but they weren't enough. They needed more. First, the masses needed to be aware of the evil. But then they needed a change of heart as well.

That's 101 for kingdom people, right? We need our stone hearts to be replaced with hearts of flesh.

Paradigm shifts are often about the heart—the seat of gut-level, intuitive decision-making—as the reality of the world impacts our emotional selves. The abolitionists knew nothing would change if the general public didn't even know about or sympathize with the plight of the abducted Africans. Hannah More needed the British people to experience a change of heart, and so she needed a story big enough to captivate them. The good news? She was one of the most prolific popular storytellers of her generation.

Now, at the same time the first abolitionist bill was failing to pass, all over England, short, inexpensive pamphlets were starting to pop up, penned by the English-born (but American revolutionary) Thomas Paine. Paine was living in France at the time, and was a key propogandist for the French Revolution. Paine's pamphlets advocated rebellion toward any authority (including God's); freedom for individuals without any restraint; as well as highlighting the "charade" of Christianity and the coming triumph of secular liberalism. Hannah More immediately sensed the danger of these sentiments for the spiritual well-being of the English people. The life Paine outlined was selfish, hedonistic, and narcissistic—pretty much the antithesis of Christianity.

If Thomas Paine's aim was to use these pamphlets to harden people's hearts, More would use the same tool for the opposite effect, and with far more success. She began to produce a series of cheap pamphlets called *Village Politics,* written specifically for "the mechanics, journeymen, and labourers in Great Britain." She wrote on the gospel, goodness, Christian virtues, and a host of other topics. As the popularity of *Village Politics* grew, a number of editions addressed the issue of Africa, slavery, and the West Indies. She wasn't going after the intellectual or social elite; she was going right after the heart of the everyday person for whom Thomas Paine was also contending.

She was fighting fire with fire.

It's hard for us, more than two hundred years later, to comprehend the popularity of these pamphlets. Sitting down at night, kicking back, and reading a good pamphlet doesn't exactly sound like bingeing on a new Netflix show. But the pamphlets were so popular, many people reproduced their own copies to give to friends and family at their own expense—and printing wasn't cheap.

From March 1795 to September 1798, there were more than one hundred editions of *Village Politics*. More wrote more than half of them and oversaw the development of the remaining half. Like any good writer attempting to reach the masses, the writing improved over time as they figured out what worked and what didn't. What did the audience connect to? What went over their heads? Each edition was like a new experiment, an iteration of the previous one: publish a new edition, then tweak, adapt, change, cut, iterate. Rinse. Repeat.

This was a mountainous undertaking, but Hannah More knew that abolition would never happen unless she swayed public opinion. She needed a movement filled with mobilized people; but until those everyday people knew about the atrocities of slavery, and their hearts were moved, the abolition didn't have a chance.

There was a twenty-year gap from the introduction of the first Parliamentary bill and the final passing of the Slave Trade Act of 1807. It took another twenty-six years before slavery was outlawed in all of the British Empire.

Hannah More, William Wilberforce, and the other abolitionists had a revelation from God—a paradigm shift in the way they saw these abducted and oppressed brothers and sisters. In order to spread that revelation as quickly as possible, they innovated with posters, plays, and pamphlets. There was no eureka moment or overnight hit. Over time, with thousands of hours of work, like Rivers Cuomo using Python on pop songs, More codified what would change hearts and minds.

5.

But how do we codify when something *isn't* working?

In the spring of 1963, the American Civil Rights Movement was *stuck*.

The problem with successful revolutions is that facts get lost to legend. As time goes by, and rough edges get smoothed out, we tend to only remember the folklore highlights: Rosa Parks on the bus, the March on Washington, the "I Have a Dream" speech, the passage of the Civil Rights Act, quickly followed by Selma and the Voting Rights Act.

In reality, it was a long road to those momentous events and pieces of legislation, and extraordinary innovation was at the heart of it all. It didn't begin with Birmingham's triumvirate of leaders and Project C, but it's as good a place as any to start.[†]

Obviously you've heard of Dr. Martin Luther King Jr. He was the face of the Birmingham push, invited by Birmingham leader Fred Shuttlesworth, a preacher whom the Ku Klux Klan had begrudgingly decided not to kill. It was Shuttlesworth who dubbed the new phase of the Birmingham struggle "Project C" (the "C" standing for confrontation). But there was a third person on the scene: Wyatt Tee Walker, Dr. King's long-time fixer and strategy-man. Together, these three leaders formed the leadership core of Project C.

Walker had a strategy in mind, and it seemed hatched from a lifetime of demonstrations-meeting-irony-meeting-publicity. A Baptist minister from Massachusetts, this was a man who, in between preaching at church services in Petersburg, Virginia, *took his family* to a whites-only public library with the intention of getting arrested. He was in violation of the segregation laws of the town, located just forty-five minutes south of the former Capital of the Confederacy.

[†] Please note that while I draw upon quite a few sources for the sections about to come on Civil Rights, the story about Wyatt Walker and Project C were shaped by the book, endnotes, and sources of Malcolm Gladwell, *David and Goliath: Underdogs, Misfits, and the Art of Battling Giants* (New York: Little, Brown and Company, 2013), chapter six, 165–193.

And because irony seemed to amuse him, upon his arrest he was holding a library book in his hand, a biography of Robert E. Lee, the confederate general and local Virginian viewed by the black community as a symbol of slavery and oppression. A picture of his arrest, book in hand, made its way into all kinds of newspapers. Walker didn't just want to get arrested and cause a scene; he wanted it served with a side of irony.

You want to know about Wyatt Walker? That story says it all.

His plan for Project C was simple, and it had three phases. Phase 1: They would lead a series of sit-ins that would draw national publicity to the problems of segregation in the specific city of Birmingham. They had to draw a media crowd. Phase 2: A coordinated boycott of businesses in the downtown district to put pressure on the white business community around the issue of segregation, making them feel it where it hurt most—their wallets. Phase 3: A series of marches designed to fill up the jails of Birmingham, because once the jails were full, the police would actually have to deal with the protestors, and the world would be watching.

Project C's biggest challenge? Its success depended on how Eugene "Bull" Connor, the bourbon-swilling Commissioner of Public Safety for the city of Birmingham, responded. Project C came at a tenuous moment in the life of the Civil Rights struggle. Dr. King and Wyatt Walker had just employed a similar strategy in a long-standing effort in Albany, Georgia, and it had gone nowhere. The Albany police chief, a man by the name of Laurie Pritchett, always let cooler heads prevail and seemed to have a rudimentary respect for King and Walker's tactics. There would be weeks at a time when Pritchett wouldn't return home and instead chose to move into a downtown motel to keep any violence at bay, even missing a wedding anniversary with his wife.

Point being? King and Walker had just left Albany in defeat. If they didn't succeed in Birmingham, the press would stop caring, stop covering the story, and the demonstrators themselves would stop turning out. As Dr. King put it, they needed Bull Connor to "tip his hand" and show all of America the ugly reality of racism, a misstep Pritchett never made.

They were stuck, and time was running out. Forget heuristic, algorithm, or code. The way forward for the Civil Rights Movement was shrouded in mystery. And you can't codify and repeat what's still mysterious.

But then Wyatt Walker had an idea.

CHAPTER EIGHT

The Revolution Will Be Televised

"NEVER DOUBT THAT A SMALL GROUP OF THOUGHTFUL,
COMMITTED CITIZENS CAN CHANGE THE WORLD; INDEED,
IT'S THE ONLY THING THAT EVER HAS."

1.

Like the English abolitionists, the leaders of Project C were attempting to help white America see the face of evil. In the early 1960s, only 26 percent of US residents felt race was a problem facing America. It meant that while people knew about segregation, restricted voting rights, and a whole host of other race related issues, the vast majority of white Americans were fine continuing with the status quo. They needed to *experience something* that would turn their hearts and their heads.

It's virtually impossible to mobilize a movement until the heart and the head meet. And that's just what the Civil Rights Movement was still struggling with.

Several weeks into Project C in Birmingham, things were not going well. Dr. King had just spoken in front of seven hundred people, trying to churn out support for the demonstrations they were planning. They had a grand total of nine volunteers. (Many of the African Americans in Birmingham were rightly concerned they'd be fired by their white employers for being associated with anything King was doing.) The next day, a different person stepped up to the platform, delivering an impassioned plea to the black community of Birmingham, and he fared even worse, recruiting only seven volunteers.

On Palm Sunday, 1963, they got a lucky break.

A grand total of twenty-two protestors were marching, but the march started an hour and a half late. While they were waiting to start, more than a thousand black spectators lined up to *watch* the demonstration. The next day, much to Walker's delight, various newspapers misreported the story. Instead of saying there were only twenty-two people marching, and a thousand onlookers, the media reported there were eleven hundred demonstrators marching on the streets of Birmingham. "They can only see through white eyes," Walker recalled. "They cannot distinguish even between Negro demonstrators and Negro spectators. All they know is Negroes."

Day after day, they kept sending a few dozen marchers down the streets of Birmingham, lined with black spectators, and day after day the news reported mass demonstrations happening in the city.

Now, Bull Connor, the Commissioner of Public Safety, had a habit of drinking bourbon in the morning at the Molton Hotel as he read his daily newspaper, and the misreporting must have driven him crazy. Eventually he decided enough was enough. Wyatt Walker explained:

> Bull Connor had something in him about not letting these n****** get to city hall. I prayed that he'd keep trying to stop us ... Birmingham would have been lost if Bull had let us go down to the city hall and pray. If he had let us do that and stepped aside, where would we be? There would be no movement, no publicity.

And with no publicity and no news coverage, America wasn't going to see the truth.

Four weeks into the protest, Walker threw out a new idea, which they immediately decided to experiment with. They needed to fill the jails, and they just weren't generating enough demonstrators to do that. They'd gotten significant traction in Phase 1 and Phase 2 of Project C, but until those jails were full, and Bull Connor had to deal with protestors he couldn't immediately lock away, they would never see the breakthrough they needed.

His idea? Invite young teenagers into the struggle. And thus start what became known as the 1963 Children's Crusade. Maybe it would work, maybe it wouldn't. But the MVP for them was obvious: Let's experiment with getting teens involved.

Here's how Malcolm Gladwell retells the story. Notice the different elements that went into their experiment:

> On the last Monday in April, [Wyatt Walker] dropped off leaflets at all of the black high schools around the county. "Come to 16th Street Baptist Church at noon on Thursday. Don't ask permission." The city's most popular black disc jockey—Shelley 'the Playboy' Stewart—sent out the same message to his young listeners: "Kids, there's gonna be a party at the park." The FBI got wind of the plan and told Bull Connor, who announced that any child who skipped school would be expelled. It made no difference. The kids came in droves. Walker called the day the children arrived "D Day."
>
> At one o'clock, the doors to the church opened and King's lieutenants began sending the children out. They held signs saying "Freedom" or "I'll Die To Make This Land My Home." They sang "We Shall Overcome" and "Ain't Gonna Let Nobody Turn Me Around." Outside the church, Connor's police officers waited. The children dropped to their knees and prayed, then filed into the open doors of the paddy wagons. Then another dozen came out. Then another dozen, and another, and another ...

That day, more than six hundred teenagers were put in jail. *The experiment worked.*

The next Friday was dubbed Double D-Day. One week after the original experiment, fifteen hundred kids skipped school and went to 16th Street Baptist. Like the Friday before, at one o'clock the kids started filing out of the church.

Soon enough the Birmingham jails were full, but the kids kept streaming out. "Do not cross," Bull Connor warned. "If you come any further, we will turn the fire hoses on you." Some of the firemen were hesitant, so Connor told the fire chief, "Turn 'em on, or go home." The hoses knocked people down, stripped the clothes from some of their bodies and cut through the crowd like a knife. "Bring

154 READY OR NOT

out the dogs," Connor ordered. The children came closer, and the dogs lunged forward, taking out chunks of flesh as they did.

The next day, the headlines across the United States carried the story of the police brutality aimed at children refusing to fight back, with powerful photographs of peaceful protesters being attacked by water hoses, billy clubs, and German shepherd dogs.

The leaders of the Civil Rights Movement codified why their strategy was working, and they mobilized more and more people.

Two years later, in March of 1965, a group of two thousand peaceful marchers attempted to cross the Edmund Pettus Bridge in Selma, Alabama. The bridge is constructed in such a way that the marchers couldn't see the armed police officers waiting for them on the other side until they reached the midway point of the bridge. Seeing what awaited them, the marchers moved forward into the jaws of certain violence. The police met them with the cavalry, and protesters were beaten, trampled by horses, and tear gassed in what became known in the US as *Bloody Sunday*.

In that day and time, the vast majority of North American households watched the evening news, and that night, people watched Bloody Sunday in absolute horror. That night, the revolution *was* televised.

2.

In 1987, an ad started airing on televisions all across the United States, in which actor John Roselius cracked an egg into a hot frying pan, watched it sizzle, and metaphorically narrated the effects of illegal narcotics on the neurons. "This is your brain on drugs," he commented, as the egg fried on the pan at lightning speed. Roselius ended the ad with a simple rhetorical device: "Any questions?"

The ad, which has been parodied to death and is probably the most famous anti-drug video of all time, is a classic example of what Dan and Chip Heath describe as "tripping over the truth." In their book *The Power of Moments*, the Heath brothers define the term this way: "When you have a sudden realization, one that you didn't see coming, and one that you know viscerally is right, you've tripped over the truth. It's a defining moment that in an instant can change the way you see the world." In Roselius' ad, viewers viscerally experienced what drugs would do to their brain; aimed at helping them "trip over the truth" and resist the temptation to experiment with narcotics.

But while it's a famous ad, studies showed it was largely ineffective. Yes, viewers might have tripped over the truth, but what was the next step? "Just say no?" Does that sound like a compelling course of action for teenagers facing peer pressure? What was going to mobilize them to make a different decision? Their minds might have been changed, but remember what we now know about shifting paradigms? The *heart* also needs to be convinced.

This is where it gets really interesting for us, and where Hannah More's story and Project C intersect: How do you get someone to see the truth of something that *you* can see, but that others can't? Because if the innovation is going to spread, we have to beat the Curse of Knowledge a second time. Like a villain in a horror movie, he keeps getting back up.

Hannah More created an innovation that worked not simply because they helped people trip over the truth cognitively, but because their *hearts* were softened. She could have shamed, humiliated, and publicly embarrassed the people of England for not immediately knowing they were disgracing the image of God in another image bearer. But in doing so, the Curse of Knowledge would have won out, again. Instead, More awakened people's hearts to the evil of the slave trade.

When we talk about "tripping over the truth" in relation to kingdom innovation, it involves a deep spiritual process. We're not just looking for people to have a shift of the mind. If an intellectual shift was all that was needed, we wouldn't need a Savior. If this is a

God-truth that we're praying people will trip over, we want it to fully intersect with the heart, mind, and spirit so it can continue to grow.

Remember the ultimatum Jonathan Brooks gave to his congregation? *Move into the neighborhood or leave the church.* Remember how *no one moved*? In the end it was the scholarship fund that God used to help people trip over the truth, soften their hearts, and create a clear pathway to mobilize the church back into the neighborhood.

More, Brooks, and Project C were all successful in helping people trip over the truth, and in doing so they created a group of willing people they could mobilize into a movement. But the secret to mobilization is giving people a next step they can easily say yes to once the heart is engaged.

After all ... getting teenagers to say no to peer pressure?

It's going to take more than a fried egg on a hot pan.

3.

Not too long ago, Derek Sivers hopped onto a TED stage and broke down the anatomy of a movement. He used grainy video footage of a spur of the moment dance party that started with one person and grew to hundreds in under three minutes. When Sivers finished his talk, he received one of the few standing ovations in TED history.

The dance party story went something like this:

On a sloped, grassy plain, one shirtless man is dancing to Santigold's song "Unstoppable." And when I say dancing, I mean he's leaving it all out there. Does he have the moves? Probably not. But he at least has confidence to spare. (You can watch this video at: DougPaul.org/ReadyorNotLab)

The first dancer is out there, all alone by himself, for quite some time. But then one person jumps up, runs over, and joins in. Let's just say he isn't the best dancer either. But what he lacks in skill he makes up for in enthusiasm.

After showing some rather acrobatic dance moves, the second dancer calls out to his friends to join, never losing step (it's debatable whether he had the steps to begin with). Just as his friend shows up to be the third dancer, the second dancer trips and takes a tumble down the hill.

So we have three dancers and none of them are bashful about dancing rather gracelessly in front of their peers. But their energy is infectious. A few more join in, and then a few more, and suddenly there's momentum.

This is where it all tips.

For a few minutes, it was just one person, and then two people, and then three. But there were large gaps of time without any additional people showing up. But where are we at now? There isn't a frame in the footage that doesn't show new people joining in.

It's become socially acceptable, and eventually, it hits a point where there's mounting social pressure for everyone to get involved. And so finally, virtually everyone does.

What Derek Sivers did so well in his TED talk was not only narrate the events, but give remarkable insights, as the dance party that starts with a "lone nut" grows into a movement. Notice what he says about the role of the second person to join—the person he terms "the first follower."

> Being a first follower is an under-appreciated form of leadership. *The first follower transforms a lone nut into a leader.* If the leader is the flint, the first follower is the spark that makes the fire. The second follower is a turning point: it's proof the first has done well. Now it's not a lone nut, and it's not two nuts. Three is a crowd and a crowd is news ... Make sure outsiders see more than just the leader. Everyone needs to see the followers, because new followers emulate followers—not the leader.

Wyatt Walker was the first follower. In a time of lynching, regular police beatings, and church bombings, Dr. King was preaching non-violent resistance. When every nerve ending in a human would be screaming to return violence with violence, King was pushing peace as the best pathway to sustainable change. In many ways, he was the lone nut. But then Wyatt Walker and Fred Shuttlesworth came along.

4.

The Greatest Showman opened in December, 2017, in the midst of a crowded field; *The Last Jedi* had opened just a few days earlier, and it's hard to imagine any *Star Wars* movie not sucking all of the air out of the room. The studio, Twentieth Century Fox, had modest expectations for the success of their musical movie, but it didn't even reach those. In its first weekend, *The Greatest Showman* brought in only $8.8 million.

In the movie industry, the opening weekend provides an indicator of how well a movie will do. If you go to a website like Box Office Mojo, they obsessively track a movie's box office ratings and are able to very accurately predict the long-term financial future of a movie after the first weekend. Typically speaking, a movie can expect a moderate-to-steep decrease in ticket sales in the second weekend.

With a whopping $84 million budget, and a measly $8.8 million takings in their first weekend, *The Greatest Showman* was facing catastrophic financial loss. After the first weekend, it seemed there was virtually no scenario in which the studio would make their money back.

Every once in a while, you'll find a movie with *only* a 30 percent decrease in ticket sales from the first weekend to the second. Usually this is caused by a combination of two factors: an increase in critical praise (as usually scored by a percentage system on the website Rotten Tomatoes), and an increase in positive audience response (often tracked through a grading system developed by the research firm CinemaScore). This isn't exactly surprising, right? If both critics and audiences love a movie, it stands to reason its mass appeal should make it successful.

The Greatest Showman did *not* have those two elements converging. Most critics despised the movie, scoring it just 56 percent on Rotten Tomatoes. The audience, however, loved it. When audiences were polled walking out of the movie, the average viewer gave it an A. Usually, a best-case scenario for the second weekend is a 30 percent decrease. But this movie? It was an anomaly. Tickets sales almost *doubled*. And the run of success continued. In the end, the movie had a global box office gross of $434 million.

Vox writer Alissa Wilkinson explained the phenomenon of *The Greatest Showman* and how it stacks up historically:

> One of [the] measures is a movie's multiplier, calculated by dividing its total domestic box office returns by its first-weekend returns. This helps demonstrate the movie's staying power with audiences past the first weekend and indicates strong word of mouth. Few films have multipliers that rise above single digits; the highest multiplier of all time belongs to *Titanic*, which opened to $21.6 million but finished its 10-month run in theaters with a multiplier of 21.

Any guess on what the multiplier might be for *The Greatest Showman*? Well it didn't quite catch *Titanic*, but it came in second *all-time* with a multiplier of 19.8. The movie went from disaster to darling in just a few weeks.

But what did the movie have that critics paid no attention to? The soundtrack was written by the writers of the Broadway musical *Dear Evan Hansen* and the movie *La La Land*. In other words, the song composers had just received a Tony and an Oscar, and this was their next big move: a musical starring Hugh Jackman about a group of misfits who become a family. Grandiose, family friendly, PG musical movies don't tend to get produced very often. This was a movie about a three-ring circus, with big song hooks, endless positivity, and bright colors everywhere. There was clearly a gap in the market, and *The Greatest Showman* filled it, whether critics liked it or not.

Part of what it means to take innovation seriously is to pilot and iterate, getting feedback from lots of people along the way, so we can defeat the Curse of Knowledge. Being able to listen to, reflect on, and absorb feedback, and then iterate, is a hallmark of great leadership. But sometimes critics can also be the carriers of the curse. Their "expertise" can keep them from seeing different ways of doing things.

What if Peter had listened to the critics and not gone to Cornelius' house? Then Christianity might still be made up entirely of ethnically Jewish people. What if William Tyndale had cowed to his critics? Then the Bible wouldn't have been translated into English as the printing press was taking off. What if John Bunyan had listened to the criticism about his "plain style?" Then *The Pilgrim's Progress* would never have become one of the most influential works of the last five hundred years. What if Hannah More heeded the criticism of conservative commentators around the topic of an unmarried woman with a voice and an agenda? Then the slave trade might not have been abolished for at least another hundred years.

Innovation will almost always happen in spite of critics. Nothing comes into the world universally praised.

The Greatest Showman didn't need a giant opening to be a hit, or for it to be critically adored. It just needed a few rabid fans who would spread the word. It's the same with kingdom innovations: most of them start small, and like a seed with forest potential, grow over time and then begin to multiply.

5.

What the lone nut and the first follower show us is the power of starting with the few to mobilize the many.

The first follower turns the lone nut into a leader, and soon after, some fast followers begin to join. A few more trickle in, and then a few more, and a few more after that. Then something else starts to happen. A small group of people, committed to the aims and purposes, start to create a *hotbed*.

A hotbed is an environment that cultivates rapid growth and development as people with similar commitments learn from each other and spring into action. It becomes an ecosystem that attracts people with similar commitments; specifically, people who have already tripped over the truth and want in on the bigger story they're all part of.

For Bill Wilson and Bob Smith, the hotbed started in Bill's living room in New York City. When Jonathan Brooks was at Tuskegee in Alabama, he learned about the hotbed in 1920s Harlem for black artists such as Langston Hughes, Paul Robeson, Josephine Baker, Zora Neale Hurston, among others. Henry Blackaby had a small church, but it was a hotbed of spiritual activity, planting churches left and right, and sending out college graduates who knew how to find and live into the will of God.

With a lone nut, one gust of wind can blow out the flame of innovation. When the first and fast followers hit the scene, it becomes a torch. It's much harder to put out the flame, but not impossible with a little effort. But the hotbed? That's like a bonfire, and it's far more difficult to extinguish. The dance party video shows us, in real time, how the first followers develop a center of gravity. Like planets drawing toward a black hole, they seem to mysteriously draw more and more people. (Though by now, I hope we are starting to grow a little suspicious about our supposed inability to decode a mystery.)

Moving Toward Scale

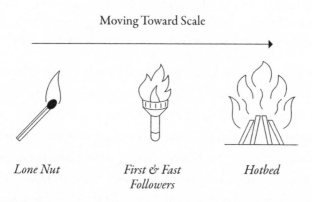

Lone Nut   First & Fast   Hotbed
Followers

In these hotbeds, iteration is happening much faster, and the learning much deeper as there is a culture committed to the same cause. If water and sunlight make a plant grow, a hotbed is like adding plant food and every nutrient you can think of. But a hotbed isn't simply a place to talk about ideas; it's a group of people putting something into action.

In the 1970s, a hotbed developed at Fuller Theological Seminary as they experimented with new forms of theological education. Peter Wagner asked John Wimber to be the founding director of the Department of Church Growth. By the early 1980s, Wimber was teaching a controversial hands-on class called "Signs, Wonders, and Church Growth." Rather than simply lecturing or using the Socratic method, students actually practiced what Jesus taught the disciples to do in Luke 10.

By the late 1990s, Dallas Willard, the brilliant University of Southern California philosophy professor, taught a two-week course each year at Fuller on life in the kingdom of God. Willard was an ardent advocate for spiritual formation, believing consistently practiced habits to engage with God changed people from the inside out. "Grace is not opposed to effort," he once said. "It's opposed to earning." In the biography *Becoming Dallas Willard*, Keith Matthews (Willard's teaching assistant), said this about the classes:

> It was as if he made a conscious effort not to be flashy or flamboyant ... He wanted to see what the Spirit would do. He wanted the class to be a laboratory for testing the notion he was giving them, that the kingdom is really here and alive. Dallas seemed to love living laboratories.

Fuller wasn't trying to be a seminary for everyone. With professors like Wimber and Willard, they were creating a school for people already open to this kind of experimentation. If you were a pastor or seminarian who wanted your theological education to be forged in the fires of a laboratory environment with a hands-on approach, Fuller was the seminary for you. They weren't trying to reach everyone. They were trying to find their first and fast followers.

6.

Think back to the instant dance party. It started with the few people who were willing to jump in. Fuller didn't need every person looking for a seminary to pick them or their innovative approach to training pastors. They only needed a few. Leadership needs the first person to stand up and start dancing, but we need the *first and fast followers* just as much. As Sivers says, "It's the first follower who transforms the lone nut into a leader." If the first and fast followers don't come along, the innovation stalls. But as more and more people join in, the hotbed develops a center of gravity, allowing the innovation to spread further and further.

The video of the dance party lasts about three minutes, and in short order, it shows us how mobilization works and how starting with a few leads to the many.

One minute into the video, there are only three dancers. That means for a third of the time, the dancers are very visible and could be feeling alone and exposed. But at the halfway point of the video, a small crowd is growing, and you're watching, in real time, the development of a hotbed and the way a center of gravity *pulls* people into it. At the two-minute mark, two-thirds of the way through, about half the people in the video frame are dancing and half are still sitting. And by the end of the video, only a few people are still sitting.

What this dance party illustrates is the *Diffusion of Innovation Theory,* the sociological principle introduced by E. M. Rogers in 1962. In it, he shows how a new innovation spreads over time into a population. For instance, there was a time when no one had a microwave, but now everyone has one. How did the appliance go from being a luxury in only a few households to being a necessity for everyone? The Diffusion of Innovation curve shows how it happens. It starts with a few and then slowly spreads over the length of that curve, eventually reaching all of the population.

Diffusion of Innovation Model

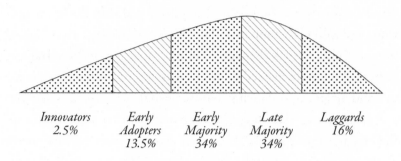

Innovators	Early	Early	Late	Laggards
2.5%	Adopters	Majority	Majority	16%
	13.5%	34%	34%	

Notice the wording on the curve, though. At the very front edge ... the original term reads *Innovators*. In 1962, when Rogers released this principle, he said that the 2.5 percent of the population who are prone to new ideas or new innovations were *Innovators*. Now this is subtle, but do you see it? What is that name implicitly communicating? It's suggesting that only 2.5 percent of the population can innovate. Once again, we see one of our great cultural myths serving as a poison pill. *Anyone* on that curve can innovate; it's simply some are more likely to try something new. (To correct this error in recent years, the term has been changed, so the 2.5 percent are now called *Radicals*.)

What we see in the curve is the codified explanation of why the dance party worked, how the abolitionists won, and why landmark legislation was passed for Civil Rights. It starts with a few people courageously and publicly trying something for long enough, and eventually—in each of these situations—it caught.

But when we look at this curve, it should come as no surprise that this is exactly how we see Jesus starting the greatest innovation (and movement) the world has ever known: the kingdom of God. More than half of his time in his three years of public ministry was spent with just twelve people, and even within that group, you have your inner core; your fast followers: Peter, James, and John.

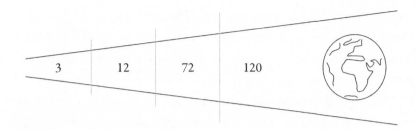

When Jesus sent out the twelve and then the seventy-two in Luke chapters 9 and 10, he doesn't tell them to go and look for as many people as possible. He tells them to do what he's already modelled for them: Look for the people in whom God is already at work—the people of peace. This is Jesus' articulation of an important principle for how we mobilize the few and reach the many: We need to *work with the willing*.

Many of us might spend 80 percent of our time on the 20 percent of people who are saying "no," rather than working with the people who have already said "yes." Working with the willing looks like flipping these ratios. What if we spent 80 percent of our time on the people who have said "yes?" What if we spent that time investing in the people who are willing to give more of themselves to the big story God is inviting them into?

As modern leaders, we are conditioned to think bigger is better, but what we see in Jesus is a wariness to this idea. Jesus, the best leader who ever lived, spent his time living out the *work with the willing* principle, and when he mobilized those closest to him, he asked them to go and do the same. He was able to navigate the crowds and lead within them, but we often forget the number of times Jesus is doing his best to get away from the crowds or bringing his disciples to places a Jewish crowd just wouldn't go. As we see with Jesus, a crowd one day is a mob the next.

Rarely, if ever, does a true innovation start with the masses. It almost always starts with the few, who codify the process, create a hotbed, and mobilize the first and fast followers.

The Greatest Showman didn't need a huge opening to eventually become a worldwide phenomenon. The lone nut started a dance party with a first follower and a few fast followers, and turned a grassy slope into a dancing free-for-all. Jesus didn't try to change the world with the masses. He started with twelve.

After all, as Margaret Mead once said: "Never doubt that a small group of thoughtful, committed citizens can change the world; indeed, it's the only thing that ever has."

Dr. King, Wyatt Walker, and Fred Shuttlesworth were the lone nut and fast followers who needed America to collectively trip over the truth. They created a hotbed that developed a center of gravity and soon enough, the willing teenagers galvanized a movement. They needed that "trip over the truth" moment to be emotional and visceral. Hannah More needed the head and the heart to align so people would *do something*. They were inviting people into a story that was so much bigger than the one they found themselves in.

But they were all doing the same thing when it came to mobilization: Codify what works. Help people trip over the truth so they want in on the vision. Identify the first and fast followers that future followers can emulate. Create a hotbed with a gravitational pull that catalyzes the innovation.

Kingdom innovation is this: *It's new, it works, and it brings glory to Jesus.*

I believe Jesus received glory when the evil of the British slave trade was destroyed. I believe Jesus received glory when segregation came to an end, and all Americans were given the right to vote. I believe Jesus received glory as people learned to live more fully in the kingdom of God as Dallas Willard trained people in his Fuller classes. And I believe Jesus received glory when millions of people were trained to experience life with God through the innovation of Henry Blackaby.

But Jesus is not done yet. In his now-and-not-yet-kingdom, he is still reconciling all things to himself. And I believe Jesus will receive glory as we innovate, start with the few, and begin to see many join us in his kingdom work.

LEADER INNOVATION LAB

KEY PRINCIPLES FROM PHASE 4: MOBILIZATION

> **Goal: Once our prototype has seen breakthrough, we need to know why and how it worked so that we can mobilize many to multiply it.**

Codification
When something is working, we try to figure out "Why does this work?" so we can repeat it.

Mystery/Heuristic/Algorithm/Code
Using Roger Martin's theory of the knowledge funnel, we're able to design a process that discovers why something happens the way it does, and how we can systematize it.

Tripping Over the Truth
The art of helping people see what's true, but through an experience that involves their heart and their head.

Lone Nut and the First and Fast Followers
When an innovation begins, it starts with a lone nut. But that person is quickly turned into a leader when the first follower and the fast followers join him/her.

Hotbed
The team that's formed around a breakthrough. Over time, they develop a kind of center of gravity that draws other people.

Diffusion of Innovation Theory
How a new idea or innovation spreads to an entire population. It starts with the few and spreads to the many. It's how we get a microwave in every house.

Work with the Willing

The decision to work with the people who have actively said "yes" and want to be part of the innovation.

The Master Tool for the Mobilization Phase: The Call to Arms Tool

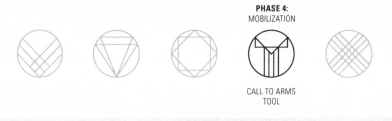

PHASE 4:
MOBILIZATION

CALL TO ARMS
TOOL

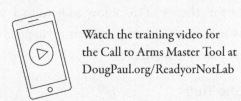

Watch the training video for the Call to Arms Master Tool at DougPaul.org/ReadyorNotLab

Nuts-and-Bolts Leader Coaching

In this chapter we revisited the Curse of Knowledge, and it's important to see the practical implications of this for helping people trip over the truth. Just because someone says they're "in" doesn't mean they are in the headspace or heartspace they need to be in.

Here's a practical example of a "trip over the truth" moment I use early on in the Disciple-Making Innovation Labs we run. (It reveals that the problem for all of us, including pastors and other church leaders, is we don't always know how fully the Curse of Knowledge affects what we do and how we lead.) We run an exercise called a crowd-source brainstorm, in which the room collects all of the *character* traits of Jesus we see in the Gospels, and puts them on giant sticky notes. (For instance, when we think of the character of Jesus, we might think of love, joy, peace, patience, etc.) Then, we crowd-source all of the *competencies* of Jesus we see in the Gospels (the things Jesus knew how to do). It only takes twenty-ish minutes to get a robust collection of character and competency traits for Jesus.

We then take the team to Matthew 28:16–20, where Jesus delivers the Great Commission and instructs his disciples to make disciples who obey everything he has taught them to do.

Then we ask the participants which is more normal in their church:

- Making disciples who look like the list we just created?
- Or forming people who participate in church programs and maybe get nicer over time?

Hopefully you see why we do this: We are helping teams trip over the truth that most churches have a discipleship process that isn't designed to help people go after the fullness of discipleship in the way Jesus planned it. We've designed a diluted version, usually because it's all we know or have experienced. That's the Curse of Knowledge. The purpose of this exercise is to not only help people trip over the truth, but to design a process that mobilizes the team into a new paradigm for what discipleship can do.

Finally, as we close this exercise, we have some heart discussion around this realization. Most leaders are seeing a gap between why they got into ministry and what they are currently doing in running the "machine" of church. There can be a sense of loss, grief, pain, or resentment in that. We've found that creating the moment for people to trip over the truth isn't just about convincing them of something in their mind, but helping them come to terms with what's happening in their heart.

As you design pathways in your context to mobilize the people God has entrusted to you, make sure it includes elements that help people trip over the truth. You want them to experience the revelation you've experienced, but not simply by them downloading the information of that revelation. It needs to involve the heart as well.

Questions to Sharpen Your Mobilization Skills

Discipleship

When someone grows from spiritual infancy to spiritual adulthood, and ultimately becomes a saint, how does it happen?

Leadership

When something multiplies in your organization, what are the essential skills of the leaders who helped that thing multiply?

Mission

What are some practical ways you can help people trip over the truth about the necessity and urgency of engaging in Jesus' mission in the world?

Worship

How can you help move people from understanding worship as "something we do in a church service" to something that they engage with in all aspects of their life?

Reconciliation

How can you help people trip over the truth that many of us have fractured and broken relationships that are left unrepaired? How can you help people trip over the truth that there are probably whole groups of people they are estranged from and to see that Jesus wasn't estranged from anyone?

Operating System

Where are the gaps in your operating system between "being" and "doing" church that aren't reflecting the call to mobilize your people into the world?

This is a Spiritual Process

One of the things we see Jesus looking for in his disciples is an increasing revelation of who he is and what he's doing in the world. And often, when they get a clearer sense of it (like the Mount of Transfiguration experience in Mark 9), he asks them to keep it to themselves until the appointed time. For the disciples, tripping over the truth of Jesus' divinity was a spiritual process, not an intellectual one.

We recognize that when something needs to align with the heart, mind, and spirit, it will take time, and in theological terms, it is the Holy Spirit leading the process of sanctification. It doesn't happen overnight. There are ways in which we need to help people live into a new way of thinking, not just think into a new way of living. But all this requires a large measure of prayer.

If this is of the kingdom, then we must recognize that we are opposed to *another* kingdom: Spiritual warfare is at the heart of kingdom innovation. While there are certainly many things we can learn to help people trip over the truth, there is wisdom and spiritual insight needed for this. We aren't smart enough to figure this out apart from Jesus, and there is an enemy opposed to the spiritual alignment of paradigm, principle, and practice. Whether it's the subtle calling of consumerism, the violent evil of slavery, or anything in between, our enemy will use every tool at his disposal to see that he doesn't lose any ground.

As a hotbed begins to develop, there is an opportunity to lean into spiritual practices of prayer and intercession, not only for those you're hoping to mobilize, but for the people you're hoping the innovation reaches. In the same way that you needed help tripping over the truth, so will future generations. As Andrew Murray wrote in *With Christ in the School of Prayer*,

> May God open our eyes to see what the holy ministry of intercession is, to which, as His royal priesthood, we have been set apart. May He give us a large and strong heart to believe what mighty influence our

prayers can exert. And may all fear as to our being able to fulfill our vocation vanish as we see Jesus, living ever to pray, living in us to pray, and standing surety for our prayer life.

Kingdom innovation requires warfare, and warfare requires power that is not our own. The only way to access that power is through prayer.

I've noticed both in myself and with others I've worked with that we can be tempted to take our foot off the gas in the Mobilization Phase, believing that the spiritual work is done; it happened in the first few phases and now we have what we need. *But you don't have it.* There is more work to be done, and it's not work that can be done apart from God. You will need his guidance, power, wisdom, and protection more than ever.

5

MULTIPLICATION

CHAPTER NINE

The Iron Triangle

"SHE GOT TOTALLY SCREWED, IF YOU WANT TO KNOW
THE TRUTH. EVEN IF IT'S LEGALLY RIGHT, IT'S MORALLY
WRONG."

1.

In 1990, the Upright Citizens Brigade (UCB) performed their first improv show at Chicago club, Kill the Poet. It was a small beginning for the ragtag group of comedians, which included the likes of Amy Poehler, Horatio Sanz, Adam McKay, and a few others who would come to fill our television screens for decades to come. Not long after this inauspicious beginning, the members of the group featured in a show on Comedy Central and were on the fast track for Saturday Night Live. Meanwhile, the UCB expanded their offerings to teach people the art of improv comedy. Over the next twenty years, thousands of aspiring creatives made their way through the UCB pipeline, including many of the top writers and comedians on SNL.

Michael Dubin was one of these creatives.

While bouncing his way through marketing and television jobs for most of the first decade of the 2000s, Dubin spent eight years sharpening his comedic skills with UCB. At a Christmas party in 2010, he got into a conversation with one of his dad's friends who had suddenly found himself in a pickle: He'd recently acquired 250,000 razors from Asia and wasn't sure what to do with them. Well, Dubin had an idea.

On March 6, 2012, a YouTube video was posted and quickly trended on Twitter and Facebook. The video starts with a straight-faced Dubin, dressed in a button-down shirt and tie, sitting behind a desk, and looking directly into the camera, making a self-serious pitch for the new Dollar Shave Club, which anyone can be part of. For one dollar a month, you can have a high-quality razor delivered right to your door. Suddenly, he pops up out of the seat, starts walking and asks, "Are the blades any good? ... No ... *they are [insert expletive] great*," he says, pointing at a sign that replicates exactly what he just said.

Journalist Joe Lazauskas describes the rest of the ad this way:

> What follows is 90 seconds of absolute absurdity that nonetheless touts all of the features of Dollar Shave Club's razors. There's a toddler shaving a man's head, polio jokes, a machete, a clumsy bear, a giant American flag, and perhaps the best "make it rain" scene of all time.

The ad is hilarious, crass, imaginative, and ridiculous. And it broke the internet. Lazauskas goes deeper into his assessment:

> Dubin knew that he had to speak to men like him. Men who were fed up with a razor monopoly that forced them to pay more than $20 for just a few blades. And so he bet big on what he does best. He created a hilarious video to connect with his target audience and cast himself as the protagonist in the Hero's Journey of his own brand.

The video was so good and so sharable, it instantly went viral. Within ninety minutes, they received twelve thousand subscriptions, and their website crashed.

2.

It's hard to pinpoint exactly when the word *scale* became part of everyday-business-speak, but Hal Plotkin's 1988 article in *Inc.* magazine seems to have played a significant role. To *scale* something is to set it up to reach its full potential as it increases in size or numbers.

Dubin wanted to get rid of those 250,000 razors, but he also wanted to *scale* far beyond that original order. He had an idea that was sticky, a market that was frustrated, a product that was cheap, and an ad that set the internet on fire. He wanted to scale the business and see it expand to its full potential. And it's fair to say he was successful. Within six years of launching the video, the business had 3.9 million monthly subscribers and sold to Unilever for one *billion* dollars.

In *The Tipping Point*, Malcolm Gladwell spent an entire book writing on why some ideas spread and others don't. He says, "The tipping point is that magic moment when an idea, trend, or social behavior crosses a threshold, tips, and spreads like wildfire." He goes on to say: "There is a simple way to package information that, under the right circumstances, can make it irresistible. All you have to do is find it."

The final phase of the process for kingdom innovation is *multiplication: Make the innovation scalable, removing as many barriers as possible, for as many people as possible, so we can invite them all into a brand new breakthrough.* Scaling something is about finding that tipping point.

We know that Scripture says that a kingdom return is thirty, sixty, one hundred-fold beyond the one seed that was planted. For in every seed lies the potential of a forest.

So here we are: The innovation is working, there's a hotbed of people who have been mobilized. The Holy Spirit is at work. We must now remove the barriers to multiplication, so the innovation can expand to reach its full potential.

3.

There's a little-known story about how two creatives, separated by a hundred years, were each swindled out of hundreds of millions of dollars.

The first story goes something like this: While we can't locate the exact origin of the phrase, the first record of it pops up with the prince of preachers, Charles Spurgeon himself, in a sermon he delivered on June 28, 1891 in London. Referencing Thomas à Kempis' spiritual classic *The Imitation of Christ* as his inspiration, several times Spurgeon asked his listeners that night a simple but sticky question: "What would Jesus do?"

Around the same time, one pulpit and a continent away, Pastor Charles Sheldon in Topeka, Kansas started to end each of his Sunday night sermons with a new innovation: He'd tell a story.

Each week he made up a different story, with a different character, in different circumstances, each facing some kind of dilemma or moral quandary. He'd then pose the question to his listeners: *What would Jesus do?* "Sheldon," journalist Karl Smallwood wrote, "would end each story on a cliffhanger ensuring the people there would come back the following week to learn what happened next."

Sheldon, it should be mentioned, was a spiritual revolutionary for his time. He despised capitalism, believing it fostered greed in Christians. He was, as Smallwood continued, "among the few white ministers of the day to not only allow, but openly invite, black people to become full members of his church; he also openly spoke out against the KKK *to their faces* and wasn't shy about slamming anti-Semites whenever he encountered them." He encouraged women in his congregation to be involved in politics and to fight for equal rights for women in the workplace.

Over time, these Sunday evening story times grew in popularity, and more and more people came to hear them. By 1896, Sheldon decided to put these stories all in one place and published the book *In His Steps*, with the subtitle, *What would Jesus do?*

In one particular story in the book, "Reverend Maxwell," the main character, comes across a homeless person, and over the course of the conversation, he challenges the right reverend to take seriously the call to imitate Jesus. The vagabond is confused as to why so many Christians neglect Jesus' call to look after the poor, saying to the reverend:

I heard some people singing at a church prayer meeting the other night,

"All for Jesus, all for Jesus,
All my being's ransomed powers,
All my thoughts, and all my doings,
All my days, and all my hours."

And I kept wondering as I sat on the steps outside just what they meant by it. It seems to me there's an awful lot of trouble in the world that somehow wouldn't exist if all the people who sing such songs went and lived them out. I suppose I don't understand. But what would Jesus do? Is that what you mean by following His steps? It seems to me sometimes as if the people in the big churches had good clothes and nice houses to live in, and money to spend for luxuries, and could go away on summer vacations and all that, while the people outside the churches, thousands of them, I mean, die in tenements, and walk the streets for jobs, and never have a piano or a picture in the house, and grow up in misery and drunkenness and sin.

Sheldon's simple story goes on to tell how a town is completely changed when all the Christians, "pledge themselves, earnestly and honestly for an entire year, not to do anything without first asking the question, 'What would Jesus do?'"

The novel was a success. By 1935, *In His Steps* had been translated into twenty-one languages and sold more than thirty million copies worldwide, making it one of the top fifty most purchased books *of all time*. This book had scaled and was close to reaching its full potential.

But something happened that allowed for this possibility. There was a hiccup with the original publisher ... mainly, that they screwed up the copyright, and a few years after the first run was published, it was placed in the public domain. This meant all kinds of other publishers picked it up, sold it, and distributed it, and they didn't owe Charles Sheldon one single dime. He didn't know it at the time, but as we'll soon discover, Sheldon accidentally lowered one of the most significant barriers in the Multiplication Phase.

The result? The author who wrote one of the highest selling books of all time made about ten thousand dollars.

4.

Rent the Runway started with a simple idea for women: What if you could *rent* (rather than buy) a designer dress for a wedding or special event? After all, an occasion dress is usually expensive, and a woman might only wear it a few times at most.

The business model and offerings have morphed and iterated since Jennifer Hyman and Jennifer Fleiss founded the company in 2009, but it continues to disrupt the $2.4 trillion fashion industry. Like Dollar Shave Club, you can now subscribe and receive a monthly revolving closet of the newest fashion trends and choices. In 2019, it received a valuation of one billion dollars, with millions of women subscribing to their monthly service.

To scale to this level, they had to create the largest dry-cleaning service in the world. They have a fulfillment center that runs stock supply, inspection, stain removal, steam cleaning, mending, and shipping.

But in October of 2019, Rent the Runway stopped accepting new customers.

Due to a breakdown in their supply chain, software issues, and a customer service meltdown, they weren't even able to fulfill orders to current subscribers in the timeframe they promised. "You rely on us for meaningful events in your life and to get dressed every day," the email from Runway said to current clients. "We realize we have let some of you down, and we need to fix it."

Rent the Runway had scaled, but it hit the ceiling of what its resources and infrastructure could handle. They eventually fixed it (by adding more resources), and today they continue their upward trajectory, with each of their founders' net worth estimated at three hundred million dollars.

Charles Sheldon, on the other hand, had one of the most successful books of all time, but, as we now know, had very little financial gain to show for it. Alcoholics Anonymous started in a living room in New York City and now, more than one hundred million people have been part of it. *Experiencing God* started in a small Canadian church and went on to sell ten million copies, significantly influencing the North American church.

These are all examples of innovations that scaled. But they are not all alike.

In healthcare and software development, there's a principle called the Iron Triangle: "Fast, good, or cheap—Pick two." As the Business.com Editorial Staff explain:

- Develop something quickly and of high quality, but it will be very costly to do.
- Develop something quickly and cheaply, but it will not be of high quality.
- Develop something of high quality and low cost, but it will take a long time.

One of the key points of the Iron Triangle is that you have to make trade-offs. A triangle works in tension with itself. Any time you lean more to one side, that means there is less of the other.

When I work with teams around scaling an innovation, I use something called the Scalability Tool, and it involves three different components:

Control: The amount of leadership power and quality control you exert as something scales.

Masses: The potential number of people the innovation can reach as it scales.

Simple: The amount of complexity needed to sustain the innovation as it scales.

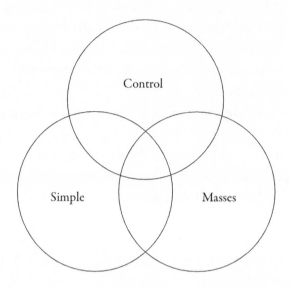

The Scalability Tool and the Iron Triangle share the same rule—you can only pick two of the three. Very rarely does an innovation violate the rules of the Scalability Tool and achieve all three. But when it does, it cannot be sustained for a lengthy period of time; there's just too much tension in the system to sustain it. Usually, all three dimensions come together in times of crisis, when individuals are more willing to surrender their own personal liberties for the sake of a greater cause. But that willingness fades away within a few months.

As a leader, you have to make choices, and it's important to make these decisions earlier on, in the Ideation and Experimentation phases, as you design with the end in mind. Every time you make a choice and say "yes" to two aspects, you're also implicitly saying "no" to one of the three components.

Paul didn't want immature churches (the Corinthian Church), or ones breeding heresy (the Colossian Church), or legalism (the Galatian Church). But he made a decision: He would take the mess of it (forgoing *control*), so that he could plant more churches (*masses*) and see the gospel extend (*simple*) much further than if he went after a purer model that was simple and highly controlled (but not able to extend to the *masses*).

Selecting two of the three components creates a particular model:

Model 1: Resourced Model

High *control* of your innovation (with centralized leadership and quality control) + reaching the *masses* = Resourced model e.g., Chick-fil-A or Life.Church.

This model can't sustain *simple* because as it expands, the system and infrastructure for sustainability becomes extraordinarily complex. The user experience might be simple, but behind the curtain, it is heavyweight and high maintenance.

Model 2: Groundswell Model

Mass influence + a *simple* model (with individuals buying in and taking ownership) = Groundswell model e.g., Alcoholics Anonymous or the New Testament church.

This model can't sustain *control* because the "center" can't keep up with or maintain quality control of the reproduction that's happening at the edges. There's a certain degree of freedom and variance from once place to another that this model is comfortable with.

Model 3: Walled Garden Model

High *control* of your innovation (with centralized leadership and quality control) + a relatively *simple* innovation = a Walled Garden model e.g., Acts 29 church planting movement or your favorite independent restaurant.

This model can't sustain reaching the *masses* because there are a great number of people who won't fit within the "box" that the walled garden creates. Some people might love their favorite restaurant because it's a raw bar, but what if you don't like seafood or uncooked food? It works exceptionally well for the niche, but not for everyone.

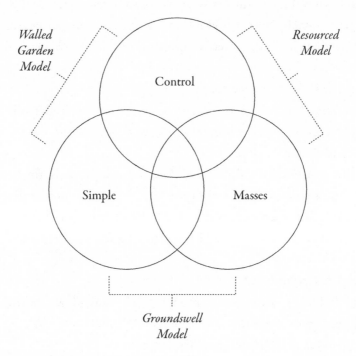

As Christian leaders, we need to discern what the Lord is calling us to. There isn't a "bad" choice, just one that God calls us to lean into. When you say "yes," you're not just saying yes to a specific model, but what is necessary for that model to succeed, as the overlap of those two components produces a unique need:

Resourced Model
Control + Masses—needs *resources* (e.g., money, time, people, infrastructure)

Groundswell Model
Simple + Masses—needs *embodied principles* (e.g., Alcoholics Anonymous meetings, sponsors, Twelve Steps)

Walled Garden Model
Control + Simple—needs *purity* (e.g., tight doctrinal statements, very specific menu)

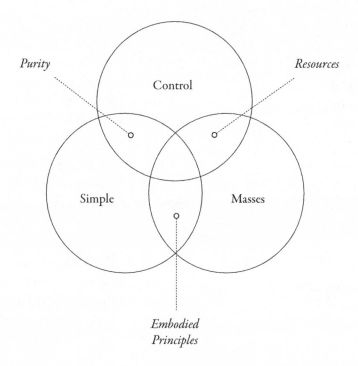

Jesus said that when we enter into any kind of spiritual conflict, we should count the cost. Choosing which model we're going after requires the same kind of cost-counting, as there will always be friction within any model we use. In fact, British statistician G.E.P. Box once ironically said, "all models are wrong, but some are useful." A model might work perfectly on a piece of paper, but once it's activated in real life, we begin to realize its imperfections, and frictions soon arise. So as we start discussing models of scalability, we acknowledge the imperfection of any model, but the usefulness that a framework can provide.

	What the Model Needs	Friction the Model Produces for Leadership
Resourced Model *Control +* *Masses*	Resources	People's desire for more freedom (people may want to change things and the 'center' only allows for one way)
Groundswell Model *Simple +* *Masses*	Embodied principles	Leader's desire for quality control (people will change and iterate in ways the leader wouldn't choose)
Walled Garden Model *Control +* *Simple*	Purity	People's desire to expand the walls (people may want to broaden the parameters and make it less niche in order to impact more people)

When we design with the end in mind through all five phases of the kingdom innovation process, we're making choices about where the "end" could be, considering what the idea might look like at its full potential.

As you're making decisions, it's helpful to imagine that your innovation has a scalability dashboard. Like a music producer setting levels, the choices you make along the way and in the Multiplication Phase determine what scaling potential your innovation has. As we set that dashboard and those various "levels," the barriers start to emerge that we're going to need to compensate for.

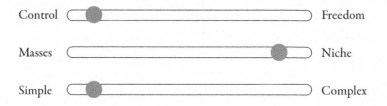

The visual of the scalability dashboard is helpful in seeing some of the "levels" we're setting, each attempting to answer a different scalability question:

- *Leadership* question: How much oversight and quality control do you want?
- *Size* question: How many people do you feel called to impact?
- *Sustainability* question: How much complexity is needed to sustain the innovation?

The diagram above illustrates the dashboard of an organization I recently worked with who felt called to build using a Walled Garden model. This kingdom innovation will have a "pure" form that concentrates on quality control and centralized leadership, but the trade-off was the masses—it could only reach a limited number of people. If they tried to expand beyond what they could control, they would lose key DNA.

As you discern which model God is calling you to, you'll want to think through the barriers each model has coming against its ability to scale. After all, just because we decide on a model, it doesn't mean it will work! All we've done is land on the ingredients necessary for scaling the innovation. So let's think about the barriers for each of the models:

	Key Requirements of Model	Barrier to Overcome
Resourced Model *Control + Masses*	Centralized leadership and quality *control* that can reach the *masses* through multiplication when it's resourced	Scarcity (achieving *control* and *masses* requires money, people, time, and infrastructure)
Groundswell Model *Simple + Masses*	*Simple* reproduction of embodied principles that can reach the *masses*	Complexity (it's difficult for the *masses* to reproduce something if it's not *simple*)
Walled Garden Model *Control + Simple*	*Control* of the ecosystem that binds "true believers" together with something simple	Diluted forms (when the leadership in *control* proposes changing something in the *simple* walled garden, people often revolt, as they no longer think it's "pure")

Remember, there isn't a "right answer." Some innovations stay relatively small and touch fewer people, but that's exactly what God intends for it. We've previously explored how something can go from the few to the many; but the "many" is always relative. It's only in comparison to what your innovation looks like at its fullest potential. We are not giving into the "bigger is always better" fallacy. But if we're to take Jesus at his word about how the kingdom works, we need to always consider looking through the filter of scale.[†]

---

† There is an hour-long training video on the Scalability Tool that goes into far more depth at: DougPaul.org/ReadyorNotLab .

5.

The place? Holland, Michigan. The year? 1989.

Janie Tinklenberg was a youth leader at Calvary Reformed Church when she picked up an old book: *In His Steps* by Charles Sheldon. In one day, she read it cover to cover. It knocked her socks off, and soon enough, she was talking about it to the teens in her youth group. She thought the question *What would Jesus do?* was an ingenious way to keep the call of Christ in front of teenagers each and every day, and she wanted to create something that would constantly draw teenagers back to this important question.

"At the time, 1989," Tinklenberg said, "beaded friendship bracelets were popular. I figured a bracelet was perfect: They could wear it all the time and it was even kind of cool." So she went to work creating a bracelet that closely resembled the design trends of the time.

The problem she ran into, however, was the phrase was a little too long to put onto a bracelet, so she did something that unwittingly was going to start a spiritual wildfire. Chances are, you know what she did: She shortened the phrase to just the first letters of each word: WWJD.

She started with an order of three hundred bracelets, but they quickly disappeared, as teens started taking them, followed by their friends and parents. So she ordered hundreds more, and then hundreds more after that.

Janie Tinklenberg created something that was *sticky* and *sneezable*. The message of WWJD is inherently sticky—like flypaper for the brain—because it asks a pretty profound question: What would Jesus do? But it's also *sneezable*—it's easy to pass the message around to others with very little resistance. When it first started, no one knew what WWJD stood for, so when everyone started wearing the bracelets in Holland, Michigan, what was the natural thing to do?

Ask what it meant.

The sneezability was built right into the innovation.

At the end of the day, an innovation that is sticky and sneezable is about *sharability*. Can people remember it and can it easily spread? When Ronald Reagan said, "Mr. Gorbachev, tear down this wall!" or Dr. King proclaimed, "I have a dream," they both spoke words with high sharability. Why was Dollar Shave Club a success? Because they created a video that was so sticky and sneezable people wanted to repost an advertisement, of all things.

Key to the Multiplication Phase is the removal of barriers, and there are a number of barriers to something being sticky and sneezable. It could be unclear, boring, ambiguous, or uninspiring. The 1980s advertisement, "This is your brain ... this is your brain on drugs," was sticky, but it wasn't sneezable. Teens didn't walk away inspired or with their heart changed. If anything, it was something they made fun of.

Quibi (combining the first few letters of "quick and bite") is a newer streaming platform that specializes in "quick bites of captivating entertainment," viewed on a downloadable mobile app. *The Verge* journalist Julia Alexander describes it like this:

> Trying to describe Quibi's essence to people is difficult. There are shows where food explodes in chefs' faces, series about flipping murder homes, and Chrissy Teigen presiding over a small claims court. Quibi's best content operates on the belief that "the more ludicrous, the better," but that's easier to show than tell.

In today's social media landscape, sharability is paramount, and it's here that Quibi seems to have made a mistake: The platform doesn't allow people to take screenshots of shows while they are playing. Why is this a big deal? Because memes are one of the easiest ways to make something sticky, sneezable, and ultimately, shareable. Experts believe one of the reasons Netflix was an early success was because people could take screenshots of a show, turn it into a meme, and it could instantly be shared on social media. By not allowing screenshots, Quibi is putting up a barrier to its own success.

Quibi raised nearly two billion dollars before it ever launched, and they went all in on an innovation strategy of *control* and *mass*, but that meant saying no to *simple*. Even with all that money and prestige behind it ... no one is talking about it. Quibi built something that scales, but one little choice made it difficult to share.

For Janie Tinklenberg, every bracelet provided the opportunity to make the sticky message sneezable. And over time, the message moved and multiplied to new youth groups and new schools. Protestant evangelicals were wearing them and Catholics were wearing them. What started with a few was starting to multiply to the many.

What Tinklenberg did was find an innovative way to develop a hotbed using a sticky and sneezable message. She did this by injecting it into a preexisting network of relationships: a local youth group. The bracelets were fairly inexpensive, so she lowered the price barrier, making it accessible for teenagers with even a little disposable income. The bracelets were on-trend for the design of that time, so she lowered the barrier of teens not wanting to wear it as a fashion accessory.

Remember how I said this is the story of two creatives who were swindled out of hundreds of millions of dollars? Well, in a strange through-line of history, the same thing that happened to Charles Sheldon also happened to Janie Tinklenberg. Before she filed a proper copyright, the company she'd hired to manufacture the bracelets saw how many she was selling and started to mass manufacture and market the product themselves. When she went to file the copyright, so the earnings could fund a non-profit youth ministry, she found out it was too late.

The uncopyrighted WWJD bracelets had become so prevalent so quickly, they were now within the public domain. This allowed for companies with scalable distribution pipelines (including clothing factories and bricks-and-mortar stores with available financial capital) to put the bracelets into the mass market. In fact, an international Christian publishing company we've all heard of (and that I won't name here) even tried to trademark it for themselves. There were hundreds of millions of dollars at stake, and Tinklenberg saw none of it. As Mike Yaconelli, the founder of Youth Specialties commented, "She got totally screwed, if you want to know the truth. Even if it's legally right, it's morally wrong."

Charles Sheldon's book *In His Steps* ended up printed and distributed by multiple publishers, allowing mass scalability in a short amount of time. The barrier Tinklenberg accidentally lowered was the same as Charles Sheldon: *mass distribution*. The sad irony is the WWJD bracelets were a phenomenon *because* there were so few barriers, and distribution across the country scaled very quickly with the financial capital (resources) Janie probably didn't have access to. It moved from one hotbed (her youth group) to multiple hotbeds (additional youth groups) with a sticky and sneezable message.

At the end of the day, Janie Tinklenberg lost out on the money, but she didn't lose out on multiplication. Now it's possible both could have happened, and there are lots of positive examples of innovation where money *is* involved. But if we want to understand how multiplication happens when you've got a new breakthrough on your hands, you start with the barriers. How can this thing multiply to as many people as possible with the least amount of barriers so it reaches its full potential?

YouVersion could charge for their Bible app, but if they were to do that, they may not have four hundred million users. The Bible Project could charge a subscription fee to watch their extraordinary whiteboard overview videos for each book of the Bible, but that immediately alienates a chunk of people. Alcoholics Anonymous has brought breakthrough to millions of people, but it's free to join. For Charles Sheldon and Janie Tinklenberg, they lost out on the money, but money wasn't the measure of success.

Success was *kingdom impact*.

6.

When Winston Churchill stood up to address the House of Commons on May 13, 1940, as the new prime minister, he spoke not as conquering politician, but as a man many opposed. He took the realm as a deeply unpopular leader, a last-gasp choice as the forces of Nazi Germany were quickly surrounding the small island nation.

In 1936, Churchill was passed over to be the minister for Coordination of Defense, leading General Ellison to quip, "Thank God we are preserved from Winston Churchill." Later that year, Neville Chamberlain, the current prime minister of Britain at the time, signed a "peace treaty" in Munich, allowing Hitler to seize control of Czechoslovakia without a single shot fired. While Chamberlain returned home proclaiming "peace in our time," Churchill held a very different belief. In writing to former prime minister Lloyd George, Churchill gave his analysis of the situation: "We seem to be very near the bleak choice between War and Shame. My feeling is that we shall choose Shame, and then have War thrown in a little later on even more adverse terms than at present."

Without knowing it, Chamberlain bought Hitler the time Germany needed to scale up for a second world war, adding an extra calendar year to stock up and plan before the fateful events of the invasion of Poland. In 1940, on the same day that the Nazis began to cut through the low country of France with a fast-track eye toward toppling Paris, and on the same day Germany invaded Belgium, Luxembourg, and the Netherlands, Winston Churchill was appointed the prime minister of Britain. He was not the first choice, but he was the right choice.

There were some in Britain who wanted to negotiate for peace with Germany, but Churchill wasn't biting. He made his now famous "Blood, Toil, Tears and Sweat" speech to Parliament on May 13, 1940, concluding with this thunderous reprise:

> We have before us an ordeal of the most grievous kind. We have before us many, many long months of struggle and of suffering. You ask, what is our policy? I can say: It is to wage war, by sea, land and air, with all our might and with all the strength that God can give us; to wage war against a monstrous tyranny, never surpassed in the dark, lamentable catalogue of human crime. That is our policy. You ask, what is our aim? I can answer in one word: It is victory, victory at all costs, victory in spite of all terror, victory, however long and hard the road may be; for without victory, there is no survival.

At the same time Churchill was calling the nation to courage and to arms, quiet plans were being put in place to avoid a full-scale collapse of allied forces. The British Expeditionary Force (BEF) deployed into France when it was invaded, but they were now trapped in Dunkirk. An overwhelming German force stood before them, on three out of four sides.

What was behind them? The English Channel, a body of water with shallows that meant naval destroyers were unable to come to their aid for an evacuation. Churchill called it "a colossal military disaster," saying "the whole root and core and brain of the British Army" was stranded in Dunkirk.

Long story short? If they couldn't evacuate the almost 350,000 soldiers stranded like sitting ducks in Dunkirk, Britain had almost no hope of surviving. As General Alan Brooke said, "Nothing but a miracle can save the BEF now."

Enter *Operation Dynamo.*

CHAPTER TEN

Operation Dynamo

"THE REVOLUTION IS NOT SOMETHING YOU ORDER TO
YOUR OWN SPECIFICATIONS. YOU HAVE TO TAKE THE
OBSTACLES WITH THE OPPORTUNITIES. THERE IS NO
PROVIDER OF REVOLUTIONARY CONDITIONS WHOSE JOB IT
IS TO SET EVERYTHING UP JUST RIGHT FOR YOU."

1.

The barriers to success for Operation Dynamo were immense. They needed boats small enough to go through the shallow waters, pick up the soldiers, and ladder them out to the larger boats sitting out in the sea like fish in a barrel. And on top of that, the Navy didn't have near enough boats to fit these specifications.

So the leaders of Operation Dynamo put a call out to the British people: *Who has a boat?* They needed as many as possible, and civilians responded in droves with everything from lifeboats to paddle steamers to barges.

Imagine the rescue mission like a relay race: On the beaches, the allied forces fought the advancing Germans, serving as a shield for the soldiers who, little by little, made their way out into shoulder-deep water and waited for a small boat to pick them up. Once they were collected, they were ferried to a larger destroyer, which then crossed the English Channel back to the British mainland. The idea was to do this over and over again. The real threat came from the Luftwaffe, the devastating German air force who looked to cut through the allied forces like a scythe, with bullets and bombs, aiming for the small boats, destroyers, and forces on the beaches. It required a superhuman effort by the British Royal Air Force. Somehow, they needed to keep the Luftwaffe from using the skies to obliterate the evacuation effort.

Neither Churchill nor the leaders of Operation Dynamo had high hopes for complete success; they believed they could rescue about forty thousand soldiers from the beaches at Dunkirk.

On the first day, only eight thousand soldiers were rescued.

But the barrier for entry was low, and a growing swell of civilian boats continued to come to their aid. In all, more than seven hundred little boats, with civilians at the helm, met up along the coast of Britain and began a nine-day evacuation that seemed impossible at best. The *Sundowner*, the small wooden motorboat owned by Charles Lightoller, the highest-ranking surviving officer of RMS *Titanic*, rescued 150 people, packed as tightly as sardines in a can. The *Medway Queen* made seven round trips, the most of any of the boats, and evacuated seven thousand soldiers, earning the title "Heroine of Dunkirk." And the *Tamzine*, the smallest boat to take part in the operation, could barely carry ten people each time.

Toward the end of May, 1940, there were almost 350,000 troops stranded in Dunkirk. Nine days later, more than 338,000 troops were saved.

On June 4, Winston Churchill stood before the House of Commons, with the whole of the British people listening, trying to understand the miracle they had all witnessed:

> We shall go on to the end, we shall fight in France, we shall fight on the seas and oceans, we shall fight with growing confidence and growing strength in the air, we shall defend our Island, whatever the cost may be, we shall fight on the beaches, we shall fight on the landing grounds, we shall fight in the fields and in the streets, we shall fight in the hills; We shall never surrender.

Soon thereafter, Operation Dynamo received another name: The Miracle of Dunkirk.

What we see in this operation is a low *barrier* for entry (bring your boat), but a high *cost* (destruction of your boat and possible death). Low-barrier entry. High-sacrifice cost. What might this principle tell us about the scalability of kingdom innovation?

2.

The Miracle of Dunkirk illustrates how a *radical minimum* is one of the most important factors in making an innovation scalable.

A radical minimum is a simple thing you ask everyone to do. Rather than asking people to do a lot of things, it's asking them to do a few things that might be more difficult. As a rule of thumb, a radical minimum is simple, but hard. For Churchill and Operation Dynamo, the radical minimum was putting your boat in the English Channel, setting sail for Ramsgate, and ultimately ending up in Dunkirk. For Charles Sheldon and Janie Tinklenberg, it was asking yourself the question "What would Jesus do?" For the Benedictines, their radical minimum was living by a rule of life. For the early Methodists, it was joining in Wesleyan Triads. For Jonathan Brooks and Canaan Community Church, it was participating in their scholarship fund. For those in Alcoholics Anonymous, it's attending meetings and walking out the Twelve Steps in a fight for your sobriety. How does

AA keep its DNA after more than eighty years? Simple. It's codified straight into their radical minimums.

A radical minimum says, "Some people might call this radical, but here, we call this normal." Now, *culture is whatever is normal for a group of people.* So when radical minimums become core practices for the culture in which they are embedded, it establishes a new normal for that culture.

In his book *The Power of Habit,* author Charles Duhigg says "keystone habits" are, "small changes or habits that people introduce into their routines that unintentionally carry over into other aspects of their lives." These habits have an outsized effect. For some people, if they go to the gym first thing in the morning, there's a very good chance they will make other disciplined choices for the day. If someone spends fifteen minutes in prayer before going to work, there's a good chance they will walk closely with the Lord the rest of the day, paying attention to what God is up to. And for kingdom innovation, a radical minimum is a keystone habit for the hotbed. It's one thing that has an outsized effect, like a little yeast leavening the whole lump of dough.

Dallas Willard wrote about this spiritual phenomenon in *The Great Omission.* He said that in order to respond to Jesus' final words—that all disciples should do everything he commanded—Christians must become more and more like Christ through what Willard calls *indirect effort.* And the way you find this kind of life is through a few simple spiritual habits and practices that activate God's Spirit within you. In other words, there are practices—radical minimums—that though small, can have an outsized spiritual impact by the way they ripple and reverberate in unexpected ways. In the same way that a spiritual discipline in the life of an individual disciple can have ripple effects across their spiritual life, radical minimums have an outsized effect in the life of the collective.

Dave Runyon and Jay Pathak developed a radical minimum, but for a very different vision. They had a sticky and sneezable idea: What if when Jesus said "Love your neighbor," he meant your actual neighbor? So twenty-one churches in Arvada, Colorado banded together, essentially forming a hotbed. What they started was a neighboring movement in their community, looking to change their neighborhoods with the gospel, one house at a time. The simple tool below served as their radical minimum:

Imagine your home is the house in the middle. You would use the sheet to write the names of your neighbors in the various houses around you and put the sheet on your fridge. The first step to loving your neighbors, after all, is getting to know their names. Runyon and Pathak don't prescribe what has to happen after that, but they do offer different resources and ideas for next steps. Today, there are more than a thousand churches committed to this radical minimum.

For a radical minimum, it isn't that the "big ask" isn't costly. It is costly! It may be simple, but it takes effort and determination. For a teenager, to publicly associate with Jesus is costly. For the British people, risking your boat and life on behalf of the nation was costly—more than a hundred boats never made it back home. For an alcoholic, trying to get sober is costly. For members of Canaan Community Church, giving money to a scholarship fund in the midst of poverty was costly. The "ask" of the radical minimum should feel costly, or else it wouldn't be radical. People are having to choose between something; after all, Jesus says we should count the cost.

In his book *Running Lean*, Ash Maurya introduces a helpful rule of thumb when considering business products and services: "You know you've come up with a good pricing model when you have a value that the customer accepts but still has some resistance." When it comes to the kingdom, people should feel there's a cost, because when they give up something, they receive something better in return. Depending on the innovation, the radical minimum might require money, time, relinquishing a carefully manicured life, or any number of things. But what we receive is better.

Radical minimums are essential to scalability, but they also remind us that there is no kingdom without a cost. We are the people who trade everything for the pearl of great price. We get Jesus.

3.

Perhaps no one shows us more about how radical minimums relate to scale than a self-avowed socialist septuagenarian from Vermont. You probably wouldn't expect to find Bernie Sanders in this book, but we'd be hard-pressed to find a better gateway for understanding this last phase of multiplication. (And his inclusion should not be mistaken for an endorsement of his policies.)

If for some reason you've been under a rock, I'll not bury the lead: Were it not for the somewhat vague (read: *sketchy*) role of superdelegates in its primary system, Bernie Sanders would almost certainly have been the Democratic nominee for president of the United States in 2016. He was a hair's breadth away from beating Hillary Clinton (and certainly had a puncher's chance of winning against Joe Biden and the rest of the primary field in 2020).

We now know that one of the key tasks in the final phase of this process is to remove the barriers that hinder multiplication. And for Bernie Sanders? There were a lot of barriers:

Barrier 1: His *politics*. Bernie Sanders is a socialist and that's not traditionally a "warmly" received ideology in American politics.

While Democratic socialism (which is the camp Bernie Sanders falls into) is quite different from actual socialism, most political scientists argue it contains significant threads that run counter to the organizing values and principles of America's continuing experiment with democracy. As Molly Ball wrote in her 2015 article for *The Atlantic*, "Even Republicans seem to see Sanders as a harmless curiosity. 'I like Bernie,' said Lindsey Graham, the South Carolina senator and 2016 GOP presidential candidate, 'but he's a socialist! If he had his way, we'd have one tank, one machine gun, and 90 percent tax rates!'"

Barrier 2: His *opponent*. Beyond his personal politics, he was running in the primary against Hillary Clinton, the front-runner and presumed nominee, benefiting from name recognition, finances, back-scratching, and all the rigmarole that comes with the Clinton political machine.

Barrier 3: His *relative obscurity*. Sanders had virtually no name recognition. Who knows who this senator from Vermont is?

Barrier 4: His *personality*. When you first listen to Sanders, what mostly comes across is a certain gruffness, with an accompanying grumpiness, as well as an intense and self-righteous demeanor. In other words? Listening to Bernie can be a tough hang for anyone.

Barrier 5: His *financial model*. Sanders had no intention of going into debt, and refused to accept money from corporate donors. Because of his organizational background, he also refused to hire almost any campaign staffers. If his campaign was going to happen, it was going to happen almost exclusively through volunteers.

The barriers to scaling this political movement were vast, but if Sanders was good at one thing, it was being able to identify the first and fast followers. At his first official rally in May of 2015, Bernie Sanders gave the line that became the rallying point of his entire campaign, the big idea that would juxtapose him against Hillary Clinton again and again: "We need a political revolution."

What Bernie Sanders had was a sticky and sneezable message that met the moment in time he found himself in. In his view, Clinton represented more of the same old political hackery. Donald Trump also capitalized on this same moment with his own sticky and sneezable message, "Make America Great Again," which similarly recognized the political climate and acknowledged the anger a certain segment of people were feeling. Revolution was in the air, and Bernie was ready to mobilize a political movement.

4.

Republican and Democrat politicos alike concede that the 2008 Obama Campaign was the gold standard for grassroots, digitally supported, and staff-led campaigns. The perfect alchemy of an inspirational figure, grassroots fundraising, discipline, innovative thinking, and volunteer mobilization; it was weaponized by a simple digital infrastructure. To put the two campaigns in perspective, the Obama state campaign headquarters in Ohio was bigger than the *entire national headquarters* of the Sanders Campaign. The 2008 Obama Campaign had launched a neighborhood strategy whereby a group of paid campaign organizers would recruit, train, organize, and deploy groups of volunteers into the various neighborhoods they were trying to reach.

Zack Exley, a professional political operative who helped lead the Sanders Campaign, chronicled its events, along with Becky Bond,

> On my very first day in DC, I fell into depression as I learned that the campaign was basically not hiring anyone. There were no solid plans to do so at any time in the future. Bernie was forcing us to rely almost 100 percent on volunteer leadership that was already out there.

Conventional wisdom would have told him it couldn't be done.

Exley was running smack into the Curse of Knowledge, wasn't he? The barriers for multiplication were mounting, and all he could see were the constraints. Stuck in the prison of his own prior experiences, he believed successful campaigns needed scads of paid staff, a large centralized structure, and a high degree of control. With more than a touch of hyperbole, he went on to say, "This is a crime against history. We're allowing the biggest opportunity for change in one hundred years to be thrown away."

That night, Exley went to bed despondent and inconsolable.

5.

Led by front man Jerry Garcia, the Grateful Dead's music is a fusion of folk, reggae, rock, country, psychedelia, jazz, funk, and probably numerous other genres mashed together. Their concerts are mythic, with jam sessions often lasting into the small hours. As an iconic band with legendary status and a legion of rabid fans, they are also filthy rich.

But unlike most rich musicians, the Grateful Dead didn't succeed because of the sheer number of records they sold. They barely had any singles that charted, with only one Top 40 record. But over the course of their careers, the band grossed more than one hundred million dollars. Why? Because for more than thirty years, they toured the country, doing what they loved, and slowly but surely, gathered a group of people who not only loved their music and their enigmatic lead singer, but also loved the experience of being at these shows *with other people who loved these shows.* Groups of fans would hop on the road and follow the band for months at a time, earning the moniker "the Dead Heads."

In Seth Godin's book *Tribes,* he writes, "A tribe is a group of people connected to one another, connected to [leaders], and connected to an idea." Little by little, what the Dead Heads were becoming over time, was a *tribe.* (I'm choosing to use this word carefully, referring to the anthropological term for a smaller grouping of human society.)

You don't need to reach the masses to be wildly successful. If you start with your first follower, then your fast followers, cultivate your hotbed and look to multiply hotbeds ... you don't need to reach *everyone.* You just need to reach *your people.* That's what happened in youth groups across the United States, with teenagers running around with WWJD bracelets. And that was what started to happen for Dave and Jon Ferguson.

When the Ferguson brothers started Community Christian Church in March of 1989, they cast a vision to plant campuses and churches in every neighborhood of the city of Chicago, but as the years went by, and they went about this work, they noticed these new churches wanted to continue to relate to each other and partner in mission together. The more churches they planted, the more churches expressed this. They weren't trying to start a new denomination or a network, but they were discovering a key element we have already seen in many of the stories of this book: a Groove of Grace. God was at work, so they should join him in what he was doing.

When the NewThing Network came into shape, it started with a single hotbed; a few churches who related to one another and had a center of gravity. But then one hotbed multiplied to another, and then another, creating a small network of hotbeds choosing to be part of the same organic tribe. Like the Grateful Dead, they didn't need to win everyone over. In fact, while NewThing is now a global network, the group started in the midwestern United States and didn't bear much resemblance to some of their more charismatic church planter contemporaries. NewThing didn't need to find the people interested in emulating those leaders. They just needed to find *their people*.

The Fergusons observed that when churches worked *together* to plant more churches, something magical was happening. There seemed to be far more power in a small network of three to four local churches than in a single church going at it alone, even if that church was part of a bigger network.

But how far could it scale?

6.

A good night's sleep did Zach Exley some good as he stepped into day two working on the Bernie Sanders Campaign:

> I woke up filled with excitement. I had been shooting my mouth off for two decades about how mass movements were supposed to be run by the people, not by mercenaries, and how there were more and better leaders among a movement's supporters than a movement could ever hope to hire. I had been lulled into a permanent dependence on staffers while working with big nonprofits and campaigns.

So on that morning, in June 2015, the ragtag underdog team went back to the drawing board. They all circled July 29 on their calendars, marking the day they'd have a massive, decentralized rally across the United States, and then they went back to building their campaign model, which would need to address the many barriers they had to overcome before that date.

Taking a closer examination of the Obama model, they discovered something: "The neighborhood team model [that the Obama Campaign had pioneered] had a limitation," Exley said. "It could only scale in proportion to the number of paid staff." At this point, the Sanders Campaign only had two full-time paid staffers. How could two people build an entire central operation, one that was supposed to catalyze a decentralized movement, using only volunteers?

The answer? The creation of a quickfire process where they could identify, train, and release *teams of volunteers.* "That was the only way to get large numbers of people doing work without direct supervision by paid staff." These teams of people, convened around an urgent cause they were passionate about, were trained, and quickly released to do the work. What they skilled these volunteers to do in organizing their local neighborhoods was the *radical minimum.*

The Obama Campaign adopted the Resourced model, scaling innovation around *control* and *mass.*

Obama Campaign

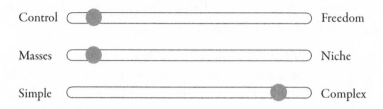

The Sanders Campaign, however, wasn't trying to be the Obama Campaign. They didn't have the resources for that when it started. They were attempting a scalable innovation around *mass* and *simple*: The Groundswell model. And in order to do that, they would need an incredibly effective radical minimum that was simple and sticky. The Sanders Campaign wasn't asking volunteers to do something only the few and the elite could do. Instead, the Campaign defined a few things that required a lot of intentionality, but that "the many" could do, such as making phone calls, door-knocking, and registering new people to vote. It didn't need to be the purest form or a perfect form; it simply needed to be a working form that could catch like wildfire and multiply—just as Hannah More and the abolitionists did with posters and pamphlets. Like the Sanders Campaign, the abolitionists chose a Groundswell model that relied on the masses to take something and run with it, with very little oversight.

Sanders Campaign

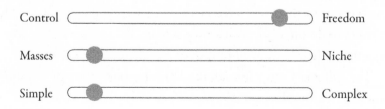

The drawback of this model is you can't control what people do, and there are a number of cringeworthy stories of how Sanders Campaign volunteers went beyond the pale in things they did or said (particularly on Twitter). But the trade-off was a campaign that went further, faster.

On July 29, 2015, the campaign livestream put the campaign's scalable model to the test. They had a sticky and sneezable message: "We need a political revolution." They'd worked with the willing, training an army of volunteers to lead out the specific radical minimums for organizing in local neighborhoods. They'd multiplied their hotbed from one central campaign office to hundreds of volunteer hotbeds around the United States. A paid campaign staff of two people, plus candidate Bernie Sanders, were looking to throw a decentralized, nationwide rally, all organized and led by groups of passionate volunteers.

And on that day in 2015, in over 2,700 different locations, more than 100,000 people met all around the country, making it the largest distributed event in political history.

Now, in political campaigns, the number of phone banks a candidate has is a good indicator of the kind of grassroots support and momentum they have. At the end of January, 2016, if you had pulled up Hillary Clinton's website and done a search of volunteer phone banks within a 250-mile range of New York City, Chicago, Los Angeles, and Austin, there were 39 phone banks listed. If you had pulled up the Sanders Campaign website and looked to find a phone bank in those same areas? There were 1,089.

In the end, the effort was just shy of enough. Sanders almost pulled off a monumental upset, but fell short, largely due to the influence of superdelegates on the Democratic primaries (which was subsequently changed). But in his loss, Sanders and his team rewrote the way modern political campaigns will function from here on out.

"The revolution is not something you order to your own specifications," Exley reminisces. "You have to take the obstacles with the opportunities. There is no provider of revolutionary conditions whose job it is to set everything up just right for you."

7.

The Ferguson brothers and their emerging tribe of churches started to discuss what it would look like for them to band together and become a church planting movement. As you might imagine, after launching the NewThing Network, they went through several iterations. But having studied network and movement theory, the radical minimums they landed on engineered scalability into the model itself, as they asked churches to commit to 4 Rs:

Relationships
Churches in their tribe would form networks of three to four churches that were close in proximity (usually the same city). They asked these churches to intentionally meet with each other once a month, and as a region once a year.

Reproducing
Rather than one church thinking about church planting by themselves, this network of three to four churches banded together to plant churches. Each year, each individual church and network completes an MRP together ... the My Reproducing Plan. These networks would reproduce churches and new networks.

Resources
Each church gives a small amount of money to the local city network, essentially funding their future church planting efforts. Interestingly, there's very little going to "the center" of the NewThing Network. The money and control is on the edges.

Residency

The key to the reproduction of churches is the reproduction of leaders, starting down at the group level. A church in this tribe agrees to have a resident at their church who they invest in and prepare for a future church plant. The residency also fosters experiences at other churches in the network who may do things differently than they do.

But would the radical minimums succeed, or would it just be movement theory that looked good on paper but didn't work in real life? After all, in movement theory, the exponential growth curve can sometimes feel like a mythical creature: Something you've heard is real, but you're never really sure if it is. It's always happening somewhere else, with other people in other places, but never with people like you. But NewThing *did* experience that growth curve, and it looked like this.

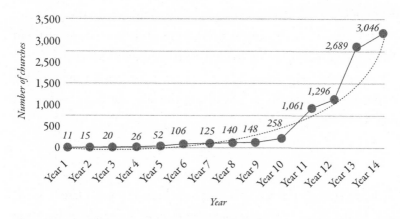

This growth curve is a picture-perfect representation of social change going to scale. Margaret Wheatley, who has a doctorate from Harvard, and Deborah Frieze, the former president of The Berkana Institute, have spent their careers researching, discussing, and ultimately training communities in how to scale social change. Wheatley and Frieze discovered what we're seeing over and over again in this chapter: "In spite of current ads and slogans," they wrote, "the world doesn't change one person at a time. It changes as *networks* of relationships form among people who discover they share a common cause and vision of what's possible." Things don't normally scale through *individuals*; they scale through *networks* of relationships.

The WWJD bracelet didn't catch on one person at a time. It caught on one *youth group* at a time. The people behind the Sanders Campaign weren't multiplying volunteers; they were multiplying decentralized *teams*. And for NewThing, they didn't hit the tipping point by simply multiplying individual churches, but by multiplying *networks*.

Now, what you need to appreciate is that, in a statistician's world, the NewThing Network growth curve is the Shangri-la of multiplication. It's the same thing the Sanders Campaign went after. Both the NewThing Network and the Sanders Campaign achieved it by finding their tribe and sticking to it, by being unrelenting in their mission, and by cultivating and iterating the experience of the tribe over a long period of time. They kept distilling their core practices until they found their radical minimums and then dropped them into a tribe of teams, spring-loaded with movement potential.

Maybe that's why Jesus, when he first mobilizes his burgeoning kingdom movement, doesn't send out the singular hero leader, but sends them out two-by-two.

8.

When we started the COVID-19 coaching groups, Daniel Yang, Todd Milby, and I were hoping we'd have somewhere between fifty churches join in. As we continued to talk with leaders of other networks, we began to realize the number might be a little bigger, but our expectations didn't massively shift.

Early on, we made a strategic choice: We decided not to brand the work under any particular organization. If we believed we were better together, it needed to function and be communicated as a collaboration. It was a trade-off: No single organization got the credit, but it meant more people (*mass*) might be part of it. So from day one, these coaching groups were a combined effort of Catapult, the Send Institute, Christ Together, and the NewThing Network—a collection of leaders who were already working together in one way or another, with each of us bringing some of our coaches to the table.

We made another strategic choice: We would not charge for participation in a coaching group. Every coach gave their time away. That made it accessible to *anyone* in the world with internet access. We offered groups on every day of the week, including some with early morning slots, to account for global time zones. We asked coaches to help lead at least two groups. This was our radical minimum. Not surprisingly, the first and fast followers of our coaches quickly turned into a hotbed with a center of gravity. And as more groups developed, more hotbeds started to emerge and multiply, and they started to share best practices. Very quickly, a tribe was developing, and it had all the relational thickness that Alan Hirsch calls *Communitas*—the friendship, community, and relational bonds formed in the fires of being on mission together.

The groups themselves happened on Zoom, so if we had five hundred people register for one time slot, the only thing keeping us from scaling was the number of coaches, because each virtual breakout room required one coach to every six to eight participants.

We started Week 1 with a few hundred churches participating in groups, and we decided to lower another barrier that might hurt scalability: We didn't close registration after Week 1. As it turns out, the experience of the first week was sticky and sneezable. We grew to 1,094 churches at the end of Week 2.

But it didn't stop after Week 2. Word got out what was happening; not only were the groups helping people stabilize and renormalize in the midst of the crisis, they were also helping leaders mobilize their people into mission. We had more and more people clamoring to get into groups.

Like Rent the Runway, we had a problem on our hands: A lot of new churches wanted to get into coaching groups, but our infrastructure was starting to creak. We were running out of coaches, the IT support needed to sustain the team maxed out, and the logistics of running that many groups, with that many people, were redlining the effort. At this point, the way we were scaling the innovation was using the Resourced model (*control* and *mass*). This was only possible because everyone was donating their time, and we were using technology already in our budget.

A number of networks, denominations, and mission agencies asked if we could start groups for churches in their tribe. There was just one problem: the infrastructure built for the Resourced model was tapped out. But if we pivoted to the Groundswell model (*simple* and *mass*)? It was suddenly scalable to a new level. However, doing this would mean sacrificing *control.*

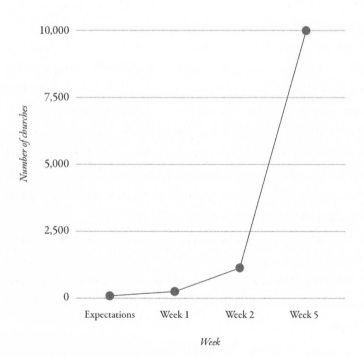

In the end, we made a choice. We gave those leaders everything we had and held nothing back: detailed notes of every session, scripts, worksheets, slides, training videos we'd recorded for coaches, video replays of each week, email templates. Everything we had, we gave it to them, free of charge. We trained the leaders of those tribes of churches, walked them through the essentials of the radical minimums and what they'd need to do. We then released them to be the yeast in the dough of their specific tribe.

The pivot worked.

At the end of Week 2 there were 1,094 churches in a coaching group. At the end of Week 5, there were more than ten thousand churches in a coaching group, spread across thirty-nine countries, speaking eleven languages.

And after that? We simply stopped counting.

LEADER INNOVATION LAB

KEY PRINCIPLES FROM PHASE 5: MULTIPLICATION

Goal: Make the innovation scalable, removing as many barriers as possible, for as many people as possible, so we can invite them all into a brand new breakthrough.

Scale
Set up your kingdom innovation to reach its full potential as it increases in size or numbers.

The Scalability Tool
Every team has to make a choice about how they want to scale and what they want to sacrifice: *control*, *masses*, or *simple*?

Radical Minimums
The simplest but most radical practice(s) you can invite people to participate in that will be normal for your innovation movement.

Sticky and Sneezable
When a message or innovation is sticky, it's memorable and sticks like flypaper in your brain. When something is sneezable, it means that same sticky message is easy to share and get in front of other people.

Tribe
The group of people you're with who are committed to the same mission and relational investment.

The Master Tool for the Multiplication Phase: The Bust the Barriers Tool

PHASE 5:
MULTIPLICATION

BUST THE
BARRIERS TOOL

Watch the training video for the
Bust the Barriers Master Tool at
DougPaul.org/ReadyorNotLab

Nuts-and-Bolts Leader Coaching

Not all kingdom innovations need to grow, spread, multiply, and scale. There are plenty of examples of significant moves of God where this didn't happen. For instance, the Clapham Sect itself didn't multiply across the Western world, but it led to significant breakthrough.

The question is where our bias is. Does our bias lead us toward innovations that are heavyweight, high maintenance, led by elite leaders, and hard to multiply? There are many remarkable moves of God that involve those things, such as seminaries, missions agencies, and denominations. But again, it's a question of locating our bias. The other bias is toward innovations that are lightweight and low maintenance, that release control, and chase after rapid reproduction. There isn't a "superior" choice here, but we need to know what our bias is, because only when we know our bias can we discern for each particular innovation whether or not God is calling us to let go of it and pick up another way of thinking.

So, the best nuts-and-bolts-coaching I can probably give you in the Multiplication Phase is to help you identify where your bias is. My observation is that the bias of most leaders is toward the status quo, which leans against multiplication, so I'd like to double-click on this bias in particular.

Here's how it can play out: A few months ago, I was working with one of the largest and fastest growing churches in the United States. And honestly? It's probably one of the most innovative churches I've ever been around. But when we started working on the Multiplication Phase and what their innovation could look like at a movement level, they hit the giant brick wall of the Curse of Knowledge. They couldn't see past all the reasons it wouldn't work, in the same way Exley couldn't see how the Sanders Campaign would ever get off the ground. One of the most imaginative leadership teams I've ever been around couldn't stop saying "It won't work here" (referring to a North American context) despite the fact that there are loads of examples of it "working here."

Our bias tends to be toward growing things that already exist and doing things by addition. That's our cultural predisposition in Western Christian leadership. Is it easier to focus only on addition? Absolutely. It's a known quantity. But what we've seen in this book again and again is if you can focus on your tribe and bake reproduction into the radical minimum, we might be surprised about what a kingdom return can look like. It doesn't mean it goes this way every time or that God wants it to go this way every time. But rather than making that decision because our bias has made it for us, what if we were open to brand new possibilities? What if our bias didn't lead us down a road of limited possibility?

When we design with the end in mind, we're circling, high-lighting, underlining, and applying a gold star to what we want to see happen when the innovation reaches its fullest potential. After working with thousands of teams in the last decade, I can't overstate the way in which our bias early on can short-circuit where things end up in Phase 5. Again, it doesn't mean that things *have* to multiply in order to be a kingdom innovation; rather, we need to challenge the bias that something at its fullest potential couldn't multiply.

Questions to Sharpen Your Multiplication Skills

Discipleship
What's a sticky and sneezable message to invite people into the giant story of being a disciple of Jesus?

Leadership
In what ways could your own ego serve as a barrier for what God wants to do through a scalable kingdom innovation?

Mission
In what ways have you inserted rapid reproduction into your radical minimums? If you haven't, why not? Does this decision reveal anything about your unconscious biases?

Worship
What are the spiritual idols that most people in your tribe are fighting against that will serve as practical barriers to multiplication?

Reconciliation
How can you bake reconciliation into all the generations that will come after you and not just the first generation?

Operating System
Is the operating system of your church or organization built for institution or scalability? What are the specific things in your operating system that are barriers to scale?

This is a Spiritual Process

The Multiplication Phase is about scaling the innovation so it reaches its full potential, removing as many barriers as we can along the way.

Here's the good news in this: *Jesus Christ is the same yesterday, today, and forever.* And our God is in the business of breaking down barriers. Jesus broke down religious barriers, ethnic barriers, and class barriers. He broke down gender barriers, racial barriers, and metaphysical barriers. And ultimately, he broke down all the barriers between humanity and God: sin, death, hell, and the grave.

Jesus Christ is the same yesterday, today, and forever. What Jesus did in his earthly life he is still doing to this day: breaking down barriers and achieving the impossible. There is no kingdom innovation without Jesus, for "apart from me you can do nothing." That means there is no kingdom scaling without Jesus, no multiplication without Jesus, and no Jesus-tribe without Jesus.

When I first became interested in movement theory and practice about fourteen years ago, I had a time of prayer with the Lord that quickly became confrontational. God asked me, "If you had to pick between leading a huge church with everyone in the wider church hanging on your every word, or be part of a team that catalyzes a movement in which you were anonymous—which would you pick?"

The problem with paradigms is they aren't about your head. *They're about your heart.* You see, in that prayer time, I knew what the right answer was, and I cognitively knew that *movement* was the right answer. But my heart was still clinging to the affirmation of fame, status, recognition, and influence. I wanted the kingdom success of movement with the worldly recognition of the megachurch sphere. Yet Jesus once said, "For what does it profit a man to gain the whole world and forfeit his soul?"

For me, whenever I hit the Multiplication Phase, the warfare over my heart goes into overdrive. My old sin patterns reappear as there are still deep roots in me that believe bigger is better; and if it's big, then people will think I'm significant. Scaling something brings up all the things I want said about me ("What you've done is significant"), but that Jesus has already given me through the gospel ("The work I accomplished through the cross and resurrection, and the invitation into my royal family, is the most significant thing you'll ever need"). There's still something in me that wants to *earn* the acceptance, earn the acclaim, earn the significance.

For me, scaling something reveals that there are still times that I want the glory.

There are two problems with wanting the glory. First, as we've identified a number of times before, all the glory of a kingdom innovation goes to Jesus. There aren't leftovers that are tossed my way. And that's as it should be! Second, it is quite rare in kingdom innovation for the leader to receive acclaim when something scales. One of the reasons it scales is because it's *not* built on one leader.

The book of Proverbs says, "Above all else, guard your heart, for everything you do flows from it." This might be the last phase for kingdom innovation, but don't switch off from the ways the enemy is quietly and subtly at work. In my experience? That war usually starts in my own heart.

How Then Shall We Lead?

Epilogue

"THEY WORK EVERY DAY EXCEPT SUNDAY AND THEY
BEHAVE IN A *MOST UNRESTRAINED WAY*."

1.

In 1736, Robert Raikes was born into a solidly middle-class family in Gloucester, England. Raikes' father was in publishing, and when he was old enough, Raikes took over the family publishing business.

While visiting a friend one day, Raikes witnessed the behavior of a rambunctious group of children and found himself shocked by their cursing, gambling, and fighting.

"This is nothing [compared] to what [happens] on Sundays," Raikes' friend advised him. "You'd be shocked indeed if you were here then. They work every day except Sunday and they behave in a *most unrestrained way*." (What a wonderfully Victorian way of saying "They're totally out of control!")

In today's Western society, child labor laws have been in force for many generations. But not in Raikes' time. It would be years before precedent-setting laws "generously" capped a child's work to *twelve hours a day*.

Many children of the poor worked horrible hours in factories during the week—often in excess of 12 hours a day. Those on the lower end of the economic spectrum often did not have access to educational opportunities due to their overburdened work schedules, which kept them trapped in a cycle of poverty.

Raikes was burdened by the plight of these kids and how their lives would be affected ten, twenty, or fifty years down the road. With his heart now broken for them, he spent the rest of his life fighting on their behalf.

When Raikes opened the doors to his first Sunday School class in July of 1780, he was not the first to try this grand new experiment. Others had attempted similar endeavors and had experienced little-to-moderate success. The core idea was simple: Use the only day off these kids have, teach them to read, and in doing so equip them for a better future. However, Raikes introduced a remarkable new paradigm. At the time, it was believed that if individuals were to attend church, they must wear their "Sunday best," and this mindset was often reinforced by the churches themselves. Raikes removed this barrier, stating that if a child's clothes were suitable for the streets, then they were suitable for his Sunday School class.

The Sunday School involved a full and rigorous day: Children showed up in the morning for educational instruction, and returned after lunch for a reading lesson, a worship service, followed by another classroom lesson. Finally, the kids were sent home at 5:30 p.m. (and instructed to "leave quietly and without making a noise").

Perhaps the most brilliant aspect of Raikes' plan was the text they used to teach literacy: the Bible.

Raikes seamlessly brought two key elements together: *Justice* and *evangelism*. And he did this without government intrusion, intervention, or subterfuge. Raikes and his colleagues advocated for child labor reform legislation, but not at the expense of the children sitting right in front of them. They believed learning to read was essential for escaping poverty, and claiming Christ as Savior was essential to life eternal.

Unsurprisingly, Raikes had his critics. Maybe he didn't have trolls on Twitter or angry emails pouring into his inbox, but his Sunday School soon became tagged as "Raikes Ragged Regiment." The movement was criticized for violating the Sabbath and for undermining home-based religious education. And more than a few people were concerned it was a funnel for political propaganda.

After three years of trial and error, Raikes published an account of his experiences (and for what it's worth, the article didn't even mention his name). Soon, other newspapers got hold of the story and began to share it. One company owner, commenting on the pupils at Raikes' school, said, "They have been transformed from the shape of wolves and tigers to that of men." The school caught the attention of William Wilberforce, the great abolitionist, reformer, and philanthropist, and he and his crew began to fund large segments of the endeavor.

In only twenty years, what started as a small group of people had grown to two hundred thousand. By 1831, just fifty years after opening the doors of Raikes' Sunday School, more than 25 percent of the entire population of England were learning to read, while learning about Jesus—*every week*. By 1850, there were two million children in Sunday School.

To this day, the Sunday School movement is not only credited for embedding the moral courage in individuals who later went on to advocate for the abolition of slavery, but also for creating the seedbeds of the great revivals of the nineteenth century. The embers of this fire also spread and caught wind in the newly forming United States.

This one, relatively simple innovation, fanned into flame by the winds of the Spirit, became a movement that changed the trajectory of two countries on two separate continents.

So why does Sunday School have such a bad rap these days?

2.

In 1956, the British Supersonic Transport Aircraft Committee met to discuss the formation of a new project. They wanted to create a new airplane that would not only fly faster than the speed of sound but would be used commercially to fly from New York City to Paris. Within a few years, engineers and companies from France joined the mix.

The original cost estimates for the supersonic Concorde were £70 million (around $88 million). But long before the project was completed, with costs ballooning and deadlines passing by, the collaborating countries realized their aircraft wasn't economically viable. There was no way the twenty commercial aircrafts they were building could possibly recoup the costs. In other words, continuing with the project would bring economic catastrophe.

In 1976, the first Concorde flight took off, and over the next twenty-seven years, it ferried wealthy passengers back and forth across the Atlantic. In the end, the Concorde cost £1.3 billion (about $1.6 billion) to manufacture and is considered one of the worst financial investments in modern history. The losses were so catastrophic and so renowned that a metaphor emerged, which is now commonly used across a range of sectors, from business to biology: *The Concorde fallacy*.

Forbes journalist Jim Blasingame describes the fallacy as "a metaphor for when animals or humans defend an investment—a policy, business, or nest—when that defense costs more than abandonment and an alternative."

It made no sense in the world for the engineers, businesses, and governments of Britain and France to continue working on the Concorde project. Even though they knew it had no financial viability long before the first flight ever took off, and despite losing money for decades, it still continued to fly commercially for more than twenty-five years.

Alan Skorkin is a software developer and writes on the evolution of software (alongside a number of other random things). He points out that even those in the tech world, generally thought to be one of the most innovative sectors, "will often stick with a technology/ library choice through thick and thin long past the time we should have abandoned it and found something that fits our needs better."

What the Concorde fallacy highlights is a unique aspect of human nature that struggles to choose a different direction, once a significant amount of time and money has been invested. Journalist Daniel Bier, using gambling as an example, explains this further with another iteration of the principle we're looking at, known as the *sunk cost fallacy*:

> Inexperienced gamblers fall inside this trap: "Sure, the house took me the last 10 hands in a row, but if I get up now, I'll have lost everything! I've got to get it back!" We tend to think of money we've already lost as being "still on the table," and if only we raise the stakes, we could get it back. To leave would force us to admit our mistake and reckon its cost.

The need for Sunday education shifted dramatically in 1870 with the passage of the Forster's Education Act. It kickstarted the modern education movement for all children in England and Wales. Likewise, similar legislation was passed in the United States. Over time, children increasingly had literacy opportunities in environments outside of Sunday School and therefore no longer needed Sunday School to learn how to read. In other words, in 1870, the world changed: Would Sunday School adapt along with it?

Well, the Concorde fallacy highlights the challenge Sunday School was facing. As Bier continues, "The more we invest in a project or a person, the harder it is to let it go. Our brain tricks us into thinking that the more energy we put into something, the more valuable it is." Sunday School had been wildly successful, with tremendous investment of time, resources, and energy. But Sunday School never "let go." As time passed, the purpose of Sunday School gradually shifted. It went from fighting injustice, creating a better future for children, and exposing them to the gospel, to *religious education for people already in the church system*.

There was still a massive opportunity (and need) to reach those far from God and to seek justice on behalf of the most marginalized. But over time, the *practice* of Sunday School won out over the *principle* and *paradigm* of why Sunday School started in the first place. The Concorde fallacy won out. For many, many congregations, Sunday School still essentially functions with the same shell that was culturally effective 250 years ago.

But time stands still for no one.

3.

It's entirely possible to have a game-changing innovation but be so committed to that specific innovation, that it becomes inflexible, refusing to change and adapt to shifting cultural realities. Remember our friend Henry Ford from the introduction of this book? His assembly line innovation pioneered the mass production of the Model T car. But eventually, as culture changed, people stopped wanting that version of the Model T. For a while, Ford struggled to innovate again after the runaway success of the first innovation. It seems he slowly began confusing the *vision* (a preferred picture of the future) with the *vehicle* (the actual thing that will move someone toward that preferred picture). Eventually, the vision simply served to prop up and sustain a vehicle that no longer resonated with the world in which Ford lived. It started to be all about making sure the original vehicle survived, even if it stopped delivering what people wanted.

When we finally see a kingdom innovation scale, it's a powerful experience. I can vividly remember the first time it happened to me and can replay it back in my mind and heart as if it were yesterday. Why? Because we attach ourselves to an innovation, emotionally and spiritually. But we have to continue to remember that no matter how extraordinary the experience of an innovation, what is working now will not work forever. Eventually, an innovation will start to stall out.

When that happens to you, will you remember to go back to the big *why* questions, or will you stubbornly stick with the *how* and the *what* of the past? When we feel successful at something, our own leadership ego can subtly insert itself into our decisions, and if ego is the enemy, it's helpful to remember that the antidote is humility. As we keep in step with the Spirit, the invitation from Jesus always looks like the path of humility.

Throughout the course of this book, I've walked through the basic principles of kingdom innovation. My deepest hope and prayer is that God uses these principles to activate a wave of innovation in your life and leadership. But if that happens, beware the Concorde fallacy.

You are not to be the *reformed*, gilding in gold the victories of the past. You are to be *reforming*: Active. Adaptive. Always listening, learning, searching, curious ... joining Jesus in what he's doing next.

This is the leadership we need for the brave new world we find ourselves in. This is how we find the future, together.

Afterword

There are not many people familiar with the Law of Involution, which is hardly surprising, given it's a theorem within Boolean algebra. But it contains one of the most important and fundamental ideas creative leaders bump against almost every single day. Transposed into a leadership context, it says this: Once an idea has been widely accepted as true, there's a window of time to prove the viability of the idea before it's rejected as a pipedream. When applied to radically innovative social movements, which require high levels of costly commitment from their followers, this "law" states that the idea must see some significant wins for the followers to remain committed to the revolution. If the movement cannot provide reasonable proof of concept, the revolution will "involute," that is, turn in on itself.

In other words, once the idea is accepted, a giant countdown timer starts to click down.

In the last fifteen years, there's been a countdown timer on ideas surrounding movement theory and the gospel. Many books have been written, much digital ink has been spilled, and a vast number of conference and workshop hours have been spent espousing these ideas. And the good news is that, as far as we can tell, for at least 16 percent of our best leaders in the Western church, the *idea* of missional movements has been accepted. This means that the critical tipping point of adoption required for an idea to be inevitable in a given population has effectively been won. But while the battle for the mind of the church may have been won, appropriate practice sadly lags seriously behind. And so in the West at least, the involution clock is ticking down, waiting for the idea to be *proved* viable.

In *The Forgotten Ways*, I (Alan) wrote about the need for Christian leaders to increasingly learn the discipline of *design thinking*. Led by the likes of IDEO's Tom Kelley, Roger Martin, or Stanford Group, design thinking is the process required to crack the code on what seems to be an unsolvable "wicked problem" and then field testing the prototypes until that problem is figured out and solved.

As leaders, it is time for us to build on our best thinking in terms of missional theology and organizational theory, and engage design thinkers to come in and tackle the Law of Involution. Right now, what we really need are some strategic practitioners who can move us from paradigm to practice, from the head to the heart and from the heart to the hand. And that's exactly what Doug Paul has done in this book.

Truth is that leaders might *want* apostolic movement—they might even dream of it—but many seem unwilling to move beyond the hegemonic structures of the existing forms of church. We've lost count of how many times we've been talking about this idea of movement and multiplication when an exasperated leader eventually pops up, "Yeah, but that won't work here. People have tried it and it doesn't work here." Perhaps even you have had that same thought.

But let us analyze some assumptions that are loaded into such statements: First, we must challenge the assumption that "movements don't work in the West." The church as movement *has* worked here in the West, and in fact represents our best hope for the advance of the cause of Christ in this time. What that leader often *actually* means is, "It hasn't worked in the way I currently understand and practice church." And this, dear reader, has to do with the core Villain in this book—the Curse of Knowledge.

Epictetus, the Greek philosopher once noted that "it is impossible for a man to learn what he thinks he already knows." Similarly, Upton Sinclair wryly noted that "it is difficult to get a man to understand something when his salary depends on his not understanding it!" The more we know about something, the more expertise we gain, the harder it is for us to see other ways of doing things. The issue at hand is not whether movemental principles work in the West. They do. The issue is whether people with the highest levels of expertise can defeat the Curse of Knowledge and see a new way of being the church that is already happening around them.

Finally—and this is something Doug repeatedly explores in this book—we want to speak to the incompleteness of the statement, "That won't work here." It's a declarative statement, which rings in absolutes. Ironically, many people who make such declarations have been successful, innovative leaders themselves. Once upon a time, others probably observed what they were trying to do and said, "But that won't work here." And yet ... somewhere along the way ... *it did work*.

And so perhaps what the statement might actually read is: "That hasn't worked here ... *yet*." When leaders say something hasn't worked, it's often that they tried an idea *once*. And that *one time* it didn't work. But as Doug has so effectively shown us, innovation doesn't happen overnight. In addressing some of the biggest challenges and myths of innovation, Doug illustrates that kingdom innovation isn't going to happen immediately, or because one miraculous idea popped up in an isolated eureka moment. It's going to come through iterating and trying over and over and over again. And this will feel costly. Many leaders in church circles resist the process of unlearning in order to relearn; many lack the courage that is needed to make those sometimes sacrificial strategic decisions and don't always have the patience that is needed for systemic change.

But what if each of us could develop these skills and attributes?

What if as Christian leaders we could develop the capacity to really learn again, to conceive of a vision that can activate a resolute determination, and become leaders who are patient enough to keep trying, to keep iterating, to keep adapting until we find breakthrough?

How might this brave new world look different?

ALAN AND DEBRA HIRSCH
Authors of numerous books on missional spirituality, leadership, and organization. Founders of Forge Missional Training Network and Movement Leaders Collective.

Take Your Next, Best Step

If you'd like to learn more about the Innovation Lab process Doug leads at Catapult, you can watch the explainer video, get more information, and download an info packet at

WeAreCatapult.org/InnovationLabs

Interested in working with Doug?

You can reach him at DougPaul.org/contact. He regularly speaks at conferences, churches, workshops and is a regular guest for podcasts and webinars.

About the Author

Doug Paul co-leads Catapult, an innovation and activation shop that helps leaders create successful ministries that scale. While he no longer works as a full-time pastor, he does continue to serve as a pastor and elder of a local church in the city center of Richmond, Virginia, where he lives with his wife, Elizabeth, their three kids, and a Great Dane. The church itself is racially and socially economically diverse, with a mission focused on two square miles of real estate holding the sixth highest concentration of poverty in the United States.

You can visit his website at DougPaul.org , and you can follow him on Twitter, Facebook, and Instagram: @dougpauljr

Acknowledgments

This project could never have happened without the belief, support, and contribution of so many people!

I want to start by thanking my wife, Elizabeth: The content of this book and the process I use for kingdom innovation is the result of a covenantal life together. We do all of this ... *together*. You've been an endless sounding board and content co-creator, and you always sharpen and challenge whatever I'm doing. You've believed in this book from the beginning, probably even more than me at points. Thank you for all your contributions and your unwavering love and faith. It's an honor to be half of "us."

My kids, Avery, Judah, and Sam: You're inheriting this world, and we're passing this faith on to you, as you choose Jesus for yourself. You and the generations to follow are why innovation is so important. And to Avery specifically, thanks for your "back cover content" contributions.

My parents: Now having children of my own, it's only more apparent how difficult it must have been to have me as someone God entrusted to you! But you were remarkable at stewarding what God gave you, and I'm eternally grateful.

Anna Robinson, my editor: What can I say? You've been ruthless with me, and I needed it. I dreaded emails and notes from you about half of the time, but I'm so very proud of what we've put into the world, and it couldn't have happened without your consistency and faithfulness to bringing the very best out of this project. You were masterful in your role.

Sean O'Brien, the cover designer: I'm so grateful you took this on. You saw a story to tell and had a heart for something that needed creative expression. Thank you so much for lending your genius eye and creativity.

Alan Hirsch: You've stayed the course with me and been a friend, mentor, and generous colleague. You've offered wisdom, insights, and personal challenge when I've needed it. You've served me incredibly well. Thank you to you and Deb for writing the afterword—it means a lot to me.

Dave Ferguson and Daniel Yang: It's been a blast working with you two, and a tremendous honor that you wrote the foreword.

Todd Milby and Andy Graham: We've been in this together from the start. You've never stopped encouraging or believing in this book, even when I felt stuck. I hope I've done you proud.

Pastor Don: You've been such an encouragement to me during this project. I don't know that anyone has ever quite believed in me like you do. All I can do is say "thank you."

Will Mancini and Dave Rhodes: You are killer toolmakers, big picture thinkers, and masterful at creating culture through language. I've learned so much from you, and this book wouldn't even exist without that learning.

To the several hundred leaders I interviewed as research for this book: thank you so much for your investment and wisdom. I hope there are evident sparks of that investment sprinkled throughout.

Notes

INTRODUCTION: THE GREAT MANURE CRISIS OF 1894

xxiv   **In fifty years," *The Times* claimed.** Ben Johnson, "The Great Horse Manure Crisis of 1894," *Historic UK*, https://www.historic-uk.com/HistoryUK/HistoryofBritain/Great-Horse-Manure-Crisis-of-1894/ . I am also grateful for the following sources on the Great Manure Crisis of 1894: David Doochin, "The First Global Urban Planning Conference Was Mostly About Manure," *Atlas Obscura*, July 29, 2016, https://www.atlasobscura.com/articles/the-first-global-urban-planning-conference-was-mostly-about-manure ; Raymond A. Mohl, *The Making of Urban America* (Maryland: Rowman & Littlefield Publishers, 2011); Elizabeth Kolbert, "Hosed," *The New Yorker*, November 9, 2009, https://www.newyorker.com/magazine/2009/11/16/hosed .
   After the introduction to this book was written, the Great Horse Manure Crisis also featured in Dan Heath, Upstream: How to Solve Problems Before they Happen (New York: Simon & Schuster, 2020) 29–30.

xxv   **The Lord brought me to 2 Corinthians 11.** 2 Corinthians 11:2–4.

xxviii   **See, I am doing a new thing!** Isaiah 43:19.

xxviii   **On earth as it is in heaven.** Matthew 6:10.

xxviii   **There is not a square inch.** Abraham Kuyper, *Sphere Sovereignty*, cited in James D. Bratt, ed., *Abraham Kuyper, A Centennial Reader* (Michigan: Eerdmans, 1998), 461.

xxviii   **Why aren't we known as creators.** Andy Crouch, *Culture Making: Recovering our Creative Calling* (Illinois: IVP Press, 2008), 118.

xxix   **"It was a cold, drizzly day," she recalled.** "The Chicken Coop Story that Led to AARP," *AARP History*, https://www.aarp.org/about-aarp/history/chicken-coop-inspires-mission/ .

xxix   **Stockily built, with short grey hair.** Ibid.

xxx   **Old age, Ethel, needs care as youth needs care.** Ibid.

xxxi   **By 1912, the number of cars.** Julia Felton, "Lessons from the Great Horse Manure Crisis of 1894," *Business Horsepower*, December 2018, https://www.businesshorsepower.com/lessons-great-horse-manure-crisis-1894/ .

xxxi   **Let me dispel with the suspense.** Patrick Vlaskovits, "Henry Ford, Innovation and that 'Faster Horse' Quote," *Harvard Business Review*, August 2011, https://hbr.org/2011/08/henry-ford-never-said-the-fast .

xxxii **Any color, so long as it's black.** John Duncan, *Any Color – So long as it's Black: Designing the Model T Ford 1906–1908* (Auckland, New Zealand: Exisle Publishing, 2011).

xxxii **Henry Ford's genius.** Vlaskovits, "Henry Ford."

xxxii **In 1908, the Ford Motor Company manufactured ten thousand cars.** Ibid.

xxxii **A Car for every Purse and Purpose.** Michael Martin, "Remembering GM's Alfred P. Sloan," June 1, 2009, in *All Things Considered*, produced by NPR, podcast, https://www.npr.org/templates/story/story.php?storyId=104797209 .

xxxiii **In 1921, more than 67 percent.** Vlaskovits, "Henry Ford."

xxxiii **In 1965, Gordon Moore, the co-founder of Intel.** Gordon Moore, "Cramming More Components onto Integrated Circuits," *Electronics Magazine*, April 19, 1965, https://newsroom.intel.com/wp-content/uploads/sites/11/2018/05/moores-law-electronics.pdf .

xxxiv **People within a delineated population.** Jane Pilcher "Mannheim's Sociology of Generations: An undervalued legacy," *British Journal of Sociology*, (September 1994), 45.

xxxiv **Pew Religious Landscape Survey.** Pew Forum editors, "In U.S., Decline of Christianity Continues at Rapid Pace," The Pew Research Center, Religion and Public Life, October 17, 2019, https://www.pewforum.org/2019/10/17/in-u-s-decline-of-christianity-continues-at-rapid-pace/ .

xxxv **Churches who love the method more than the mission will die.** Carey Nieuwhof, "5 Reasons Charismatic Churches are Growing," *Church Leaders,* November 2018, https://churchleaders.com/outreach-missions/outreach-missions-articles/336975-5-reasons-charismatic-churches-are-growing-and-attractional-churches-are-past-peak-carey-nieuwhof.html/2 .

xxxv **If the 1950s came back, many churches are ready.** Ed Stetzer "Missing the Mission: Looking for the Right Results While Loving the Wrong Things," *Christianity Today*, May 2013, https://www.christianitytoday.com/edstetzer/2013/may/missing-mission-looking-for-right-results-while-loving.html .

xxxv **Our current forms of "doing church" can only reach about 40 percent of the population.** Alan Hirsch and Dave Ferguson, *On the Verge: A Journey into the Apostolic Future of the Church* (Michigan: Zondervan, 2011), 27.

xxxvi **If you love the form.** Scott Erickson, (@scottthepainter), "If you love the form, you have everything to lose. If you love What gives it its form, you're free to receive whatever it is turning into," Twitter, May 17, 2018, 2:33 p.m. Used by permission.

CHAPTER ONE: ARCHIMEDES' REVENGE

3   Young men capable of close observation. Susan Cheever, *My Name is Bill: His Life—And the Creation of Alcoholics Anonymous* (New York: Washington Square Press, 2005), 88.

5   It tasted so good. Ibid, 75.

6   If there be a God. Ibid, 118.

7   Give me a place to stand, and I will move the earth. T. L. Heath ed., *The Works of Archimedes with the Method of Archimedes* (New York: Dover Publications, 1953), xix.

7   Displace more water than its pure gold counterpart. David Biello, "Fact or Fiction? Archimedes Coined the Term 'Eureka!' in the Bath," *Scientific American*, December 8, 2006, https://www.scientificamerican.com/article/fact-or-fiction-archimede/ .

8   The historian Vitruvius. M. H. Morgan ed., *Vitruvius: The Ten Books on Architecture* (New York: Dover Publications, 1960).

9   A scientist of Archimedes' stature. Biello, "Fact or Fiction?"

9   The volumetric method works in theory. Ibid.

9   The enduring power of the story. Ibid.

10   "The trick," he says. Steven Johnson, *Where Good Ideas Come From: The Natural History of Innovation* (New York: Riverhead Books, 2011, 41.

10   As human connectivity has increased. Ibid, 46.

11   When innovators are asked how they came up with their idea. Scott Berkun, *The Myths of Innovation* (Beijing: O'Reilly, 2007), xxx.

11   Steven Johnson builds on this idea with the concept of the "slow hunch." Johnson, *Where Good Ideas Come From*, 77.

12   In the 1980s, Tim Berners-Lee was a computer scientist and engineer. Stephanie Sammartino McPherson, *Tim Berners-Lee: Inventor of the World Wide Web (USA Today Lifeline Biographies)* (Minneapolis: Twenty-First Century Books, 2009).

13   He "applied [those theories] to his alcoholic followers." Cheever, *My Name is Bill*, 136.

14   Armed with the knowledge of his previous failures. Ibid, 136.

CHAPTER TWO: WHEN EXPERTS STOP ASKING

19   Paul and his companions. Acts 16:6–8.

20   After receiving a vision of a Macedonian man. Acts 16:9.

21   On the Sabbath. Acts 16:13–15.

24   The problem, according to Sinek. Simon Sinek, *Start with Why: How Great Leaders Inspire Everyone to Take Action* (New York: Penguin, 2009), 173.

26   W. Edwards Deming, the American engineer. Megan MacDavey, "System Redesign Part I: Why It Matters," *The Tower Foundation*, April 2018, https://thetowerfoundation.org/2018/04/26/system-redesign-part-i-why-it-matters-html/ .

27   He was water skiing on a lake. Warren Berger, *A More Beautiful Question: The Power of Inquiry to Spark Breakthrough Ideas* (New York: Bloomsbury Publishing, 2016), 11.

27   There was an empty spot. Ibid, 12.

28   This "new best friend." Ibid, 11

28   Tripped on a pebble the size of a pea. Ibid, 11

28   I bit my tongue. Ibid, 12.

28   Phillips exhibited one of the telltale signs. Ibid, 12.

28   In a time when so much. Ibid, 13.

28   Polly Labarre, writing for the *Harvard Business Review*. Polly Labarre, "The Question That Will Change Your Organization," *Harvard Business Review*, November 2011, https://hbr.org/2011/11/whats-the-question-that-will-c .

29   If you have hard, cynical eyes. Alan Hirsch, *5Q: Reactivating the Original Intelligence and Capacity of the Body of Christ* (Atlanta: 100 Movements Publishing, 2017), xii.

29   If they can put a man on the moon. Berger, *A More Beautiful Question*, 11.

29   The more Phillips learned. Ibid, 35.

30   "A journey of inquiry," Berger comments. Ibid, 33.

30   Perhaps that's why Albert Einstein said. Matthew Radmanesh, *Cracking the Code of Our Physical Universe: The Key to a World of Enlightenment and Enrichment* (AuthorHouse, 2006), 97.

30   The Jewish theologian. Abraham Joshua Heschel, *The Prophets* (New York: Harper, 1962), xv.

30   When you consider retooling [the organized church for mission]. Will Mancini and Cory Hartman, *Future Church: 7 Laws of Real Church Growth* (Michigan: Baker Books, December 2020). Forthcoming title, used by permission.

31   Christian leaders will need soft eyes. Hirsch, *5Q*, xxi.

32   Instead of a traditional L-shaped lower leg and foot. Berger, *A More Beautiful Question*, 35

32   Drawing of prosthetic design. Recreation of drawing in Ibid, 35.

32   Using Phillips' creation. Ibid, 37.

PHASE 1 LEADER INNOVATION LAB

36   **Steven Johnson shares this practical piece of advice.** Johnson, *Where Good Ideas Come From*, 246.

38   **God set aside "good works."** Ephesians 2:10.

40   **As Paul said.** Galatians 5:25.

40   **In the downloadable Case Studies for the Identification Phase.** Go to DougPaul.org/ReadyorNotLab

CHAPTER THREE: THE CURSE COMES CALLING

45   **Opportunity knocked for twenty-three-year-old Richard Warren Sears.** I am grateful for the following sources on Sears Holdings Corporation: Boris Emmet, *Catalogues and Counters: A History of Sears, Roebuck & Company* (Chicago: The University of Chicago Press, 1954); Michael Klepper and Michael Gunther, *The Wealthy 100: From Benjamin Franklin to Bill Gates—A Ranking of the Richest Americans, Past and Present* (New Jersey: Carol Publishing Group, 1996); Robert Passikoff, "A Love Song To Mr. Sears & Mr. Roebuck, Who Could Use One About Now," *Forbes*, January 22, 2014, https://www.forbes.com/sites/robertpassikoff/2014/01/22/a-love-song-to-mr-sears-mr-roebuck-they-could-use-one-about-now/#13fede6c1f68 .

47   **By 1931, Sears made more money through its stores than through its catalogues.** Shoshanna Delventhal, "Who Killed Sears? Fifty Years on the Road to Ruin," *Investopedia*, July 1, 2019, https://www.investopedia.com/news/downfall-of-sears/ .

47   **By 1969, it was the largest retailer in the world.** Ibid.

48   **Dear Chicago Summer.** Chance the Rapper, "Dear Chicago Summer," *Back to School Pack*, Mixtape Coalition, 2013, track 3, https://soundcloud.com/chancetherapperfans/dear-chicago-summer .

49   **I felt a deep pit in my stomach.** Jonathan Brooks, *Church Forsaken: Practicing Presence in Neglected Neighborhoods* (Illinois: InterVarsity Press, 2018), 20–21. I am also grateful to the personal communication I had with Jonathan Brooks on November 29, 2018, which informed my writing.

49   **I was offered the position for two reasons.** Ibid, 20.

50   **I am offering you the position today.** Ibid, 21.

50   **I could see a young man from the neighborhood.** Ibid, 32.

51   **In 1990, a famous study was conducted.** Elizabeth Newton, "Overconfidence in the Communication of Intent: Heard and Unheard Melodies," PhD diss., Stanford University, 1990.

52   **Once we know something.** Chip Heath and Dan Heath, *Made to Stick: Why Some Ideas Survive and Others Die* (New York: Random House, 2007), 20.

52   **The more expertise and experience people gain.** Adam Grant, *Originals: How Non-conformists Move the World* (New York: Viking, 2016), 41.

53   **In 2006, the combined profits of Sears and Kmart was $1.5 billion.** Delventhal, "Who Killed Sears?"

54   **I saw the mothers, wives, and daughters.** Brooks, *Church Forsaken*, 32.

55   **"Babe," Brooks said to his wife.** Ibid, 45.

56   **Come ... help us.** Acts 16:9.

56   **There are no God-forsaken places.** OMF International US (@ omfus), "There are no God-forsaken places, just church-forsaken places." Twitter, April 15, 2012, 9 a.m., https://twitter.com/OMFUS/status/191511422394576896 .

CHAPTER FOUR: THE MOONSHOT RULE

59   **We choose to go to the Moon in this decade.** John F. Kennedy. "Moon Speech." Rice Stadium, Houston, Texas, September 12, 1962.

60   **Apart from me you can do nothing.** John 15:5.

60   **But he said to me, "My grace is sufficient for you."** 2 Corinthians 12:9–10.

62   **Fertile, enabling, desirable.** Adam Morgan and Mark Barden, *A Beautiful Constraint: How To Transform Your Limitations Into Advantages, and Why It's Everyone's Business* (New Jersey: John Wiley & Sons, 2015), 2.

64   **This is a natural constraint of the digital age.** Research has been done into U.S. Bible reading habits commissioned by the American Bible Society: Barna Group, "State of the Bible: 2017 Top Findings," *Barna Group*, April 4, 2017, https://www.barna.com/research/state-bible-2017-top-findings/ .

64   **Unlike other companies when we started.** Nir Eyal, *Hooked: How to Build Habit-forming Products* (New York: Penguin Portfolio Press, 2014). You can also read about YouVersion in Nir Eyal's article, "The App of God," *The Atlantic*, July 24, 2013, https://www.theatlantic.com/technology/archive/2013/07/the-app-of-god/278006/ .

64   **We originally started as a desktop website.** Eyal, *Hooked*, 243 (also quoted in article).

64   **#shereadstruth "turned into the fastest growing Bible-reading community."** Kate Shellnutt, "She Reads Truth: Why Women Will Lead the 21st-Century Bible Resurgence," *Christianity Today*, October 2016, https://www.christianitytoday.com/women/2016/october/she-reads-truth-why-women-will-lead-21st-century-bible-resu.html .

65   **The medium is the message.** Marshall McLuhan, *Understanding Media: The Extensions of Man* (New York: McGraw Hill, 1964), 9.

65   **A tentative assumption made in order to draw out and test.** *Merriam-Webster.com* "Hypothesis," accessed June 2020, https://www.merriam-webster.com/dictionary/hypothesis .

70   You'll find yourself frequently shifting gears. Tom Kelley in IDEO.org, *The Field Guide to Human-Centered Design* (California: IDEO, 2015), 13.

70   Clayton Christensen is a legend in the field of innovation. Clayton Christensen, *The Innovator's Dilemma: When New Technologies Cause Great Firms to Fail* (Massachusetts: Harvard Business Review Press, 1997).

70   In Walter Isaacson's seminal biography on Apple founder, Steve Jobs. Walter Isaacson, *Steve Jobs* (New York: Simon & Schuster, 2011), 939.

70   90 percent of the successful ones. Christensen, *The Innovator's Dilemma*.

71   The odds of producing an influential or successful idea. Dean Keith Simonton, "Creative Productivity: A Predictive and Explanatory Model of Career Trajectories and Landmarks," *Psychological Review* Vol.104 (1) (1997), 66–89.

71   This kind of communal process. 1 Corinthians 14.

72   In a 2009 article in *Bloomberg*. Jessie Scanlon, "How Whirlpool Puts New Ideas Through the Wringer," *Bloomberg*, August 3, 2009, https://www.bloomberg.com/news/articles/2009-08-03/how-whirlpool-puts-new-ideas-through-the-wringer .

75   I've adapted some of these ideas from Will Mancini's book. Will Mancini, *Innovating Discipleship: Four Paths to Real Discipleship Results: Volume 1* (CreateSpace Independent Publishing, 2013).

PHASE 2 LEADER INNOVATION LAB

86   My friends Steve Cockram and Jeremie Kubicek talk about. Jeremie Kubicek and Steve Cockram, *5 Gears: How to Be Present and Productive When There is Never Enough Time* (New Jersey: John Wiley & Sons, 2015).

CHAPTER FIVE: THE GENIUS OF BURL CAIN

91   The slave breeder who owned the plantation believed. Chris Frink, "Breaking into Prison," *Christianity Today*, May 2004, https://www.christianitytoday.com/ct/2004/may/4.36.html .

93   He grew almost immediately impatient. Lacey Rose, "Bill Simmons Breaks Free," *The Hollywood Reporter,* June 2016, https://www.hollywoodreporter.com/features/bill-simmons-espn-hbo-900291   . I am also grateful to the following source: Jack Hamilton, "How Bill Simmons Changed Sportswriting," *Slate*, May 2015, https://slate.com/culture/2015/05/bill-simmons-getting-booted-by-espn-is-the-best-thing-that-could-happen-to-the-sports-guy.html .

94   The day after The Dooze left us. Bill Simmons, "One Final Toss for The Dooze," *ESPN Page2*, January 2009, http://www.espn.com/espn/page2/story?page=simmons/090122 .

95   **Almost nothing Grantland published could have appeared in print.** Alex Shephard and Mark Krotov, "A Eulogy for Grantland," *The New Republic*, October 2015, https://newrepublic.com/article/123312/eulogy-grantland .

95   **This is sports writing for grownups.** Stephen Carter, "Oh ESPN, why did you have to kill Grantland?", *Chicagotribune.com*, December 2015, https://www.chicagotribune.com/news/sns-wp-blm-grantland-comment-4acc8d94-8163-11e5-8bd2-680fff868306-20151102-story.html .

97   **I couldn't believe this dumpy broken-down church building.** Richard Blackaby, personal communication with author, August 14, 2018.

97   **So we prayed for a university ministry.** Ibid.

98   **He never had the same notes.** Ibid.

98   **I think part of Dad's genius.** Ibid.

98   **In the 1970s, people were very much wanting.** Ibid.

99   **In 1988, I was in seminary in Texas.** Ibid.

100   **Eventually Avery Willis from Lifeway publishing.** Ibid.

101   **In 1990, *Experiencing God* was published.** Henry Blackaby and Claude King, *Experiencing God: Knowing and Doing the Will of God* (Lifeway Christian Resources, 1990).

102   **A long obedience in the same direction.** Originally quoted by Nietzsche but popularized in recent years through Eugene H. Peterson's book of the same title. Eugene H. Peterson, *A Long Obedience in the Same Direction: Discipleship in an Instant Society* (Illinois: InterVarsity Press, 2000).

102   **The new Jim Crow:** Michelle Alexander, *The New Jim Crow. Mass Incarceration in the Age of Colorblindness* (New York: The New Press, 2012).

104   **The Atlantic not only ran a feature article.** Lifeway publishing, "Experiencing God: Angola," Echo Light Studios, *GodTube*, 2016, https://www.godtube.com/watch/?v=YLYPL7NX . You can find this short, powerful video on the *Ready or Not* website (www.DougPaul.org/ReadyorNotLab).

104   **The Atlantic reported.** Jeffrey Goldberg, "The End of the Line: Rehabilitation and Reform in Angola Penitentiary," *The Atlantic*, September 9, 2015, https://www.theatlantic.com/politics/archive/2015/09/a-look-inside-angola-prison/404377/ .

105   **When I see the hands of men raised in worship.** John Yeats, "At Angola prison, pastors see God's Hand," *Baptist Press*, March 28, 2008, http://dev.bpnews.net/27721/at-angola-prison-pastors-see-gods-hand .

CHAPTER SIX: APOLLO BURNS

107 **He knows the results before the report is released to the public.** Matt Bonesteel, "Bill Simmons once again took a shot at Roger Goodell. Was it the last straw for ESPN?," *The Washington Post*, May 8, 2015, https://www.washingtonpost.com/news/early-lead/wp/2015/05/08/bill-simmons-once-again-took-a-shot-at-roger-goodell-was-it-the-last-straw-for-espn/ .

108 **This site had a pretty different direction.** Bill Simmons, "The Colangelo Saga and the NBA Finals Best Narratives," May 31, 2018 in *The Bill Simmons Podcast*, produced by The Ringer Podcast Network, https://www.theringer.com/the-bill-simmons-podcast/2018/5/31/17415042/the-bryan-colangelo-story-and-an-nba-finals-preview-plus-rich-kleiman-on-kd-jay-z-and-superstardom .

109 **This time around.** Ibid.

109 **You just never know what's going to happen.** Ibid.

109 **The faster you can move.** Eric Ries, *The Lean Startup: How Today's Entrepreneurs Use Continuous Innovation to Create Radically Successful Businesses* (New York: Crown Business, 2011), 112.

110 **Everyone's got a plan until.** Albert Breer, "With Coronavirus Outbreak During Peak NFL Travel Season, League Office Has to Lead," *Sports Illustrated*, March 12, 2020, https://www.si.com/nfl/2020/03/12/coronavirus-nfl-peak-travel-season .

111 **Fail often to succeed sooner.** Tom Kelley and Jonathan Littman, *The Ten Faces of Innovation: IDEO's Strategies for Beating the Devil's Advocate & Driving Creativity Throughout Your Organization* (New York: Currency/Doubleday, 2005), 42.

111 **In the initial stage of validating an idea.** Ash Maurya, *Running Lean: Iterate from Plan A to a Plan That Works* (California: O'Reilly, 2012), 16.

112 **Instead of machines that looked like.** Steve Wilson, "My Trip to Stanford Design Thinking Bootcamp," *Citrix Blog Home*, September 17, 2014, https://www.citrix.com/blogs/2014/09/17/my-trip-to-stanford-design-thinking-bootcamp/ .

113 **Effective innovations start small.** Peter Drucker, "The Discipline of Innovation," *Harvard Business Review*, August 2002, https://hbr.org/2002/08/the-discipline-of-innovation .

113 **Rarely do we get it right on our first try.** IDEO.org, *The Field Guide to Human-Centered Design* (IDEO, 2015), 21.

113 **Tom Kelley, IDEO's founder, also emphasizes this in an unusual story of a baseball team.** Kelly and Littman, *The Ten Faces of Innovation*, 42.

117 **I encourage leaders to escape the expert expectation.** Tod Bolsinger, *Canoeing the Mountains: Christian Leadership in Uncharted Territory* (Illinois: InterVarsity Press, 2018), 213.

119   **In every seed is the potential for a tree.** Alan Hirsch and Dave Ferguson, *On the Verge: A Journey into the Apostolic Future of the Church* (Michigan: Zondervan, 2011), 45.

120   **Especially me. I was there from minute one.** Simmons, "The Brian Colangelo Saga," podcast.

121   **Currently, there are *one hundred million downloads*.** Ashley Carman, "Spotify needed a huge podcast, and it just bought one of the biggest," *The Verge*, February 5, 2020, https://www.theverge.com/2020/2/5/21124201/bill-simmons-the-ringer-spotify-acquistion-podcast-purchase .

121   **In February 2020, Spotify purchased The Ringer.** Todd Spangler, "Spotify Is Paying Up to $196 Million in Cash to Acquire Bill Simmons' The Ringer," *Variety*, February 12, 2020, https://variety.com/2020/digital/news/spotify-acquires-the-ringer-196-million-cash-bill-simmons-1203502471/ .

124   **Alpha can be summed up as rationalistic conservatism.** Rob Warner, *Reinventing English Evangelicalism: 1966—2001* (Oregon: Wipf & Stock Publishers, 2008), 122.

PHASE 3 LEADER INNOVATION LAB

127   **Scott Belsky outlines the need for putting together a team.** Scott Belsky, *Making Ideas Happen* (New York: Portfolio/Penguin, 2010).

130   **Christian leadership is a strange beast.** Mark Sayers, *Facing Leviathan: Leadership, Influence, and Creating in a Cultural Storm* (Illinois: Moody Publishers, 2014), 120-121.

131   **God needed to intervene and reveal the wisdom.** James 3:17.

131   **But fortunately, as the song says.** Sinach (2015), "Way Maker," *Way Maker—Live,* produced by Mayo and Sinach.

131   **In his book *The Culture Code*.** Clotaire Rapaille, *The Culture Code: An Ingenious Way to Understand Why People Around the World Live and Buy as They Do* (New York: Broadway Books, 2006).

CHAPTER SEVEN: THE SECRET TRICK TO HACKING A HIT

135   **Hannah More was born into humble circumstances in 1745.** Eric Metaxas, *Seven Women: And the Secret of Their Greatness* (New York: Thomas Nelson, 2016). I am also grateful to the following source: Karen Swallow Prior, *Fierce Convictions: The Extraordinary Life of Hannah Moore—Poet, Reformer, Abolitionist* (New York: Thomas Nelson, 2014).

136   **That an unmarried woman via her own talents and efforts.** Metaxas, *Seven Women*, 115.

137   **The only time I could write songs.** Kate Rockland, "Student with a Past," *The New York Times,* February 6, 2016, https://www.nytimes.com/2006/02/16/garden/16weezer.html .

138   **The Weezer frontman has long used algorithms.** Gab Ginsberg, "Rivers Cuomo on His Data-Driven Approach to Weezer," *Billboard,* March 1, 2019, https://www.billboard.com/articles/columns/rock/8500614/weezer-rivers-cuomo-data-driven-approach-interview .

138   **I wrote a program to get all the information from Spotify's API.** Ibid.

138   **Cuomo estimates he drew on thousands of riffs.** Dan Hyman, "How Weezer's Rivers Cuomo Used Google Sheets to Make Ambitious New Album," *Rolling Stone,* October 5, 2017, https://www.rollingstone.com/music/music-features/how-weezers-rivers-cuomo-used-google-sheets-to-make-ambitious-new-album-205947/ .

139   **They have 1.4 *billion* on-demand streams.** Ginsberg, "Rivers Cuomo."

139   **The ridiculous song "Beverly Hills"?** "Weezer—Beverley Hills (Official Music Video)," *YouTube,* uploaded by Weezer, June 16, 2009, https://www.youtube.com/watch?v=HL_WvOly7mY (last accessed June 11, 2020).

139   **Over the course of time, phenomena enter our collective consciousness.** Roger Martin, *The Design of Business: Why Design Thinking is the Next Competitive Advantage* (Massachusetts: Harvard Business School Press, 2009), 7.

140   **"Heuristics," Martin says, "are rules of thumb."** Ibid, 8.

140   **In the modern era, a fourth important step has been added.** Ibid.

141   **The difference between them is the difference between one-hit-wonder Don McLean.** Ibid.

144   **"Most of Hannah's readers," Eric Metaxas writes.** Eric Metaxas, *Seven Women,* 124.

146   **Poster and medallion of a slave in chains, with the question emblazoned beneath.** "Am I Not a Man and a Brother?", 1787 medallion designed by Josiah Wedgwood for the British anti-slavery campaign. Public domain. https://en.wikipedia.org/wiki/Abolitionism#/media/File:Official_medallion_of_the_British_Anti-Slavery_Society_(1795).jpg .

146   **We need our stone hearts to be replaced with hearts of flesh.** Ezekiel 36:26.

146   *Village Politics,* **written specifically for "the mechanics, journeymen, and labourers in Great Britain."** Ibid, 127.

150   **As Dr. King put it, they needed Bull Connor to "tip his hand."** Malcolm Gladwell, *David and Goliath: Underdogs, Misfits, and the Art of Battling Giants* (New York: Little, Brown and Company, 2013), 178.

CHAPTER EIGHT: THE REVOLUTION WILL BE TELEVISED

151 **In the early 1960s, only 26 percent of US residents felt race was a problem facing America.** Andrew Cohut, "Despite mixed views on civil rights in 1965, Americans largely supported Selma marchers," *PBS News Hour*, March 5, 2015, https://www.pbs.org/newshour/nation/integration-moved-fast-many-americans-according-1965-poll . I am also grateful to the following sources on the Civil Rights Movement. Taylor Branch, *Parting the Waters: America in the King Years 1954–63* (Simon and Schuster, 1988); Ben Cosgrove, "Civil Rights: Preparation and Protest, Virginia, 1960," *Time Magazine*, https://www.life.com/history/life-and-civil-rights-anatomy-of-a-protest-virginia-1960/ ; Kim Gilmore, "The Birmingham Children's Crusade of 1963," *Biography.com*, January 28, 2020, https://www.biography.com/news/black-history-birmingham-childrens-crusade-1963; Diane McWhorter, *Carry Me Home: Birmingham, Alabama; The Climactic Battle of the Civil Rights Revolution* (Touchstone, 2002); Howell Raines, *My Soul Is Rested: The Story of the Civil Rights Movement in the Deep South* (Penguin, 1983); Hansi Lo Wang, "50 Years Ago, Freedom Summer Began By Training For Battle," June 14, 2014, in *NPR Weekend Edition*, podcast, MP3 audio, https://www.npr.org/sections/codeswitch/2014/06/14/318917992/50-years-ago-freedom-summer-began-by-training-for-battle .

152 **They can only see through white eyes.** Michael Cooper Nichols, "Cities Are What Men Make Them: Birmingham, Alabama, Faces the Civil Rights Movement 1963," Senior Thesis, Brown University, 1975, 286.

152 **Bull Connor had something in him about not letting these n****** get to city hall.** Ibid.

153 **On the last Monday in April, [Wyatt Walker] dropped off leaflets.** Gladwell, *David and Goliath*, 184–185, quoting James Forman, *The Making of Black Revolutionaries: A Personal Account* (Macmillan, 1972), 114–118, and Nichols, "Cities Are What Men Make Them," 286.

153 **Do not cross.** Nichols, "Cities Are What Men Make Them," 286.

154 **In 1987, an ad started airing on televisions.** "Your Brain on Drugs," *YouTube*, uploaded by Egallity, September 16, 2008, https://www.youtube.com/watch?v=3FtNm9CgA6U .

155 **In their book *The Power of Moments*, the Heath brothers define.** Dan Heath and Chip Heath, *The Power of Moments: Why Certain Experiences Have Extraordinary Impact* (New York: Simon & Schuster, 2017), 103.

156 **Derek Sivers hopped onto a TED stage and broke down the anatomy of a movement.** Derek Sivers, "First Follower: Leadership Lessons From A Dancing Guy," *Derek Sivers*, February 11, 2010, https://sivers.org/ff .

156 **He used grainy video footage.** "Sasquatch music festival 2009 – Guy starts dance party," *YouTube*, uploaded by dkellerm, May 26, 2009, https://www.youtube.com/watch?v=GA8z7f7a2Pk .

156 **Santigold's song "Unstoppable."** Santigold (2008), "Unstoppable," *Santigold*, Schoolhouse, Downtown, track 9.

159 **Being a first follower is an under-appreciated form of leadership.** Derek Sivers, "First Follower."

160 **In its first weekend, *The Greatest Showman* brought in only $8.8 million.** Alissa Wilkinson, "How The Greatest Showman rewrote the stars to become a monster success", *Vox*, March 12, 2018, https://www.vox.com/2018/3/9/17029684/greatest-showman-musical-success-explained-efron-jackman-box-office-circus-musical . See also, Scott Mendelson, "Box Office: 'The Greatest Showman' Became One Of The Leggiest Movies Ever," *Forbes*, July 19, 2018, https://www.forbes.com/sites/scottmendelson/2018/07/19/box-office-greatest-showman-legs-hugh-jackman-zendaya-zac-efron-mamma-mia/#1f23c904568a ; Michael Ordona, "'La La Land' songwriters change their tune for risky new musical 'The Greatest Showman," *The Los Angeles Times*, November 3, 2017, https://www.latimes.com/entertainment/movies/la-ca-mn-sneaks-greatest-showman-songs-20171103-story.html .

161 **One of [the] measures is a movie's multiplier.** Wilkinson, "How The Greatest Showman."

164 **In the 1970s, a hotbed developed at Fuller Theological Seminary.** Healing and Revival editors, "Biography of John Wimber," *Healing and Revival*, https://healingandrevival.com/BioJWimber.htm . See also, Bill Jackson, *The Quest for the Radical Middle: A History of the Vineyard* (Cape Town, South Africa: Vineyard International Publishing: 1999).

164 **Grace is not opposed to effort.** Dallas Willard, *The Great Omission: Reclaiming Jesus's Essential Teachings on Discipleship* (New York: HarperCollins, 2006), 34.

164 **It was as if he made a conscious effort not to be flashy or flamboyant.** Gary Moon, *Becoming Dallas Willard: The Formation of a Philosopher, Teacher, and Christ Follower* (Illinois: IVP Books: 2018), 196.

165 **It's the first follower who transforms the lone nut into a leader.** Sivers, "First Follower."

165 ***Diffusion of Innovation Theory*, the sociological principle introduced by E. M. Rogers in 1962.** E. M. Rogers, *Diffusion of Innovations* (New York: Free Press, 2003). See also, Leif Singer, "On the Diffusion of Innovations: How New Ideas Spread," *Leif.me*, https://leif.me/2016/12/on-the-diffusion-of-innovations-how-new-ideas-spread/ ; Boston University School of Public Health editors, "Diffusion of Innovation Theory," *Boston University School of Public Health*, http://sphweb.bumc.bu.edu/otlt/MPH-Modules/SB/BehavioralChangeTheories/BehavioralChangeTheories4.html .

167   When Jesus sent out the twelve and then the seventy-two. Luke 9:1–6
       and Luke 10:1–17.

168   Never doubt that a small group of thoughtful, committed citizens
       can change the world. Donald Keys, *Earth at Omega: Passage to
       Planetization* (Massachusetts: Branden Pub Co, 1982), 79.

PHASE 4 LEADER INNOVATION LAB

173   Mount of Transfiguration experience. Mark 9:2–12.

173   May God open our eyes to see what the holy ministry of interces-
       sion is. Andrew Murray, *With Christ in the School of Prayer* (Merchant
       Books, 2013), 3.

CHAPTER NINE: THE IRON TRIANGLE

180   On March 6, 2012, a YouTube video. "DollarShaveClub.com—Our
       Blades Are F***ing Great," *YouTube*, uploaded by Dollar Shave Club,
       March 6, 2012, https://www.youtube.com/watch?v=ZUG9qYTJMsI .

180   What follows is 90 seconds of absolute absurdity. Joe Lazauskas and
       Shane Snow, *The Storytelling Edge: How to Transform Your Business, Stop
       Screaming into the Void, and Make People Love You* (New Jersey: Wiley:
       2018), 76. See also, Steven Davidoff Solomon, "$1 Billion for Dollar Shave
       Club: Why Every Company Should Worry," *The New York Times*, July 26,
       2016,   https://www.nytimes.com/2016/07/27/business/dealbook/1-
       billion-for-dollar-shave-club-why-every-company-should-worry.html   ;
       Kris Frieswick, "The Serious Guy Behind Dollar Shave Club's Crazy Viral
       Videos," *Inc.*, June 4, 2016, https://www.inc.com/magazine/201604/
       kris-frieswick/dollar-shave-club-michael-dubin.html ; Barbara Booth,
       "What happens when a business built on simplicity gets complicated?
       Dollar Shave Club's founder Michael Dubin found out," *CNBC*, March
       24, 2019, https://www.cnbc.com/2019/03/23/dollar-shaves-dubin-
       admits-a-business-built-on-simplicity-can-get-complicated.html .

180   Dubin knew that he had to speak to men like him. Lazauskas, *The
       Storytelling Edge*, 75–76.

180   Hal Plotkin's 1988 article in *Inc.* magazine. Merriam-Webster editors,
       "What Does 'Scale the Business' Mean? How a common word became
       a staple of business jargon," *Merriam-Webster*, https://www.merriam-
       webster.com/words-at-play/scale-the-business-meaning-origin .

181   The business had 3.9 million monthly subscribers. Erica Sweeney, "Dollar
       Shave Club's inclusive campaign, space contest lather up results," *Marketing
       Dive*, October 26, 2018, https://www.marketingdive.com/news/dollar-
       shave-clubs-inclusive-campaign-space-contest-lather-up-results/540655/ .

181   The tipping point is that magic moment. Malcolm Gladwell, *The
       Tipping Point: How Little Things Can Make a Big Difference* (New York:
       Little, Brown and Company, 2013), 69.

181 **There is a simple way to package information.** Ibid, 232.

181 **Scripture says that a kingdom return is.** Matthew 13:8.

181 **Charles Spurgeon himself, in a sermon.** Charles Spurgeon, "The Agreement Of Salvation By Grace With Walking In Good Works," *Christian Classics Ethereal Library*, Sermon no. 2210, June 28, 1891, https://www.ccel.org/ccel/spurgeon/sermons37.xxix.html .

182 **"Sheldon," journalist Karl Smallwood wrote.** Karl Smallwood, "The Fascinating Story of how the WWJD Slogan Came About," *Today I Found Out*, June 6, 2014, http://www.todayifoundout.com/index.php/2014/06/origin-jesus-slogan/ .

182 **Among the few white ministers of the day.** Ibid.

183 **I heard some people singing at a church prayer meeting.** Charles Sheldon, *In His Steps: What Would Jesus Do?* (CreateSpace Independent Publishing Platform: September 2010), 20.

183 **Pledge themselves, earnestly and honestly.** "What would Jesus do?: The rise of a slogan," *BBC News*, December 8, 2011, https://www.bbc.com/news/magazine-16068178

184 **In 2019, it received a valuation of one billion dollars.** Yola Robert, "Rent The Runway Joins The Unicorn Club At A $1 Billion Valuation," *Forbes*, March 25, 2019, https://www.forbes.com/sites/yolarobert1/2019/03/25/rent-the-runway-joins-the-unicorn-club-at-a-1-billion-valuation/#71a401db5f0c .

184 **You rely on us for meaningful events in your life.** Jason Del Rey, "Rent the Runway stops accepting new customers as operations melt down," *Vox*, September 27, 2019, https://www.vox.com/recode/2019/9/27/20887017/rent-the-runway-new-customer-freeze-subscribers-delivery-delays-warehouse-issues .

185 **Develop something quickly and of high quality.** Business.com Editorial Staff, "Fast, Good or Cheap—Pick Three?" *Business.com*, April 14, 2020, https://www.business.com/articles/fast-good-cheap-pick-three/ .

186 **Paul didn't want immature churches (the Corinthian Church).** 1 Corinthians 3:1–3.

186 **Or ones breeding heresy (the Colossian Church).** Colossians 2:8.

186 **Or legalism (the Galatian Church).** Galatians 3.

189 **Jesus said that when we enter into any kind of spiritual conflict.** e.g., Luke 14:25–33.

189 **All models are wrong, but some are useful.** G. E. P Box, "Science and Statistics," *Journal of the American Statistical Association*, (1976), 71.

193 **"At the time, 1989," Tinklenberg said.** Smallwood, "The Fascinating Story."

194 **Trying to describe Quibi's essence.** Julia Alexander, "It's impossible to screenshot a Quibi show, and that's detrimental to its success," *The Verge*, April 8, 2020, https://www.theverge.com/2020/4/8/21211463/quibi-screenshot-streaming-netflix-disney-tiktok-instagram-viral-tiger-king .

194   **Experts believe one of the reasons Netflix was an early success.**
        Kathryn VanArendonk, "Let Me Screenshot Your Quibi Show,
        Cowards," *Vulture*, April 17, 2020, https://www.vulture.com/2020/04/
        let-me-screenshot-your-quibi-show.html .

194   **Quibi raised nearly two billion dollars.** Julia Alexander, "Quibi has
        raised close to $2 billion, and it hasn't even launched yet," *The Verge*,
        March 4, 2020, https://www.theverge.com/2020/3/4/21165312/
        quibi-funding-investors-jeffrey-katzenberg-launch-date-price .

195   **She got totally screwed, if you want to know the truth.** Smallwood,
        "The Fascinating Story."

197   **Thank God we are preserved from Winston Churchill.** Richard M.
        Langworth, "Churchill and the Rhineland," *International Churchill
        Society*, https://winstonchurchill.org/publications/finest-hour/finest-
        hour-141/churchill-and-the-rhineland/ .

197   **We seem to be very near the bleak choice between War and Shame.**
        Richard M. Langworth, ed., *Churchill by Himself: The Definitive
        Collection of Quotations* (New York: PublicAffairs, 2008), 257; also
        cited in Richard M. Langworth, "Churchill's words: Choosing between
        War and Shame—and getting both," *RichardLangworth.com*, October
        11, 2019, https://richardlangworth.com/war-shame .

197   **We have before us an ordeal of the most grievous kind.** Winston
        Churchill, "Blood, Toil, Tears and Sweat: May 13, 1940. First Speech as
        Prime Minister to House of Commons," *International Churchill Society*,
        https://winstonchurchill.org/resources/speeches/1940-the-finest-
        hour/blood-toil-tears-and-sweat-2/ .

198   **Churchill called it "a colossal military disaster."** Winston Churchill,
        "We Shall Fight on the Beaches," *The Guardian*, April 20, 2007,
        https://www.theguardian.com/theguardian/2007/apr/20/
        greatspeeches1#:~:text=The%20whole%20root%20and%20core,an%20
        ignominious%20and%20starving%20captivity.

198   **Nothing but a miracle can save the BEF now.** James Moore and Reiss
        Smith, "The miracle of Dunkirk: 40 facts about the famous evacuation,"
        Express.co.uk, May 23, 2017, https://www.express.co.uk/news/
        world/578885/Dunkirk-evacuation-World-War-Two-Germany-Britain .

CHAPTER TEN: OPERATION DYNAMO

200   **In all, more than seven hundred little boats.** Moore and Smith, "The
        miracle of Dunkirk."

201   **We shall go on to the end.** Winston Churchill, "We Shall Fight on the
        Beaches: June 4, 1940: House of Commons," *International Churchill
        Society*, https://winstonchurchill.org/resources/speeches/1940-the-
        finest-hour/we-shall-fight-on-the-beaches/ .

202 **Charles Duhigg says "keystone habits" are.** Charles Duhigg, *The Power of Habit: Why We Do What We Do in Life and Business* (New York: Random House, 2012), 13.

202 **Dallas Willard wrote about this spiritual phenomenon.** Dallas Willard, *The Great Omission: Reclaiming Jesus's Essential Teachings on Discipleship* (New York, HarperCollins, 2006). See also Dallas Willard "Spiritual Formation in Christ: A Perspective on what it is and how it might be done," *Journal of Psychology and Theology*, (2000), Vol. 28, #4.

202 **Dave Runyon and Jay Pathak developed a radical minimum.** Jay Pathak and Dave Runyon, *The Art of Neighboring: Building Genuine Relationships Right Outside Your Door* (Michigan: Baker Books, 2007).

203 **Jesus says we should count the cost.** e.g., Luke 14:25–33.

204 **You know you've come up with a good pricing model.** Ash Maurya, *Running Lean: Iterate from Plan A to a Plan That Works* (California: O'Reilly, 2012), 260.

205 **Even Republicans seem to see Sanders as a harmless curiosity.** Molly Ball, "There's Something About Bernie," *The Atlantic*, July 29, 2015, https://www.theatlantic.com/politics/archive/2015/07/theres-something-about-bernie/399740/ .

206 **On my very first day in DC.** Becky Bond and Zack Exley, *Rules for Revolutionaries: How Big Organizing Can Change Everything* (New York: Chelsea Green Publishing, 2016), 18–19.

207 **This is a crime against history.** Ibid, 19.

207 **A tribe is a group of people connected to one another.** Seth Godin, *Tribes: We Need You to Lead Us* (New York: Portfolio, 2008), 13.

208 **When the Ferguson brothers started Community Christian Church.** Dave Ferguson and Jon Ferguson, personal interview, November 21, 2018.

209 **I woke up filled with excitement.** Bond and Exley, *Rules for Revolutionaries*, 19.

209 **The neighborhood team model.** Ibid, 27.

211 **At the end of January, 2016, if you had pulled up Hillary Clinton's website.** Ibid, 15.

211 **The revolution is not something you order to your own specifications.** Ibid, 20.

212 **They asked churches to commit to 4 Rs.** Dave Ferguson and Jon Ferguson, personal interview.

213 **In spite of current ads and slogans.** Margaret Wheatley and Deborah Frieze, "Using Emergence to take Social Innovations to Scale," *MargaretWheatley.com*, 2006, https://www.margaretwheatley.com/articles/emergence.html .

214 **But sends them out two-by-two.** e.g., Mark 6:7 and Luke 10:1.

215 **Alan Hirsch calls *Communitas*.** Alan Hirsch, *The Forgotten Ways: Reactivating Apostolic Movements*, 2nd ed. (Michigan: Brazos Press, 2016).

PHASE 5 LEADER INNOVATION LAB

222 Apart from me you can do nothing. John 15:5.

222 For what does it profit a man. Mark 8:36 (ESV).

223 Above all else, guard your heart. Proverbs 4:23.

EPILOGUE: THE CONCORDE FALLACY

227 This is nothing [compared] to what [happens] on Sundays. T. B. Walters, *Robert Raikes: Founder of Sunday Schools* (London: The Epworth Press, 1930), 32. I am also grateful to the following source: Michael Peters, *Robert Raikes: The Founder of Sunday School 1780, The Story of How Sunday School Began* (Washington: Pleasant Word-A Division of WinePress Publishing, 2008).

228 Many children of the poor worked horrible hours in factories. Aaron Earls, "How the Forgotten History of Sunday School Can Point the Way Forward," *Lifeway Facts and Trends*, July 17, 2018, https://factsandtrends.net/2018/07/17/sunday-school/ .

228 Leave quietly and without making a noise. J. Henry Harris, *Robert Raikes: The Man and His Work* (New York: E. P. Dutton & Co, 1899), 69.

229 Raikes Ragged Regiment. Ibid, 14

229 They have been transformed from the shape of wolves and tigers to that of men. Ibid, 312.

230 In 1956, the British Supersonic Transport Aircraft Committee met to discuss the formation of a new project. Jim Blasingame, "Beware of the Concorde Fallacy," *Forbes*, September 15, 2011, https://www.forbes.com/sites/jimblasingame/2011/09/15/beware-of-the-concorde-fallacy/#1e979a954e22 .

230 Forbes journalist Jim Blasingame describes the fallacy. Blasingame, "Beware of the Concorde Fallacy."

231 Will often stick with a technology/library choice through thick and thin. Jose Betancur, "Beware of the Concorde Fallacy," *BrickStartUp*, September 2, 2017, https://brickstartup.co/beware-of-the-concorde-fallacy-d8462d3449d4 .

231 Inexperienced gamblers fall inside this trap. Daniel Bier, "The Concorde Fallacy: Why We Can't Quit Losing Battles," *The Foundation for Economic Education*, May 22, 2015, https://fee.org/articles/the-concorde-fallacy-why-we-cant-quit-losing-battles/ .

231 The more we invest in a project or a person, the harder it is to let it go. Ibid.

Made in the USA
Monee, IL
29 October 2020